Journey to the West

The Civilization of the American Indian Series

Journey to the West

The Alabama and Coushatta Indians

Sheri Marie Shuck-Hall

The University of Oklahoma Press : Norman

Library of Congress Cataloging-in-Publication Data

Shuck-Hall, Sheri Marie, 1972–
Journey to the west : the Alabama and Coushatta Indians / Sheri Marie
Shuck-Hall.
p. cm. — (The civilization of the American Indian series ; v. 256)
Includes bibliographical references and index.
ISBN 978-0-8061-3940-1 (hardcover : alk. paper) 1. Alabama Indians—
Migrations. 2. Alabama Indians—History. 3. Koasati Indians—Migrations.
4. Koasati Indians—History. I. Title.
E99.A4S48 2008
976.10497′38—dc22
2008010716

Journey to the West: The Alabama and Coushatta Indians is Volume 256 in
The Civilization of the American Indian Series.

1 2 3 4 5 6 7 8 9 10

For Tom

Contents

Illustrations

Figures

Maps

Acknowledgments

This project has been a ten-year journey, and I could not have completed this work without the support of many to whom I would like to express my appreciation.

I would like to acknowledge and thank Edward Ingram, editor of the *International History Review*, and Gregory Waselkov, guest editor of the *Gulf South Historical Review*, for publishing parts of chapters 4 and 5 of this book in their respective journals.

Various grants and fellowships aided significantly in the research and writing of this book. Specifically, I would like to extend my gratitude to the American Philosophical Society and the Phillip's Fund for Native American Research; the Clements Center for Southwest Studies' DeGolyer Research Grant; Auburn University's Marguerite E. Scharnagel Fellowship and Milo B. Howard Research Fellowship; and Christopher Newport University and the University of Alabama in Huntsville's faculty research grants.

While researching this project, I depended on the expertise and assistance of many archivists and librarians and would like to thank the staff of the following institutions: the Center for American History at the University of Texas, Austin; the

Clements Center for Southwest Studies at Southern Methodist University, Dallas; the Williams Research Center and the Historic New Orleans Collection, New Orleans; the Ralph Brown Draughon Library at Auburn University, Alabama; the Texas State Library and Archives Commission, Austin; the Center for Louisiana Studies at the University of Louisiana, Lafayette; the British National Archives (formerly the Public Record Office), London; the Manuscript Division of the Library of Congress, Washington, D.C.; the P. K. Yongle Library at the University of Florida, Gainesville; the South Carolina Department of Archives and History, Columbia; and the Alabama-Coushatta Indian Reservation, Livingston, Texas.

To the anonymous reviewers who gave the manuscript a critical eye and challenged me to delve further into the analysis and broaden the approach, I want to extend my great appreciation for making this book stronger. I also wish to express my gratitude to the editorial staff at the University of Oklahoma Press, especially Alessandra Jacobi Tamulevich, who provided invaluable encouragement and advice in the various stages of writing and revising.

Many friends and colleagues have made a direct impact on my work through the years, and I wish to give special thanks to Greg O'Brien, Robbie Ethridge, and James Carson; their input and support have been essential in converting this work from a dissertation into its current form. I also greatly appreciate those who have provided thoughtful suggestions to the manuscript in its various parts, including Greg Waselkov, Daniel Usner, Allan Gallay, Edward Ingram, F. Todd Smith, Charles Hudson, Steven Hahn, Josh Piker, Robin Fabel, Tony Carey, and Kathryn Braund. To my colleagues in the Department of History at Christopher Newport University and Andy Dunar and Philip Boucher, thank you for your collegiality and support through the years. I owe particular recognition to my former mentors who gave me the necessary tools to become a responsible historian and scholar: my ever-encouraging adviser, Robin Fabel, Tony Carey, John Cottier, Donna Bohanan, Larry Gerber, and Jonathan Atkins.

My greatest supporters have been my family, and I would like to give a very special acknowledgment to my parents, Jim and

Judith, and my brother James, who have always been supportive of my endeavors. To my newborn son, Lochlan, who has read this book with me on more than one occasion, thank you for coming into my world. More than anyone else, I give my complete gratitude and admiration to my husband, Tom, who has provided constant encouragement and understanding from the very beginning. With love, I dedicate this book to you.

Journey to
the West

Introduction

Long ago, three Alabama and Coushatta boys talked about traveling west when they grew up, so that they could see where the sun disappeared into the earth every night. After many years passed, they reunited at the village square ground and decided to begin their journey the next morning at sunrise. They packed deerskin bags with food, blankets, knives, bows, and arrows. Dangers awaited them as they trekked through unknown lands. The three young men encountered dense forests and wild animals, including a black bear that metamorphosed into a hairy black caterpillar. Along the path a giant eagle attacked one warrior, but he defeated the great bird by driving a knife through its heart.[1]

After safely crossing a plain, they entered a dense, dark forest full of thousands of agitated rattlesnakes, yet the young men persevered. A vast body of water soon appeared in the distance, too wide to cross. They almost lost hope, until a red-, yellow-, and black-ringed horned serpent—as large as a tree trunk with fiery scales—emerged from the water. They tricked the serpent with food and jumped on its back, riding it to the other shore. Many years passed, and the men became old, but they ardently continued on their journey. One day they heard a repeating, thunderous clash, and as they got closer expected a great conflict. They had reached the end of the earth where the sky fell up and down, striking the ground as if in an eternal battle.[2]

One of the friends tried to convince the others that if they ran under the opening between the earth and sky, they would find a "new world." Indeed, two men ran through successfully, timing their leap to avoid the periodic impact of the sky on the earth. One of the friends, however, hesitated, realizing he could not go back through the woods alone. He had waited too long; because of his delay, the sky fell and crushed him when he crossed. The two survivors, however, jumped on the sky and discovered a beautiful country full of peaceful people, animals, and bountiful vegetation, forests, and meadows. There was no pain, hatred, or suffering. It was similar to, if not better than, life on earth.[3]

Upon their arrival, the men investigated the new ground. Aba Mikko, the Great Creator, provided them with seeds for beans, watermelons, potatoes, and barley. Aba Mikko then invited the travelers to a comfortable cabin where they slept. When they awoke the next morning, they were surprised to see familiar cabins. They had in fact returned to their ancestral village. The adventurers, now old, told their kinspeople about their mystical journey and gave them the new seeds for cultivation.[4]

This story, "Journey to the Sky," derives from the oral tradition of Alabama and Coushatta Indians. It echoes themes of rebirth and renewal, both characteristic of their historical experiences; it can be interpreted as a metaphoric representation of their westward journey over three centuries and their cohesiveness as a diasporic community. This book is a study of the Alabamas and Coushattas' migration and diaspora; it is a history of a coalescent people who created and re-created their world. They fled their ancestral homelands to seek refuge and crossed the great Mississippi River in search of open, fertile land where they could clear the ground, construct villages, and cultivate their fields. Along the way, the Alabamas and Coushattas encountered new peoples and cultures unknown to their old world. Indeed, their oral tradition describes how contact with an unexpected stranger led to exchanges of goods and new additions to their crops, such as barley from Europe and watermelon from Africa. Such changes to Alabama and Coushatta society occurred throughout their long journey.

Each time the Alabamas and Coushattas chose to migrate farther west, they remade what they knew, replicating their previous world. Even far from their villages, their ties to their homeland called them back, as the end of "Journey to the Sky" reveals. Some Alabamas and Coushattas described their chosen path as an adventure. The oral tradition refers to traveling to *ihaanitókpa*, a faraway land, or their world in another place. Nevertheless, to others, this distant destination was a dangerous place where hope could be lost easily. The faraway land represented the precarious balances between nature and human life and between chaos and order. Ihaanitókpa was for the intrepid and not for the weak. Just as in their ancestors' journey to the sky, only the determined survivors reached their final space and discovered a new world.

Who are the Alabamas and Coushattas, and why have they been overlooked in American history? The Alabama and Coushatta historical experience has been plagued with misinformation perpetuated for centuries, and this may explain why few scholars have attempted to craft a history of these people from the earliest times to the late nineteenth century.[5] Misunderstanding began when Europeans settled North America and lumped together many peoples in the Southeast, referring to them collectively as "Creek Indians." They likely gave them this name because of the numerous small streams and rivers near the Indian towns. The Creeks, as they became known, included distinct communities of Alabamas, Coushattas, Abhikas, Yuchis, and Cowetas, among others. By the eighteenth century these groups joined flexible alliances to protect their collective interests. The renowned chief Alexander McGillivray later formalized this fluid alliance and declared in 1790 that he was the leader of a united Creek Nation.[6] The Creek Nation's confederation led many Europeans in the Southeast to identify Alabamas as Creeks, perpetuating the difficulty of distinguishing the groups from each other. To complicate matters, British traders in the eighteenth century labeled the

Indians living above the confluence of the Alabama and Talla-poosa rivers the "Upper Creeks" (which included the Alabam-as and Coushattas) and referred to those peoples farther south on the Chattahoochee and Flint rivers as the "Lower Creeks."

This study focuses on the Alabama and Coushatta towns and villages, clearly identified in the historical record, that com-prised their community. Joshua Piker, Jason Baird Jackson, and Steven C. Hahn have recently taken a similar approach in studying the Abhikas' colonial experience in the town of Okfuskee, the Yuchi community and ceremonial life, and the Cowetas' leadership and invention of the Creek Nation, respec-tively. They have made a significant contribution to our under-standing of these diverse peoples.[7] Moreover, recent histories have shed light on the ordeals of the Louisiana and Texas tribes and their experiences in the West. This work aims to supple-ment and extend this growing body of scholarship.[8]

My motivation for writing this book was not only to explore the early history of the Alabamas and Coushattas, but also to examine how migration and diaspora shaped a people's world-view, knowledge, and identity. "Diaspora" (an ancient Greek term meaning to sow or scatter) is defined as the dispersion of a people or group from an original homeland to another space. Diaspora can be a result of forceful expulsion by an external power or a voluntary movement in order to improve economic or political circumstances of a people, or a com-bination of both external and internal forces. Diasporic com-munities often maintain a collective memory or myth of their ancestral place and seek to rebuild former spaces elsewhere. Groups may participate in a return movement to the homeland and reconnect with those who may have stayed behind. Al-though this connection to the "stayers" is important, the stron-gest bond is created among the migrants, who form an identity and solidarity through shared diasporic experiences. Migration to another space is not without difficulty. Dispersion is trau-matic and may threaten stability. Native occupants or resident governments may not welcome a migrant group; violent con-flict may erupt. Despite these challenges, diasporic commu-nities often enjoy success in their new space. Indeed, some diasporic groups become more successful at surviving than those who stay behind, in part because of the migrants' ability to accommodate and adjust to change.[9]

The study of diasporic communities has recently gained considerable attention from scholars, particularly the study of African diasporas in North America under slavery, postcolonial European diasporas, and the formation of transnational communities in modern times.[10] Surprisingly, very little attention in the growing diasporic literature has been afforded to American Indians, who experienced migration and diaspora as much as any group. By considering the American Indian experience through the lens of diasporic analysis, we can better understand several recurring issues that arise among groups or communities that have experienced this process, irrespective of time and space. Why, for instance, does a community migrate and become part of a diaspora? How does a diasporic community create new sacred spaces and interact with new peoples it encounters? How does migration and diaspora change people's lives and their connection to each other and those around them? How are ideas of identity and sovereignty linked with diaspora? Does a diasporic community become more resilient over time? This study seeks to answer these questions by examining the Alabama and Coushatta migrations over three centuries.

In *New Diasporas: The Mass Exodus, Dispersal and Regrouping of Migrant Communities*, Nicholas Van Hear states, "Diaspora populations tend to have among the most complex migration histories."[11] This statement rings true when applied to the Alabama and Coushatta experience. The Alabamas and Coushattas saw a history of migration, diaspora, and recreation. They had origins in present-day Tennessee, Alabama, and Mississippi, but they quit these homelands for central Alabama to escape the ramifications of European contact and settlement between the late sixteenth and seventeenth centuries. By the late seventeenth century the surviving Alabamas and Coushattas had created a coalescent community along the Alabama River. Their diaspora and union became part of their oral traditions and the building blocks of creating a collective identity. Their new homeland became a sacred space— an area that physically and emotionally connected them to the land. By 1700, they had established towns and villages and made economic, political, and social exchanges and networks with their new multiethnic neighbors.

In the eighteenth century, rival European colonial powers battled for control over the southern interior of North America, affording the Alabamas and Coushattas political and economic opportunities. Once the winner among the European powers emerged, however, the Alabama and Coushatta position as balancers among contentious empires was lost. Many Alabamas and Coushattas therefore began a gradual westward exodus, one that would last until the mid-nineteenth century.

Their migrations had both voluntary and involuntary dimensions. They chose when to leave and where to move because of their own internal political decision-making process, yet external circumstances prompted their decisions. They made difficult choices to migrate away from their ancestral lands, but with the goal of preserving and re-creating their world on their own terms between larger groups or empires. In their journey west to Spanish Louisiana in the early 1800s and then to East Texas in the 1820s, they in essence created new spaces in which they stood at the center, permanently etching their experiences into memories and oral traditions. They encountered new cultures and peoples that changed their ethos, concepts, and relationships.

Not all left for the west, however. Some Alabama and Coushatta families chose to stay behind in both Alabama and Louisiana. Despite the separation, migrants continued to connect with the stayers; they maintained economic, social, and personal relationships with each other. Stayer communities also provided Alabama and Coushatta migrants with a place of refuge when a retreat from the chaotic borderlands became necessary. A people's solidarity can be lost in the process of separation, relocation, accommodation, and settlement into new communities, but the Alabamas and Coushattas were able to build and maintain their sovereignty and identity despite five hundred years of trauma and change.

Like many scholars who have undertaken similar projects, I have adopted in this book a thematic rather than a strict chronological approach. In this study, I often describe the

Alabamas and Coushattas as an entire group when individual names are absent from records. Because they kept few written records in the early period, namely from the sixteenth to the eighteenth centuries, I have relied on Spanish, French, British, Mexican, and Anglo-American documents.[12] To mitigate errors from these sources, I crosschecked disputed or unclear information and based my analysis on the best information available. This study captures the attitudes, emotions, worldviews, thoughts, and actions of the Alabamas and Coushattas by embracing ethnohistorical methodology. To balance and supplement written documents, I incorporate the Alabama and Koasati languages, anthropological analysis, and archaeological findings. Throughout the text, I have also included examples of Alabama and Coushatta oral traditions, recorded and compiled by Howard Martin in the 1930s and 1940s on the Alabama-Coushatta Indian Reservation in Texas. According to Martin, the elder storytellers he interviewed remembered oral traditions that had remained largely unaffected by the cultural changes resulting from pressures to assimilate in the twentieth century. Whether or not their memories were completely accurate, these recordings are invaluable as they reveal Alabama and Coushatta perspectives and voices.[13]

By tracing their history over many centuries, this book examines how the Alabamas and Coushattas developed and retained their identity and sovereignty through their western migrations. Chapter 1 explores Alabama and Coushatta origins from ancient Mississippian chiefdoms, their respective development in the Southeast, and their initial migration and diaspora in the wake of European contact and disease and American Indian slavery. It traces how they merged as a diasporic community and together created a new sacred space in central Alabama. Chapter 2 follows the Alabamas and Coushattas' new vision of their world after their migration and contact with Europeans. It examines how new ideas and relationships— political, economic, and social—developed as the Alabamas and Coushattas established a center for trade in the heart of their territory. Chapter 3 explores the political landscape of the Southeast as European and American Indian peoples struggled for hegemony over the territory. This chapter discusses how the Alabamas and Coushattas took advantage of their position in between colonial rivals, yet began a second migration when their status declined. Chapter 4 traces how the Alabamas and Coushattas re-created another homeland in Louisiana and explores their relationships with American Indian, European, and Anglo neighbors. This chapter also examines the motivations behind the third migration of the Alabamas and Coushattas. Chapter 5 details the nineteenth-century Alabama and Coushatta community in East Texas and its alliance with neighboring emigrant peoples. It also examines how the Alabamas and Coushattas played contending powers off each other on the eve of the Texas Revolution in their efforts to remain on their lands. Finally, Chapter 6 explores the end of their migration and journey west. It examines how they faced head-on pressures of western expansion and how, despite extreme hardship, Alabama and Coushatta leaders negotiated permanent title to land.

History is replete with episodes of forced and voluntary migrations and diasporas in Africa, Asia, Europe, and the Americas. Destabilization or depopulation of a community can be the result of changes in the environment, such as flooding, depletion of game, or deforestation. These can in turn lead to disease, increased warfare, or threat of military conquest. Those who survive may either migrate in large groups, as extended families, or as individuals scattered among a number of destinations. Many survive these unpredictable situations and stay in their new homeland for an extended period, establishing lasting connections. Yet many others, whose new host communities or countries are hostile to migrants, may be forced to flee again. Such events occur in all regions and cultures of the world to this day.

This study considers American Indian migration and resettlement as a series of diasporas. Exploring the early history of the Alabamas and Coushattas as a microcosm of larger, multi-ethnic diasporas throughout history can help us better understand the complexities of human movement, the internal and external relationships of migrant peoples, and the meaning of social and political relationships within families, clans, and communities. The Alabamas and Coushattas are a unique people with a distinct history and culture worthy of study in its own right. This book, however, is not only a study of an American Indian people, but it is also part of an ongoing global history of diaspora and coalescence, migration and settlement, continuity and change, and survival.

1
Mississippian Origins and the Postcontact World

Alabama and Coushatta oral tradition describes how Aba Mikko created the Alabamas and Coushattas from clay in a cave deep beneath the earth. The Alabamas and Coushattas lived protected underground for a very long time, until one day they decided to explore the world above them. As they began the long journey upward, they stopped three times to make camp and rest. They eventually reached the entrance of the cave, where a magnificent tree grew. At nightfall, the Alabamas emerged from one side of the tree's root, and the Coushattas left from the other. Upon surfacing, they heard an owl hooting. Many of the Alabamas and Coushattas, frightened of the strange noise, returned to the security of the cave and never left again. This explained why their numbers were so few.[1]

While this recollection describes the beginnings of the Alabama and Coushatta people, it may also provide insight into their historical past by recalling their ancestors who built monumental clay mounds—sacred spaces where ancient ceremonies of birth, renewal, and purification took place. Their exit from the underground cave symbolized being born from Mother Earth and starting a life that was dependent on cultivation and bountiful harvests. The Alabamas and Coushattas developed separate societies in the Southeast, yet they shared similar roots in their early history; they came out of the same tree, but in opposite directions.

What they both experienced after the European encounter in the sixteenth century would shock their world. Their people dispersed after disease, depopulation, and slave raids ravaged their communities. This began the Alabama and Coushatta diaspora. Their long journey ahead was arduous and not for those who lacked courage. As the oral tradition recalls, some of their people returned to the cave after hearing the hooting of an owl, a symbol of the challenges of the European encounter that lay ahead. The Alabamas and Coushattas who were scared of hooting owls did not survive in the new world.

Alabama and Coushatta Ancestors

Like many indigenous southeastern peoples, both Alabama and Coushatta ancestors originated from the Mississippian culture that existed between 1000 to 1600 C.E.. The Mississippian period defined peoples who dominated the Southeast and Midwest prior to European contact. These civilizations organized their social and political worlds into chiefdoms—ranked, centralized societies consisting of numerous towns and villages controlled by a hereditary chief or elite group. Chiefdoms ranged from simple to complex: simple chiefdoms had one decision-making level over the town, whereas complex chiefdoms had two- to three-tiered hierarchies that ruled over a community, at times numbering in the tens of thousands. Paramount chiefdoms were types of complex chiefdoms in which control had expanded to reach a wider range of territory and the people that occupied it.[2]

Settlements within chiefdoms were largely self-sufficient. In complex chiefdoms, the chief who led the population may have been considered semidivine. Leadership also was more centralized, and the material wealth and status between the chief and the rest of the population was more pronounced. For example, the chief siphoned all surpluses, including labor, in order to fund public works, military expeditions, and feasts (both public and private). In simple chiefdoms, however, the gap between the chief and the commoners would have been small: the chief would have to produce his own food, and his wealth would have been similar to that of the rest of the population. In recent years, scholars have questioned the chief's absolute control over chiefdoms. Most now believe that although the chief led his community, he often received support and advice from nobles and had to receive general support from the commoners, irrespective of the size of the chiefdom. After European contact, the power of the chief depended on his political maneuvering and his ability to lead.[3]

Like other Mississippian peoples, the ancestors of the Alabamas and Coushattas settled near rivers or streams, where they built plazas, temples, ceremonial centers, and villages of clustered wattle and daub houses. Each town or village within the chiefdom specialized in the production of various foodstuffs, especially maize, beans, and squash. Hunting and gathering remained important, but maize was the staple food. Flat-topped, pyramidal earthen mounds were main features of their settlements. Surrounded by open plazas where social and religious activities occurred, the great mounds often served as residences for chiefs, storage sites for the skeletal remains of former leaders, and temples for worship. Ceremonial life centered on activities located near or atop the mounds. These earthen pyramids represented the community's social identity and symbolized the overall health and strength of the chiefdom.[4]

Could the Alabama and Coushatta caves described in their creation story represent their historical roots as mound builders in the days of chiefdoms? Indeed, it is a possibility.[5] From oral history and archaeological evidence, we know that the ancient Alabamas and Coushattas both had roots in Mississippian chiefdoms and shared similar political and socioeconomic characteristics, yet they lived hundreds of miles apart and developed quite separately.

The historic Alabamas were most likely a part of the Moundville complex chiefdom that dominated western Alabama and eastern Mississippi for almost five hundred years prior to European contact (1000–1450 C.E.).[6] Moundville initially developed out of the Shiloh chiefdom in the western Tennessee Valley.

Shiloh then cycled (known as the Moundville variant), and part of its inhabitants migrated to the Tombigbee and the Warrior river valleys sometime between 1050 and 1100 C.E. and developed simple to complex chiefdoms from which later Alabamas originated.[7]

Moundville was a paramount chiefdom in the region by 1300, extending 50 kilometers along the Black Warrior River. The center of the chiefdom was located near present-day Tuscaloosa, Alabama, and it encompassed over three hundred acres of fertile floodplain. The terrain consisted of various hardwoods, including sweet gum, black gum, bald cypress, holly, hickory, chestnut, and oak. The floodplain also had an abundance of edible plants, seeds, and fruits. It was an ideal location for cultivating corn; the high water table preserved crops during droughts. Moundville's inhabitants also had a variety of fish and game animals to hunt, principally deer, turkey, and rabbit.[8] Moundville's chiefs and nobles strictly controlled the nonelite, who were responsible for providing surplus food as tribute.[9]

The social and political landscape included twenty-six earthen mounds, a central plaza, a palisade, and scattered settlements throughout the valley. Moundville towns were square, with the length of each side measuring about four hundred feet long. Surrounding the villages along the river's bank were defensive palisades to protect the occupants from intruders. Outside the main villages were numerous homesteads up and down the river. Among the artifacts found in the villages during various archaeological expeditions spanning over 150 years were shell gorgets, ornate copper pendants, manufactured greenstone axes, elaborate stone discs, and decorative pottery. Outside of pottery, most of the goods were not of Moundville manufacture; their economy depended on trade with other polities. Between 1200 and 1350 C.E., the Moundville chiefdom underwent a period of military expansion. Smaller and weaker chiefdoms located north near the upper Black Warrior River and the Tennessee River fell to Moundville domination or relocated.[10]

During its paramountcy between 1300 and 1450 C.E., the chiefdom's center began showing signs of stress. Long-distance exchange started to decline, and soil depletion and exhausted resources further strained the exposed community. These factors may have led to the Moundville inhabitants' out-migration from the center to the hinterlands. By 1450, settlement patterns began reverting to nuclear villages increasingly independent of Moundville.[11]

It was during this period of instability and decentralization that simple chiefdoms emerged, a common fissioning or cycling process under chiefly polities. These simple chiefdoms, controlled by a single-level elite subgroup, established smaller, nonpalisaded towns and villages. The groups included Alibamus and Miculasas on the Tombigbee River and Taliepacanas, Moclixas, and Apafalayas on the Black Warrior River; the historic Alabamas most likely came out of these simple chiefdoms. Unlike the inhabitants of Moundville, they relied more heavily on wild foods rather than on the large-scale production of maize. By the sixteenth century these simple chiefdoms suffered from a general decline in health resulting from malnutrition, and in this weakened state, they first encountered the Spaniards.[12]

The historic Coushattas most likely were once part of the more distant Coste chiefdom, whose main town was on Bussell Island in the Little Tennessee River (associated with the Hiwassee Island Focus).[13] Coste was a simple chiefdom closely affiliated with the larger and powerful Coosa paramount chiefdom. Coste incorporated peoples who lived along the Tennessee and Hiwassee rivers and their tributaries in modern-day Tennessee. Its inhabitants had large sedentary communities near the banks of rivers or on large islands and supported an agricultural economy; they cultivated corn, hunted game animals, and gathered wild plants and fruits. Closely surrounding the houses and buildings were stockades, allowing little space for cornfields or gardens. Coste dwellings circled an open-air ceremonial court, public buildings, and other community structures atop earthen mounds, comparable to those found at Moundville.[14]

Recent archaeological studies have linked the two chiefdoms, suggesting that Coste also may have originated from the Shiloh chiefdom in western Tennessee and its Moundville variant. Instead of budding and migrating to the Black Warrior and Tombigbee river valleys, as had the Alabamas' ancestors, Coushatta ancestors moved to the north and created the Coste chiefdom in the eastern Tennessee Valley sometime between 1050 and 1100 c.e. Moreover, archaeologist Ned Jenkins has argued that the ancient connection between the Coushattas and the Alabamas is evident considering the same "spaghetti style" shell gorget found in both Koasati ceramics (Dallas/Koasati phase) in eastern Tennessee and those found in Moundville (phase II–III) in the Warrior Valley.[15]

The Eve of Diaspora

The simple chiefdoms that would eventually form the historic Alabamas and Coushattas all experienced the impact of Spanish conquistador Hernando de Soto, who dropped anchor in present-day Tampa Bay, Florida, in 1539. In his quest for gold and slaves, he brought with him over six hundred soldiers, slaves, and priests, as well as 240 horses and an uncounted number of mules and dogs (namely bloodhounds for tracking down Natives). Soto's actions, followed by European settlement, forever changed the lives of southeastern peoples.[16]

Inhabitants of the Coste (Coushatta) chiefdom first met the Spaniards on July 1, 1540.[17] The chief of Coste "came forth to receive them in peace" and invited the Spaniards to take shelter in one of the villages.[18] The meeting quickly turned sour when Soto's men, without permission of the chief, took corn from some *barbacoas* and searched through houses, confiscating what they found valuable.[19]

Unnoticed by the Spaniards, the chief left to gather and arm his men at the main town on Bussell Island at the mouth of the Little Tennessee River. The island was difficult to reach, but the Spaniards found Lenoir's Shoal that stretched across the river. Upon their arrival, the Spaniards faced 1,500 armed warriors, who violently threw their fists up into the air while yelling and shouting insults; they wanted retribution for the Spaniards' blatant disrespect for their leader and their property. A group of Coushattas charged onto the plaza with their bows and arrows and clubbed five or six Spaniards. According to one Spanish account, the Coushattas were "so bold and anxious to fight that there was not a single Indian who in speaking with a Spaniard did not boast that he would scratch out his eyes, and they would have done so."[20] They quickly proved to the Spanish soldiers that they were fearless and convinced Soto that any action taken against their people would be reckless. Completely surrounded by enraged warriors, Soto surprisingly turned against his own men; he suddenly displayed his anger as he yelled at fellow Spaniards for their carelessness and beat a few of them with a warrior's club, showing the townspeople that he disapproved of his soldiers' thievery. Soto had to avoid a battle because he and his men were poorly armed and his support troops were back at the camp.[21]

The chief believed that Soto wished them no harm, so he and twelve of his council members conceded and escorted the Spaniards back to camp on the island's savannah. After they were out of sight from the armed warriors of Coste, Soto seized the chief and his principal men, placed them in chains and collars, and threatened to burn them all alive because they had "laid hands on the Christians."[22] The Spaniards stayed for several days and left only when the chief met Soto's demands for a guide and porters on July 9, 1540.[23]

Soto later traveled through the territory along the Black Warrior River that the Alabamas' ancestors claimed prior to European contact. On November 18, 1540, the Spaniards approached the remnants of the Moundville chiefdom, including Taliepacana. The main town had twenty households surrounded by the White Mound; its inhabitants had fled, so Soto and his men stayed there for a few days. Soto described the neighboring Moclixa chiefdom as situated nine miles north, with the main village located along a high bluff facing the Black Warrior River. The people of Moclixa had evacuated with their food supply, but later harassed and unsuccessfully invaded the Spaniards camped there. Days later, Chief Apafalaya, who controlled one of the largest mound centers of the same name in the valley outside of Moundville (at the Snow's Bend site), met Soto. Though Chief Apafalaya controlled fortified and abundantly supplied nuclear settlements in the surrounding area, Soto took the chief as a prisoner, demanding that he act as an interpreter and guide as the Spaniards left for the Tombigbee Valley.[24]

The chiefs of Alibamu and Miculasa who controlled settlements along the Tombigbee River met Soto when he entered the chiefdom of Chicaza in the winter of 1541. After considerable delay, the chief of Chicaza agreed to meet the Spaniard on January 3. The chief, accompanied by two tributary chiefs of Alibamu and Miculasa, appeared before Soto on a litter held up by his subjects. Archaeologists have not found Miculasa's location, but Alibamu was northwest of Chicaza near Line Creek (close to the present-day state line between Alabama and Mississippi and near the former boundaries of the Moundville and Tombigbee chiefdoms) and included numerous small towns each with at least fifteen households. After Soto battled with the Chicazas (which likely included warriors from both Miculasa and Alibamu), the inhabitants of Alibamu led the Spaniards into a trap on April 25, 1541.[25]

They had valuable provisions that Soto's men needed, but messengers from surrounding towns warned those at Alibamu of Soto's location, so they hid their foodstuffs.[26] Consequently, Soto found little maize after ransacking one of the villages. According to Spanish accounts, the Alibamu's fortification was square and had three doors that were too small for a man (let alone his horse) to enter. Near the top of the palisade stood three hundred armed warriors (outnumbering Soto's men) painted in stripes of black, white, yellow, and red, which made them appear as if they wore breeches and doublet. After they daubed red ochre over their bodies, they painted their faces black with red circles around their eyes to frighten their enemies. Some added feathers and threatening horns on their heads.[27]

As soon as Soto's men approached, the warriors beat their drums and shouted a call to war. A battle ensued after one hundred of Soto's men attacked the fort and broke through the door. Alabama warriors aimed at the Spaniards' legs and shot effectively with flint-barbed arrows; if the arrows failed to wound the Spaniards mortally, the edges severely cut them. One arrow struck a Spanish general's helmet and "flew up more than a pike's length in the air."[28] They killed between eight and fifteen of Soto's men and wounded another twenty-five. When the Spaniards reached the innermost palisade, the warriors fled from the structure and escaped across footbridges over a creek; the bridges' tricky footing, however, led some to suffer injury or death as they tried to cross. Spanish soldiers tried to pursue the warriors, but failed when their horses were unable to cross the steep-sided creek. The Spaniards searched for food and supplies within the fort but found nothing. Soto's poor military strategy sealed his defeat, and he left the province of Alibamu empty handed on April 30, 1541.[29]

The encounters with Hernando de Soto confirm the political and social transformation of Native communities from the Mississippian period to the historic one. Alabama and Coushatta ancestors who appear in the historical records left by Soto's men revealed that their respective settlements along the Black Warrior, Tombigbee, and Little Tennessee rivers all had characteristics of simple chiefdoms. The large number of warriors that the Spaniards confronted is evidence that both the Alabama and Coushatta chiefdoms supported a considerable population, albeit smaller than those found under the Moundville chiefdom at its peak in the 1300s. Soto met with their chiefs directly, not groups of noble representatives. There is also no description of these communities treating the chiefs as divine and peerless, such as those found in the paramount chiefdom of Coosa. Indeed, it is likely that the chiefdoms of Coste and the chiefdoms of Alibamu and Miculasa were under the subjection of their neighboring paramount chiefdoms, the Coosa and Chicaza, respectively. Descriptions also demonstrate that their settlement patterns were those of less-populated nuclear households, often surrounding a mound, and sometimes fortified; absent were the grand plazas and centers for trade. This was the political and cultural landscape of the Alabama and Coushatta ancestors on the eve of their diaspora and coalescence.

The Plague

The Alabamas and Coushattas survived initial contact with the Spaniards, but the ramifications of European encounters were extensive: exploitation ravaged postcontact American Indian society. They initially fought against the Spanish and attempted to expel them from their lands. Southeastern peoples quickly learned from these encounters that the invaders wanted to annihilate them. The incredible violence laid against their people left an imprint in their minds. The Spaniards raped and enslaved their women, cut off the noses of men and sent them to neighboring towns to convince others to submit, released their vicious hounds to mangle, dismember, or kill anyone who resisted, and looted and pillaged their towns. The barbarity and greed of Soto probably seemed incomprehensible to many Natives, yet the Spaniards acted with an air of superiority and believed that Providence was on the side of the Spanish, especially as European diseases crippled these southeastern communities.[30]

Even before Soto arrived in the Southeast, European diseases had already spread through American Indian populations. Earlier conquistadors (Ponce de León in 1513, Pedro de Salazar in 1514, Diego Miruelo in 1516, Lucas Vázquez de Ayllón in 1521, and Pánfilo de Narváez in 1528) had ventured to the Floridas and along the Atlantic coastline. Most were on a quest for riches or slaves, but some, like Ayllón, traveled to the Florida coast to establish a Spanish colony. These men, like countless others, unwittingly brought Old World diseases—smallpox, influenza, typhoid, and strains of the bubonic plague—that inflicted high mortality rates among American Indian communities. Massive epidemics eventually spread throughout the South and rapid depopulation of southeastern peoples quickly followed. Some scholars have estimated that up to 90 percent of the original American Indian population died from disease. Many who survived initial outbreaks died later of complications, exposure to new strains and epidemics, or starvation.[31]

After Soto's attempted conquest of the Southeast, Alabama and Coushatta ancestors may have suffered from the devastating effects of introduced European diseases. Although there is neither documentary nor archaeological evidence for disease epidemics in the interior South before 1696, the oral tradition of the Alabamas and Coushattas recounts how disease spread through their communities long before European settlement in the Southeast.[32] According to their memory, disease befell their people, "causing much trouble and grief everywhere."[33] Their ancestors met in a council and agreed to take the disease from the earth to the sky where it would remain; they gathered all of the sickness and placed it in a clay pot. Who would take it away? It was an impossible task for a man or woman, as they were unable to fly, so a snipe spoke: "I will take sickness so far into the sky that it can never return to earth." The chief then tied the pot of sickness to the snipe's legs as it took flight. To the people's disappointment, the snipe came back to earth with the clay pot; the bird's effort had failed. The end of the story proves ominous when the bird dropped the clay pot. When it shattered on the ground, "sickness scattered to all parts of the world again."[34]

This memory may echo the early tragedy and suffering from epidemic diseases brought by Soto and other Spaniards. The Alabamas and Coushattas could no longer contain sickness that inevitably spread suffering and hardship. Even before the bulk of European settlers made contact with the Alabamas and Coushattas, pestilence damaged their weakened chiefdoms. Though the Alabama and Coushatta ancestors who survived the epidemic diseases that swept through their communities maintained their settlements in eastern Mississippi, western Alabama, and eastern Tennessee, they were considerably weakened and more fragmented; it would take a generation to rebuild their strength.

Diaspora and Coalescence

A few decades after Soto's *entrada*, southeastern peoples witnessed a second phase of European contact. The Spanish Crown had staked its claim in the Americas and in 1565 ordered Pedro Menéndez de Avilés to explore and to settle the Floridas. By September 1565, Spain funded the construction of its first fortified settlement at St. Augustine, and one year later established Santa Elena (present-day Parris Island); these coastal outposts facilitated Spanish forays into the interior. The Juan Pardo expedition, launched from Santa Elena in 1566, traversed present-day Georgia, North Carolina, South Carolina, and eastern Tennessee. Pardo's journey initiated the arrival of Spanish colonists and soldiers in the region. Franciscans soon followed and constructed missions in northern Florida, and members of coastal chiefdoms settled within these missions.[35]

The Spanish colonization of the Southeast paled in comparison to the more successful English colonization, especially as England stepped up its efforts in penetrating the region. After many failed attempts and financial disasters in the Americas, England finally founded the southern colonies of Jamestown, Virginia, in 1607, and Charles Town, Carolina, in 1670. Settlers in Charles Town recognized that their colony was a buffer to Spanish Florida, and they courted American Indian allies in order to buttress their military presence against the Spanish. More importantly, the English Crown expected the colony to extract and export local raw materials and resources to London. These resources included American Indian slaves, and Charles Town soon became a commercial center for the slave trade.[36]

Indian slaves were one of the most sought-after commodities throughout the seventeenth century. Alan Gallay has analyzed how various Native communities quickly adapted to this new market. The English, like most Europeans at the time, viewed slavery as a moral, socially acceptable, and legal institution; they deemed it suitable to American Indians, even as an alternative to genocide. Natives, too, understood slavery to be an accepted social institution; under chiefdoms, American Indians owned slaves and considered them as a sign of wealth and strength. Yet with the arrival of a European market for slaves, Indian groups began to consider slaves a commodity that could be exchanged for trade goods, a mind-set that bore full fruit much later when profits from the deer trade declined in the eighteenth century.[37] Prisoners of war were no longer subject to conventional rules of warfare and captivity. Instead, American Indians brought captives to Charles Town and sold the prisoners to the English in exchange for trade goods, such as textiles, metals, weapons, and alcohol. The English then sent the slaves to planters in the North American colonies and the West Indies.[38]

Many American Indians profited from slaving, but many also feared that they too would be vulnerable to slave raids. As the slave trade widened into the interior Southeast, the Alabamas' ancestors were among many who suffered from its expansion. Their simple chiefdoms on the Black Warrior and Tombigbee rivers—including the Alibamu, Miculasa, Taliepacana, and Moclixa—began to break apart sometime in the seventeenth century, most likely because of the disruptions from Soto's entrada, disease, and slaving. In this area, the premier slavers in the middle to late seventeenth century were the Chickasaws, who by this time had moved away from the Tombigbee River and were living at present-day Tupelo, Mississippi. They had earlier established a lucrative relationship with traders in Charles Town, and English agents armed Chickasaw warriors with muskets and led some slaving expeditions against enemy towns.[39] Chickasaw men actively raided Native communities in and around the Mississippi River Valley, as far south as the Gulf of Mexico, and perhaps as far east as the Black Warrior River.[40] In 1699, French explorer and later founder of Louisiana, Pierre Le Moyne d'Iberville, noted that the Chickasaws "were going among all the other nations to make war on them and to carry off as many slaves as they could, whom they buy and use in extensive trading, to the distress of all these Indian nations."[41] The Chickasaws' years of successful slaving had convinced the French that they were the dominant American Indian force in the Southeast.

Indian slavery also had an impact on the people of the Coushatta chiefdom of Coste on the Little Tennessee River. After the paramount chiefdom of Coosa fell in the sixteenth century, the Coste chiefdom also shifted to a smaller community organization. Later documentation described Coste as a small town, devoid of the large-scale organization that characterized their previous chiefdom, which likely left them more vulnerable to slave raids.[42] The group that threatened Coste was, undoubtedly, the Westos, who had moved to the Savannah River sometime in the 1660s. The Westos had established a profitable slaving partnership with Virginia and Carolina traders. Westo warriors relentlessly raided communities throughout the Lower South, and they quickly became the enemy of the Florida mission Indians, the coastal Indians, as well as interior groups such as the Cussetas, Cowetas, Cherokees, and Savannahs (who later helped annihilate the Westos in 1682).[43] The Westos' aggressive participation in the capture and sale of Indian slaves led many groups, including the Coushattas, to fear their very name.[44]

After the Westos were eliminated from the interior slave trade, the Coushattas then had to fight off raids by Cherokee slavers, who occupied territory in the Appalachian Mountains in Tennessee and western South Carolina and apparently became involved in the slave trade soon after the Westo monopoly shattered. The Coushattas' dwindling population at Coste was especially vulnerable to enemy raids. Throughout the late 1680s, the Cherokees repeatedly captured the greatly outnumbered Coushattas and sold them to Carolina traders.[45]

Slavers mainly targeted and captured women and children; enemy warriors often tortured and killed men that survived the attacks. The frequency of slave raids, coupled by losses from disease, was the breaking point for many of the Mississippian chiefdoms, including those of the historic Alabamas and Coushattas.[46] They had great difficulty protecting their communities from attack, forcing them to reassess their situation. These people began to break apart and flee from affected areas; in all cases, they quit their ancestral lands for safer ground where they could regroup and revitalize their severely damaged populations. Indeed, this migration was reminiscent of the actions of their ancient Mississippian ancestors; chiefdoms (including Moundville) often fissioned and reorganized when communities suffered from instability or decline. It is understandable, then, that the Alabamas and Coushattas chose a path of diaspora not only to escape, but also to shape a new landscape on their own terms.

Sometime in the seventeenth century, the Alabamas' ancestors from the chiefdoms of Alibamu and Miculasa on the Tombigbee, and the peoples of Taliepacana, Moclixa, and perhaps Apafalaya on the Black Warrior, migrated to the northern Alabama River, near its confluence with the Coosa and Tallapoosa

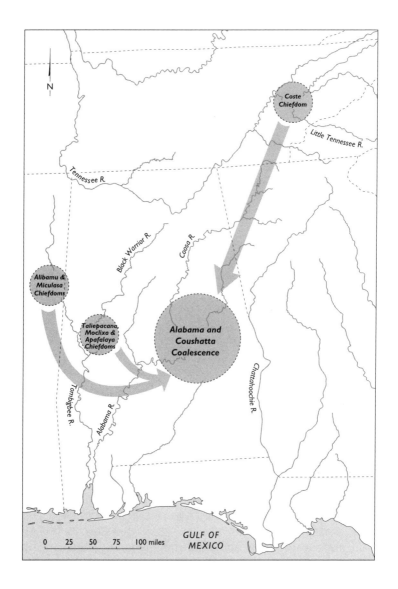

Alabama and Coushatta diaspora and coalescence

rivers (near present-day Montgomery, Alabama).[47] This group became known collectively as the Alabamas. The Coushattas, who may have followed the southward path of the scattered Coosas after the collapse of their paramount chiefdom, also quit their homeland in Tennessee and migrated to the same location as the Alabamas sometime in the seventeenth century. According to reports by Spanish explorer Marcos Delgado in 1686, the Coushattas had already settled among the Alabamas.[48]

Both the Alabamas and Coushattas were drawn to the upper Alabama River valley. The new location along protective bluffs near the confluence of the Alabama, Coosa, and Tallapoosa rivers provided a better position for the Alabamas and Coushattas to make alliances with their western neighbors who were coalescing into the Upper Creeks. The Alabamas and Coushattas now comprised a larger polity, and they were less vulnerable to raids. They also were better located for trading with the English, and later the French, by the start of the eighteenth century.

The exact dates and details of the Alabama and Coushatta diaspora and coalescence are unknown, but we can find their voice through oral tradition, which not only preserved beliefs and values, but also recorded history.[49] The story "The Origin of the Alabama and Coushatta Tribe," sheds light on these two peoples who migrated from their ancestral homelands and formed a new American Indian community in the Southeast. Alabama and Coushatta storytellers passed down through generations a memory of their ancestors traveling deep beneath the earth before reaching the surface. After much time had passed, they emerged at opposite ends of a tree's root. The tree represented the Cosmic Tree (Tree of Life), where life for the Alabamas and Coushattas began. Once they saw the light of day, their ancestors discovered the Alabama River. The Alabamas and Coushattas established their villages in two bodies. Though they had different origins, they had "always remained near each other."[50]

Although separate people, the origin story places them as close entities; they both emerged from the Cosmic Tree, symbolic of their creation and the center of their world. Their people crossed paths along their journey and emerged separately, yet joined in a diaspora and re-created their world along the Alabama River. It marked the beginning of their new existence bound together. To outsiders, they became known as the Alabamas and Coushattas. Over the next century, their bond distinguished them from other southeastern peoples. While some of their practices and beliefs were generally similar to their southeastern neighbors, based on common Mississippian roots, there were enough differences to set the Alabamas and Coushattas apart.

Linguistic evidence supports this origin story, as the Alabamas and Coushattas shared a similar language, undoubtedly owing to their Mississippian origins. Alabama and Coushatta (Koasati) languages are part of the eastern Muskogean language family (whose speakers include the Apalachees, Mikasukis, Hitchitis, Creeks, and Seminoles); the western branch includes the Choctaw and Chickasaw languages.[51] Although Alabama and Koasati are different, many linguists describe them as pairs of dialects, or a subdivision of a single language.[52] These shared linguistic links based on their common ancestry in the early Mississippian period (the Shiloh/ Moundville variant, 1050–1100 c.e.) allowed the Alabamas and Coushattas to communicate and to connect socially and politically. More importantly, these linguistic similarities would have been a "pull factor" for the Coushattas as they left the Little Tennessee River.

Based on oral history and records of European observers, the Alabamas and Coushattas created an alliance in central Alabama by the start of the eighteenth century. We know why they left their homelands, but what motivated the people to unite after their diaspora? Diaspora communities throughout history have a common characteristic: vulnerability. Migrants often encounter indigenous groups that have prior claims to territory; newcomers are not always welcome. Developing connections with other like-minded migrants not only facilitated the re-creation of home, but also aided in protection. Perhaps the immediate reason for the Alabama and Coushatta union is that they found safety in numbers. The Alabamas and Coushattas were in the same situation: they were both diasporic communities forced to migrate by larger, more powerful groups. They had relatively small populations compared to their enemy neighbors like the Chickasaws, Choctaws, and Cherokees. Alliances were critical to survival in a new environment and were products of diaspora. As they crossed paths in their migrations, the unification of their people equaled strength. An alliance provided them with increased military power and the ability to confront their enemies; it was a necessary plan in the postcontact world.

Creating a Community

Alabama and Coushatta migrants established towns and villages along protective bluffs near the river as they had under chiefdoms. The land they chose provided abundant fertile soil, and according to eighteenth century traveler Caleb Swan, it had ample natural resources "capable of producing everything necessary to the comfort and convenience of mankind."[53] The banks of the rivers rarely flooded as canebrakes and thick cypress trees covered the flood plain. The land offered both meadows and woods, including pine, wild cherry, mulberry, red oak, sassafras, basswood, beech, elm, and hickory trees.[54] It was a comparable environment, if not better, to the land they left behind.

A people's connection to the land often describes the development of a sacred landscape—a place where they not only dwelled, but also associated with their creation. Alabama and Coushatta creation stories described their people emerging together from the Tree of Life, the *axis mundi*, along the Alabama River. Their history as a coalescent people began here. The Alabamas and Coushattas developed the southern landscape to mimic their old homeland. They sought to create not just a new life, but also a new sacred space. The Alabamas and Coushattas performed ancient rites to sanctify new land, such as the ceremony called *polohpokí*, which likely originated in the days of the Mississippian chiefdoms. The ritual, practiced through the nineteenth century, blessed new fields by assembling the townspeople who sat in a circle while leaders consecrated the untouched ground. Afterward, according to ancient traditions, it became part of their sacred landscape recognized by their own people as well as outsiders.[55]

Examining the Alabama and Koasati languages reveals this connection to their sacred spaces and their environment. In the Alabama language, the term *ihanni*, or land, was equivalent to "whole world," or *ihanni onáami*, translated as "entire land." As the Alabamas and Coushattas coalesced, they emerged from the center of the world. It was a place that they created and claimed together.[56] Their very names reflected their relationship with the land; "Alabama" means "vegetation gatherers," and "Coushatta," or "Koasati," is translated as "white cane." Both illustrate the environment in which they lived and worked.[57]

"Land" in Koasati translates as "high spot of land in a swamp," "salt land where no trees grow," and "to be on rolling land." The Alabamas had similar words including descriptions for "bottom, or black land," "dry land," and "hilly land."[58] These illustrate their occupation in the southern woodlands, with similar terrain, soil, flora, and fauna. The Alabamas and Coushattas also had words to describe arable land (*ihaanikáano*), cleared land (*tamüoyha*), and cultivated land (*alchiiya*). The Koasati expression, "to dwell on a piece of land" (*pa:á:tan*) is related to *pa:atínnin*, meaning, "to burn the ground clear of brush," the key action in order to produce a productive crop. The Alabamas and Coushattas also used words to mark their space, including land posts *ihaani ittatipkachi* in Alabama, and *ihá:ni tipkací* in Koasati. Interestingly, the first term means "earth, land, ground, country," whereas the second refers to "divider."[59] At each point of settlement in their diasporas, these expressions portray their experiences of creating new sacred landscapes by clearing the land, building towns and dwellings, making trails to hunting grounds and trading posts, and denoting territorial boundaries of their spaces.

The Alabamas and Coushattas proved that they could adapt to their new surroundings. As observed by Spanish explorer Marcos Delgado in 1686, the Alabamas and Coushattas built a prosperous, interlocking community of towns and villages that covered central Alabama. The main Coushatta town was known as Coosada (which also included the village of Little Coosada). First recognized as the town of Coste (or Acoste, taken from the remnant chiefdom of the same name), it was later known as Cussawtie by the English, or Conchaty by the French. Marcos Delgado reported that its members supported over five hundred warriors, but his estimates failed to include the number of women and children, who were a substantial part of the population. Part of this same group founded the town of Tubani, nine miles northwest of the main forks of the Alabama River; Delgado noted that they had around two hundred warriors. Taskigi (Tuskegee) was another Coushatta town located near Tubani.[60]

The Alabamas supported more towns compared to the Coushattas, and in the late seventeenth century had over five hundred warriors.[61] Delgado identified the Alabama town of Pagna (Pakana) at the forks of the Alabama River. This town, in the heart of the Alabama Nation, proved to be a major diplomatic player in the eighteenth century (in 1760, it had fifty gunmen). Many chiefs from this town consequently provided important leadership for the Alabamas and Coushattas and their Creek neighbors. The most notable leaders from Pakana included Opoyheatly (known as the Grand Chief of the Alabamas) and Captain Pakana (a distinguished war chief).[62]

Delgado also mentioned the town of Culasa (possibly the same as the later-known town Mucclassa), located south along the Coosa River. By 1702, this village had 150 warriors and had relocated closer to the confluence of the Alabama River (possibly on the Tallapoosa). Mucclassa, an influential town, was on the Tallapoosa River near Harwill Mill Creek as early as 1686. Mucclassa had thirty warriors in 1761, and by 1764, they had increased to fifty. The influential leader The Wolf King, or The Wolf, hailed from this town.[63]

Tawasa (listed as "Tuave" by Delgado or "Tuasi" during the Soto entrada) was located near the juncture of the Alabama River system and had approximately one hundred warriors in the late seventeenth century. Delgado also listed "Aymamu" (Alibamu) as another town, but records of this town, as well as archaeological findings, are absent. An explanation may be found in Charles Levasseur's account of his travels to Alabama in 1700. Levasseur identified the town of Little Okchai (Hookchoieooche) as another Alabama town, possibly part of

The Alabama Nation, 1717

the original Alibamu town that was located at Okchai on the east side of the Coosa River shortly after 1686. It had different locations and branch-settlements along the lower Coosa River (above the forks of the Alabama River), the lower Tallapoosa River, and Hillabee Creek. Little Okchai became a significant town in the Alabama Nation by the mid-eighteenth century. The esteemed leader The Mortar resided in Little Okchai, but also spoke on behalf of the town of Okchai as well; Alabamas and Coushattas resided in both towns (in 1760 they had twenty gunmen there). Later both Okchai and Little Okchai always negotiated together with Europeans as part of the Alabama Nation. Levasseur also identified Tompowa as an Alabama town, located near the juncture of the Alabama River system. In 1760, the French listed seventy warriors there.[64]

One Shawnee village, Chaouanons, located near Coosada on the east bank of the Alabama River also became part of the Alabama-Coushatta community. Between 1729 and 1750 the Coushattas welcomed Shawnee refugees from the North, approximately 180 adult males and an undisclosed number of women and children. Many Shawnees kept their own identity, but others amalgamated into the Alabama and Coushatta culture, probably through intermarriage.[65] This incorporation added to the overall strength of the Alabamas and Coushattas by increasing the availability of warriors.

The Alabamas and Coushattas, like many migrants, quickly re-created not only their physical world, but also their social and political one. Not surprisingly, town organization and construction mimicked those of the chiefdoms. Individual houses surrounded the town, and most households had summer and winter homes as well as storage buildings. At the center of the town were public buildings and a carefully maintained main plaza, where all ceremonies, dances, games, and rituals took place. Within the ceremonial plaza was the chunkey yard where warriors played games; it was a cleared area often sunken two to three feet into the ground. In the center of the yard stood a thirty- to forty-foot pole that men and women used for this single-pole ball game once practiced by their ancient ancestors. To exhibit military prowess, corners of the yard often had slave posts on which the skulls and scalps of enemies hung.[66]

Although Alabama and Coushatta towns usually acted cooperatively, each was autonomous and ruled by a *miko*, or leader (usually referred to as a "chief" in the nineteenth century), a council of elders, and a *tastanaigi* (head warrior). The miko often spoke on behalf of the town, but rarely dictated authority over the town council. Some Alabamas upheld a caste system allowing for hereditary mikoships like those found under chiefdoms, but council members usually selected a town's miko and had the authority to replace the miko at anytime. Though government rested on consensus, the miko represented and led the town, and sometimes spoke for multiple towns and villages, which was reminiscent of leaders under the chiefdoms. The Alabama and Coushatta political world, like so many others of southeastern peoples after European contact, was autonomous on a local (or village) level, with shared decision making in order to incorporate diverse diasporic groups.[67]

The overall picture that emerges from the earliest historical documents and maps is of small Alabama and Coushatta communities that merged and relocated frequently. Marcos Delgado recognized the coalescence and union of the Alabamas and Coushattas as early as 1686, but his references to them clearly indicated two entities. About twenty years later, the English and the French referred to both groups collectively as the "Alabama Nation"; the Coushattas were often absent in written records. What can explain their absence from many of the documents? One can speculate that the Alabamas, who supported more towns and warriors, acted more as a chiefdom to the Coushattas by the eighteenth century. The Alabamas seemed to have placed the Coushattas in a more subordinate position, at least politically, within the newly formed polity. For example, Alabama mikos in the early eighteenth century, such as Deerfoot and Opoyheatly, were among those whom the Europeans primarily negotiated with for trade and diplomacy within the Alabama Nation. The Coushattas certainly benefited from such relations, but they seem to have had a reduced political role in the first decades of the eighteenth century.[68] Despite the possible unequal balance of power between the Alabamas and Coushattas, town leaders acted cooperatively and generally benefited from sharing common interests. This characteristic would have resembled, though on a much smaller scale, the macrosocial organization of the Mississippian chiefdoms.[69]

Bonds of Kinship

As they created a new community, Alabama and Coushatta men and women secured their alliance through intermarriage, gradually creating extensive kinship ties. Indeed, kinship ties with residents of Alabama and Coushatta towns were common; many shared both Alabama and Coushatta family members. It is not clear when Alabamas and Coushattas first began to inter-marry, but it is likely that it occurred after their diaspora and increased over decades of living in close proximity to each other. Alabama and Coushatta *ayiksa* (matriclans traced through the mother's family) coalesced, just as the people had after their diaspora.[70] Alabama and Coushatta clans represented a totemic system in which family groups believed that their clan originated from ancestors representing female animals, insects, plants, or natural phenomena. Each clan held its animal or phenomenon as a sacred entity, and clan members discouraged hunting or eating their clan animal. According to oral tradition, the Alabama and Coushatta clans originated when a dense fog left their ancestors blind to their surroundings, forcing them to use their sense of touch to locate food. While hunting, the Alabamas and Coushattas became separated into small groups but stayed within shouting distance. As time passed, one of the groups saw a great eastern wind sweep the fog away from their lands. The group who had first seen this wind adopted the Wind clan. The remaining groups took the name of the first animal that had appeared to them after the fog cleared. Each group thereafter belonged to a clan symbolizing their ancient ancestors.[71]

Clans common to both the Alabamas and Coushattas included the Beaver, Wildcat, Lion or Panther, Bear, Alligator (now extinct), Turkey, and Daddy Longlegs. The Alabamas' clans also included the Wolf (now extinct), Bird, Skunk, Salt, and Wind (Chief John Abbey, who died in 1910, was the last Wind clan member), all found in the southern woodlands.[72] Clans comprised many different families who were not necessarily "blood" relatives. Clan members often had no specific genealogical connections to each other. Genealogical relationships were possible, but unimportant. Clans were exogamous; members married outside their own clan and lineage. Thus, Alabamas and Coushattas often intermarried—a tradition that they still practice today—as long as they were members of different clans. This intermarriage tied the Alabamas and Coushattas together and reduced the likelihood of marriage between cousins.[73]

Each Alabama and Coushatta clan also belonged to one of two moieties: *hathagaigi*, or "white people" (also known as "those who stick together"), and *tcilokogalgi*, or "people of a different speech" (often associated with "reds"). The distinction between moieties is believed to be analogous to the differences between four-legged animals and birds. Since the days of the Mississippian chiefdoms, southeastern peoples associated the color white with purity, peace, and unification. These "white" clans were responsible for maintaining peace among the people. The designated tcilokogalgi clans, on the other hand, were associated with war, fear, disunity, and conflict. These divisions also applied to Alabama and Coushatta towns; certain towns were "white," others "red." Moreover, the miko from a white town was from a white clan, and a miko representing a tcilokogalgi town was from a red clan. This type of dual organization was common among southeastern peoples.[74] Moieties represented natural order and balance and, considering their separate development, provided stability among the Alabamas and Coushattas.

Clans were the most important social unit among southeastern peoples; they held this kinship system sacred for it guaranteed individual rights within the community. Kinship also defined legal duties. John Phillip Reid described it as "more than a family, the clan was a corporate entity based on kinship. . . . It was an arm of government to which all police power was entrusted."[75] Alabama and Coushatta clan law set boundaries through sanctions in order to provide stability in society. These public and private clan laws included responsibilities, from punishment of crimes such as murder, to the regulation of marriages and children's education. The goals were collective, and each clan member enforced clan law out of obligation.[76]

Like many southeastern peoples, the Alabamas and Coushattas drew strength, stability, and cohesion from their complex kinship systems that had originated from the Mississippian period. Kinship ties allowed the Alabamas and Coushattas to maintain common bonds despite their differences. Merging Alabama and Coushatta ayiksa was one mechanism of coalescence, a way to weave gradually disparate people into one. Moreover, it counteracted the disruptive effect of their migration and diaspora.

The Alabamas and Coushattas were different peoples in ancient times. Their ancestors had common origins in the Mississippian chiefdoms that dominated southeastern American Indian civilizations, but they had developed separately and lived a great distance apart. In the postcontact world, the Alabamas and Coushattas were subjected to a litany of afflictions: Soto's attempted conquest of the Southeast, massive depopulation after exposure to European diseases, and slave raids from enemy neighbors. To avoid these external pressures, the Alabama and Coushatta survivors began migrations in the late 1500s in search of safer ground—their first diaspora.

As their respective migrations ended in present-day central Alabama, they created a new sacred landscape by clearing the land and establishing settlements in the same way their ancestors had. Kinship ties between Alabama and Coushatta towns soon followed. An Alabama and Coushatta alliance meant that they had a stronger negotiating position vis-à-vis the encroaching European powers. They had carried out a survival plan in the postcontact world. The experiences recollected in their oral traditions describe the space from which they emerged as a united people, working together as a group with similar interests. These links built a permanent bridge connecting the two peoples, and the Alabamas and Coushattas relied on this solidarity when European contact presented new challenges.

« »

2

New Encounters and Worldviews

The ancestors of the Alabamas and Coushattas lived underground, venturing forth from their sacred cave only after dark. One night, a white man found their footprints near a tree and wanted to catch them. He left a barrel of whiskey at the tree trunk and waited. When Alabama and Coushatta men and women emerged, nobody went near the strange object at first. Eventually, one man was curious enough to drink some of the barrel's liquid. He started to dance around and sing joyfully. The others followed his lead and became very drunk, so drunk that the white man easily captured all of them. From that day forward, the Alabamas and Coushattas never returned to their ancestral cave and remained on the surface of the earth.[1]

Their ancestors' memory of the encounter with Europeans is one of trickery and imprisonment. The white man's drink made them vulnerable and led to their capture. The entrapment symbolizes both the pleasures and the hazards of contact with Europeans. Yet the Alabamas and Coushattas willingly consumed the white man's possessions, albeit with some hesitance. The liquor proved too tempting to ignore, and once one man drank it, others followed. The consequences of their actions symbolized their battle with the ill effects of trade with Europeans. The Alabamas and Coushattas' dealings with the whites left them exposed, and exchanges and frequent interactions with colonists meant that they could no longer live in the security of their cave. They were beginning a new phase of their history: they no longer lived in what they perceived as protected innocence.

Instead, the Alabamas and Coushattas faced the very real social and economic forces that went hand-in-hand with European settlement of the southeastern interior. As foreign intruders threatened their new life along the Alabama, Coosa, and Tallapoosa rivers, Alabama and Coushatta bonds were tested; the landscape was changing. New people arrived at the start of the eighteenth century and began to shape their sacred space. A new world of possessions and ideas lay before them, and all communities had to learn how to cooperate and relate with each other if they were to survive. War, trade, and new personal relationships forever altered the Alabama and Coushatta concept of the world.

Establishing New Trade Links

The Alabamas and Coushattas, who had migrated from a landscape of chaos, rampant with disease and slave raids, shared a common goal: to create new trade networks and alliances that would promote order and stability, power and sovereignty. Like many diasporic groups that find refuge in new spaces, the Alabamas and Coushattas faced possible hostility or attack from their new neighbors. Yet many peoples who bordered the Alabama Nation—including the Tallapoosas, Abhikas, Cowetas, and Cussitas (collectively known as the Creeks)—were in a similar situation. They, too, had fewer numbers and sought alliances to protect their autonomy, especially as the English expanded their interests into the southern interior. This situation may have been the genesis of the close relationship that later developed between the Alabamas and Coushattas and the Creeks.

Before their coalescence in the seventeenth century, the Alabamas and Coushattas lived separately and were weak and vulnerable to attacks and slave raids. During the first decade of the eighteenth century, however, the united Alabamas and Coushattas turned the tables and, ironically, reaped rewards from the Indian slave trade. They demonstrated to potential rivals that they were a dominant force in the Southeast. Indeed, the Alabamas and Coushattas were among many migrant newcomers who saw opportunity in the slaving expeditions against Spanish Florida.

Alabama and Coushatta participation in the slave trade had social, political, and economic dimensions. Because slaving was a part of warfare, warriors could build experience in battle and exercise their military prowess, as well as establish good relations with other allied Creek warriors. Moreover, given the snowball effect of slaving, it was important for warrior-slavers to establish preeminence in the southern interior, especially because there was additional incentive to exchange captives for trade goods.

Though little evidence remains, one can speculate that those who were not sold into slavery may have been incorporated into the Alabama and Coushatta community to strengthen their numbers, as the Iroquois did through the mourning wars. As historian Paul Kelton suggests, by the late seventeenth century, American Indian communities had been devastated by the Great Southeastern Smallpox Epidemic (1696–1700) and then by the disease episodes that followed the slaving paths.[2] The Alabamas and Coushattas were on the lower path of the pathogens, so they undoubtedly were among those affected (though they had probably suffered from some European diseases before this period). The Alabama and Coushatta slave raids, then, would have been motivated by a four-pronged incentive: to replace the trade networks previously lost after the collapse of the Mississippian world; to solidify their relationship with their Creek neighbors; to establish hegemony over surrounding territory in central Alabama; and to replace gradually their population loss from the smallpox epidemic by prisoner-adoption.

Based on documentary evidence, the primary targets of the early-eighteenth-century slave raids were the missionized Apalachees of Spanish Florida. The Apalachees, once part of a powerful chiefdom, were especially vulnerable after disease and enemy attacks repeatedly devastated their community in the late seventeenth century.[3] Just as slavers had once raided Alabama and Coushatta settlements in the late seventeenth century, Alabama and Coushatta warriors attacked Apalachee communities between May and September of 1702. A combined Indian force of 3,000 warriors quickly overwhelmed a small Spanish garrison and the Apalachee warriors, according to Don Hyacinthe Roque Perez, a Spanish officer stationed on the Gulf Coast deep in Apalachee territory. Armed with English muskets, the slavers included the united Alabama-Coushattas, Cherokees, Tallapoosas, Abhikas, and Cowetas.[4] The allied warriors eventually forced more than 2,000 Apalachees to surrender. The raiders took the survivors to Carolina's coast, presumably to sell them to English slave traders. A year later, on September 15, 1703, Carolina governor James Moore called for the organization of "our Fri[e]ndly Indians to our interest, and ye gaining others thereunto, as well as Encouraging our fri[e]nds, & destroying our enemies."[5] For at least five more years, the Alabamas and Coushattas continued to join these allied raids against Florida's coast, including an attack on the Spanish fort at Pensacola.[6] In Don Hyacinthe's words, "All these nations gathered together had caused tremendous havoc in the province."[7]

The Alabamas and Coushattas had demonstrated to potential rivals and especially to other slavers that they were a powerful force: they feared no one. Indeed, the seeds of the play-off system that would later characterize Indian-European trade relations throughout the Southeast in the eighteenth century were sown at this time. During Queen Anne's War (1702–13), the English worried that the Spanish agents in St. Augustine would "incite our Indians to trade with them" and that "our Indians are in Love with their liberality and Conversation."[8] European fears such as this one, coupled with the increasing leverage of Indian communities, especially the Creek Confederacy, would only grow in the following decades.

The Assessment

Alabama and Coushatta ventures with their Indian allies and the English created beneficial trade relations with Charles Town traders, especially when a new market quickly emerged for deerskins. Surpassing England's expectations, from 1699 to 1705 the English colony of Carolina prospered when they annually exported over 45,000 dressed deerskins to London. By 1716, American Indians who traded at Charles Town received up to five shillings per pound for white deerskins and five shillings per piece for raw buckskin.[9] Trade alliances with southeastern peoples were therefore an integral part of England's success in both the expanding deerskin market and the Indian slave trade. England's reliance on local American Indians for trade was a weakness, especially when they had to compete with other European nations desiring the same opportunities.

The French knew of England's designs for empire in North America but lagged behind in the contest. In 1684, King Louis XIV of France selected René Robert Cavelier, sieur de La Salle, to explore the Mississippi River and to establish a settlement with the aim of eventual colonization. When La Salle's mission failed, the French Crown sent Pierre Le Moyne d'Iberville to "select a good site that can be defended with a few men, and block entry to the river by other nations."[10] In 1702, Iberville established Fort Louis along the Mobile River, twenty-seven miles from Mobile Bay; it was ideally situated to prevent English encroachment southward and to facilitate communication with the peoples of the southern interior. France's ultimate goal was to limit English expansion from the Carolinas and Spanish expansion from Florida by controlling the fur trade in the Mississippi Valley and along the Gulf Coast.[11] The Alabamas and Coushattas soon realized that their lands were juxtaposed between two rising imperial powers: England and France.

The Alabamas and Coushattas stood to benefit from French interest in the Gulf South. The French eagerly sought the friendship of the Alabamas and Coushattas, who they knew as the Alabama Nation. Alabama and Coushatta leaders learned that Iberville wanted to trade with them to prevent English monopoly in the Southeast. Iberville had recognized the strength and importance of the Alabama Nation: their people claimed prime territory along the junction of the Alabama, Coosa, and Tallapoosa rivers and had towns consisting of over four hundred families and a substantial number of armed warriors. The Alabama Nation also was close enough to Mobile (roughly a five-day trip in a dugout canoe) to be either dangerous or beneficial to the French.[12] If Iberville convinced the Alabamas and Coushattas to leave English friendship behind in favor of the French, they would be valuable partners.

Following suit, on May 12, 1702, eight Alabama mikos traveled to Fort Louis in Mobile on an invitation to meet Iberville's brother, Jean-Baptiste Le Moyne de Bienville (who later became governor of French Louisiana). Bienville requested that the Alabama Nation make peace with their enemies the Mobilians and Tohomés, who were French allies. After the meeting, the mikos received blankets, beads, and bells, but obtained neither guns nor ammunition. In exchange, the mikos agreed to delay temporarily their raids. That October forty Alabamas, including Deerfoot, whom Bienville vaguely referred to as the principal headman of the Alabama Nation, returned to Fort Louis. Deerfoot, like the leaders of simple chiefdoms, probably represented both the Alabamas and Coushattas. A calumet ceremony followed that was presumably similar to an earlier ceremony recorded by Iberville. According to the practice, the men would sit on cane mats and smoke the peace calumet that "rested on two forked sticks two feet high in the middle of the assembly."[13] Afterward, the Alabama mikos expressed their willingness to promote peace and regional tranquility.[14] The exchange that transpired during the calumet ceremony is a good example of misinterpretation between cultures. Bienville mistakenly believed that by smoking the peace calumet he had cemented a permanent friendship and future alliance: "that we were from now on one."[15] Europeans made this blunder frequently when interacting with American Indians. The French failed to realize that the calumet ceremony never symbolized a permanent agreement. The ceremony had to be constantly renewed, often involving a lot singing, eating, dancing, and, most importantly, gift giving.[16]

So what could have motivated Deerfoot and other mikos to have the calumet ceremony with the French, whom they likely viewed as intruders in their new homeland? They probably accepted the invitation and traveled to Mobile to gather information about their new neighbors. As one of the respected leaders of the Alabama Nation, Deerfoot wanted to assess France's strengths and weaknesses, including the size of the garrison at Fort Louis and its overall condition. The mikos likely thought that the French, while giving them good presents, were not as generous as the English. The French had to earn their friendship, and gift giving was only the start; they needed to demonstrate that they could provide trade and presents to appease the powerful Alabama Nation. Deerfoot also likely compared the objectives of the new foreigners to those of the English. The French made clear that they wished to obtain an alliance with the Alabama Nation at the expense of the English. Yet Deerfoot and his companions had no intention to commit their people so early in the game—to do so would destroy any potential advantage they had between the English and the French.

The meeting provided the mikos with much to discuss when they returned to their towns. Seven months later, in May 1703, Deerfoot and his men returned to Fort Louis. Deerfoot observed that the French had only a limited amount of food and small supplies of weapons and ammunition and were vulnerable to attack. He suggested that the French visit their towns where they could purchase corn and poultry for a reasonable price. Deerfoot also told Bienville that the Englishmen had already left the Alabama Nation so the French could arrive without a confrontation (indicating that he was well aware of the Franco-English rivalry). Having few alternatives, Bienville accepted the invitation and sent a man named Labrie and four French Canadians to travel with Deerfoot and his men to Alabama territory.[17]

On the twentieth day of the journey, the party reached close to present-day Montgomery, Alabama, the heart of the Alabama Nation. Unbeknownst to the Frenchmen, Deerfoot sent an envoy to the town of Coosada with news about their location. Coushatta warriors arrived that evening and quickly left with their Alabama kinsmen by nightfall. The Alabamas had told the Frenchmen that they needed to go to their village that night in order to prepare for their visit, and the Frenchmen had no reason to suspect their actions. At dawn, Coushatta and Alabama warriors ambushed the Frenchmen with English muskets and lances. The warriors killed three and wounded the two other Frenchmen. One survivor named Charles escaped by jumping into the river—despite suffering from a broken arm and a hatchet wound to his shoulder—and fled to Fort Louis at Mobile.[18]

It was a well-coordinated attack. Deerfoot obviously had considered the plan carefully, but we can only speculate as to why he ordered the ambush in the first place. We know that the townspeople already had a profitable relationship with the English in the deerskin and slave trades. Deerfoot may have considered Bienville's request to end all hostilities against their neighbors as not only presumptuous, but also as an attempt to end their lucrative slave raids. They likely decided to attack based upon evidence of French weakness. Both Iberville and Bienville planned to establish hegemony over the Southeast, including land that the Alabama Nation controlled. Their desire for power over the English was apparent, and it may have led to resentment. In the Alabama and Coushatta perspective, then, it was the perfect time to rid their lands of the French presence.

Another factor likely aiding their decision was a visit from English Indian agent Thomas Nairne, a frontier Scotsman appointed by the South Carolinian Assembly to regulate trade. Nairne encouraged the Alabamas and Coushattas and their Abhika and Tallapoosa neighbors to make war on the French. Nairne had visited them earlier to discuss the new English trading policy, intending to curtail trading abuses. He stressed to leaders like Deerfoot that the English soon would expel the French from the Southeast and that English goods were far superior.[19] Nairne made a good case: he seemed to understand that Alabama and Coushatta trade relationships were ephemeral and had to be maintained with great care. With his people's best interests in mind, Deerfoot probably agreed to continue trade with the English because agents distributed many gifts and had access to quality goods. The French, on the other

hand, had fallen behind on their gifts and the calumet ceremony had not been renewed. Deerfoot and town representatives made the most of their options; it mattered little with
whom they traded as long as it was a reliable network.

It is safe to say that the Alabama and Coushatta warriors
knew the consequences of attacking the French: war. Both
Bienville and Iberville viewed the incident as a sign of Deerfoot's duplicity, although Deerfoot had never promised perpet-
ual allegiance or friendship. The governor organized a punitive
campaign against the Alabamas and Coushattas that would last
seven years. In addition to launching retaliatory raids, Iberville
communicated the hostilities to the enemies of the Alabamas
and Coushattas. Soon, the Mobilians, Tohomés, Choctaws,
and other rivals learned that the French would arm any who
aided their campaign against the Alabamas and Coushattas.
French observer André Pénicaut noted that 1,800 warriors
along with seventy Frenchmen participated in an expedition
against them. Led by Bienville and a fellow officer, St. Denis de
Tonty, they set out in September 1703. After six days, however,
the Mobilians—either through fault or design—managed to get
hopelessly lost and eventually abandoned the French-led war
party altogether.[20]

Some Mobilian warriors who quit the expedition explained
to the Frenchmen that they were "friends and allies of the Alibamons," and no longer wished to fight against them.[21] Although the Mobilians and the Alabamas were traditionally
enemies, some intermarriage between the two groups had occurred. Based on the traditional practices of many southeastern peoples, the only way a captured enemy could escape
torture, enslavement, or death was if a clan adopted the prisoner. In most cases, an Alabama or Mobilian clan adopted
female prisoners of war, creating kinship ties. One example
was when Bienville presented Alabama slaves as gifts to the
Mobilians later that year. According to Bienville, the Mobilians
had asked for the enslaved women and children, "as these
captives were their kin."[22] André Pénicaut, who recorded the
warfare between the two groups, noted that only two Mobilians
(likely former captives) had married Alabamas and were living

with them. Interestingly, when the two heard of Deerfoot's plan to attack their people, they escaped to Mobilian territory to warn them. Their actions show that they maintained loyalty to their own people despite their intermarriage with the Alabamas.[23] Pénicaut confirmed the problems of fidelity when he noted that despite some kinship ties, the Alabamas and Mobilians remained enemies.[24]

Each remaining day of Bienville's expedition brought more deserters. By the seventeenth day, so few allied warriors remained that the French returned to Fort Louis. Several days later, Bienville organized a new sortie, wisely including only French soldiers. The party eventually spotted fourteen canoes ten leagues from an Alabama village, a clear sign that they had found the Alabamas' location. A large group of Alabamas settled down there for the night after the men had hunted game. They were unaware that Bienville's men planned to ambush them while they slept, but the dry cane cracked as the attackers moved along the riverbank. One Alabama heard the coming French, and gave a warning shout. As the French fired weapons, Alabama women and children who accompanied the hunting party quickly fled. The warriors held back and fought, killing two Frenchmen before withdrawing to their canoes to escape. Once they reached safer ground, a medicine man, or *ahissí:cí*, would treat war wounds (especially those made from gunshots) by collecting at sunrise bark from black gum, red maple, and elm trees. After he boiled and mixed it in an earthenware jug, men both drank the concoction and applied it to their wounds. They treated other injuries with pine resin, to clot the bleeding. Luckily, the Alabama party survived, and Bienville and his men returned to Fort Louis after running low on supplies.[25]

The attack caused Alabama and Coushatta townspeople to be constantly on their guard against further hostilities by the French and their American Indian allies. Their fears were justified; French raiders caught yet another hunting party unawares later that December. Along the Alabama River, seventy leagues upstream, the French attacked and killed all of the Alabama warriors there and took the Alabama women and children to Mobile as slaves.[26]

Warfare with the French and their Indian allies continued for years. Bienville fueled such aggression by offering rewards for Alabama and Coushatta prisoners, dead or alive. In 1703, Bienville proclaimed to all southeastern peoples that for every such scalp or live prisoner delivered to him at Fort Louis, he would give them ten crowns. His plan worked. Twenty Chickasaw warriors arrived at Fort Louis in March 1704 with five Alabama scalps. For each scalp, the warriors each received a musket, a small amount of powder, and five pounds of bullets. Several months later Bienville rewarded twenty Choctaws the same for three Alabama scalps.[27] Having these greater incentives, the enemies and rivals of the Alabamas and Coushattas increased their attacks.

Such actions taken against the Alabamas and Coushattas led Deerfoot to seek temporary military alliances. Deerfoot approached the Cherokees, Catawbas (a people who had territory in the Carolinas and spoke a Siouan dialect), and neighboring Abhikas to unite and attack the French and their Indian allies, principally the Mobilians. Additional warriors would be necessary to defeat their enemies, so Deerfoot negotiated short-term alliances to accomplish these goals, a strategy his people would employ throughout the eighteenth century. In 1708, Alabama warriors and their Cherokee, Catawba, and Abhika allies organized an attack. According to André Pénicaut's journals, the alliance numbered more than 15,000 warriors. To show their strength, the Indian alliance burned Mobilian huts, captured thirty women and children, and pillaged some settlements near Fort Louis.[28]

According to ancient practices, Alabama and Coushatta men would prepare for battle by performing a ceremonial purification ritual, completed by fasting and internal cleansing. This took place in the woods over a period of four days. During this time warriors drank a medicine (referred to as "black drink") each morning, inducing them to vomit; it purified their bodies and brought knowledge. Men also carried medicine bundles that they believed protected them from harm in battle. Warriors often prepared to attack at night, waiting for the enemy to emerge. After the battle, scalps from vanquished opponents would be carried back to the village and used in a ceremonial dance. According to oral tradition, only when a boy claimed his first enemy scalp did he become a man and join in the dance. Thomas Campbell confirmed this practice when he traveled through Alabama territory in 1764, noting that, "no Indian is looked upon as a man till he has killed and scalped."[29] Warriors also received social distinction and war titles after fighting bravely. Titles usually included a first word representing a clan animal or the warrior's town. The second word often described the warrior's bravery, such as *hadjo*, meaning fearless or crazy in battle.[30]

The successful Alabama and Coushatta attacks against the Mobilians alarmed the French. Bienville appealed for aid, reporting to his superiors that Fort Louis was weak and desperately needed gunpowder.[31] While Deerfoot's strategy temporarily succeeded, the bounty on Alabama and Coushatta scalps increased the frequency of warfare. Hunting expeditions became more dangerous. In retaliation, a combined force of French, Mobilians, and Tohomés killed thirty Alabamas, wounded seven (whom they scalped like the rest), and took nine prisoners back to the fort and later violently burned them alive. During these raids, women and children were continuously captured and later sold in the Indian slave trade.[32] The persistent raids and ambushes against the Alabamas and Coushattas during hunting trips exacerbated attempts to locate food and furs for trade with the English in Charles Town. Once confined exclusively to spring and summer, warfare now occurred year-round and consequently took an exhausting toll on Alabama and Coushatta townspeople.

Reassessment

In 1713, ten years after the attack on the Canadians from Fort Louis, the Alabamas and Coushattas opened another war, this time against the English. André Pénicaut reported that they attacked forces in Charles Town "without ever being incited by the French."[33] What factors, then, drove the Alabamas and Coushattas to reassess their relationship with the English and to embark on a war against their former trading partners?

One of the main reasons for the hostilities was the building resentment of the Alabamas and Coushattas toward Carolina traders and their fraudulent practices. On July 9, 1712, the Carolina Commissioners of Indian Trade (who met regularly in Charles Town) acknowledged that trade with American Indians required increased supervision and reform as reports of corruption spread. They sent Indian agent John Wright, who had replaced former agent Thomas Nairne, to travel to the Alabama Nation and renew their friendship. Alabama and Coushatta leaders immediately complained to Wright that trading abuses were rampant throughout their territory and wanted the problems resolved. The main complaints alleged rum debt and physical abuse. They accused English traders of smuggling rum into the towns and selling large quantities to men, who then incurred a substantial debt while getting drunk. Neighboring Creek towns also reported incidences of English traders who had physically beaten and whipped their men, captured and raped their women, and enslaved both male and female relatives for unpaid debts.[34]

These scandalous practices were commonplace in Yamasee and Creek towns. To resolve the disputes, mikos of the Alabama Nation requested that Wright cancel all rum debts because the traders had taken unfair advantage of their men and women. Wright's initial response was short: he told them that they should prevent their men from buying rum. Wright failed to understand, however, that mikos lacked authoritarian power; the young men could do as they pleased. Alabama and Coushatta, Yamasee, and Creek towns threatened to quit the English over charges of corruption. The commissioners had good reason to worry about the mikos' complaints. In July 1712, they learned that the Alabamas and Coushattas had contemplated "deserting or endeavoring to desert this Government."[35] Considering this potential disaster of Indian relations, the commissioners ordered Wright "not to hinder any Time but make all the Speed you can to the Al[a]bamas."[36] According to the commissioners' instructions, Wright's duties were to heal the conflict between the townspeople and the English and to show "tender Regard the Government hath for their Welfaire [sic]."[37] Moreover, he was given specific instructions while visiting the Alabama Nation: "You are strictly to enquire into their

Greivances and to doe [sic] them immediate and impartial Justice on all Traders that have abused them."[38] The commissioners thought it was critical that Wright assure the Alabamas and Coushattas that the English would "redress all their Greivances," deter "any Manner of Injustice to be done," and regulate the traders "so that they give not the Indians Offence and Scandal."[39] Wright also planned to distribute presents to the mikos in an attempt to bring them back into the English fold. Despite these promises and grand gestures, the Carolina commissioners had great difficulty enforcing laws, including the revised American Indian Trade Act of 1711, which amended the 1707 act and included stricter trading regulations and more severe penalties against trader abuse.[40]

The Alabama and Coushatta mikos were not impressed with the reforms and began to reassess their connection to the English. The Alabama and Coushatta community took offense to rampant trading abuses and incompetence, especially by John Wright. In one incident, Wright bungled the delivery of goods and presents. Alabama and Coushatta townspeople had expected the shipment, but it was sent by mistake to Dawfusky, a Yamasee village. Wright also had other problems. John Muscrove, an Indian trader and translator among the Cowetas and neighboring towns, charged Wright with selling Ahele, a Creek freed woman, into slavery. Many Carolina traders had a reputation of illegally capturing and selling free American Indians into slavery, which had become a widespread practice by 1710. Moreover, in June 1713 Wright bought two slaves and later gave several slaves to another man for debts owed. Apparently, the slaves were not his to give away, and like other accusations before this one, the status of the slaves was questionable. The details of the case were unclear and unresolved, but according to the Commissioners of Indian Trade these incidents involving Wright were "the true Cause of the Al[a]bamas deserting to Mobele [sic]."[41]

Angered by corrupt English trading practices and Carolina slavers, Alabama and Coushatta warriors again joined their Catawba and Abhika allies in a war party of 3,000 men, who together pillaged Carolina settlements and captured many English men and women and Africans. Alabama and Coushatta warriors later joined another temporary alliance with neighboring towns and attacked Charles Town in 1715. According to reports, American Indian groups who previously had good relations with the English turned against them and killed those associated with the Indian slave trade in an incident later known as the Yamasee War. The Yamasees, who had settled near the Savannah River, were distant kin of the Muskogean peoples. They had also fallen victim to Carolina traders who enslaved their men, women, and children. The war cut down Charles Town and severely damaged British hegemony in the Southeast. Both southeastern peoples and the French took advantage of England's weakness. The Alabama and Coushatta mikos found new opportunities awaiting them.[42]

The Invitation: Fort des Alibamons

The Alabama and Coushatta attack on the English and their long-standing conflict with the French left them in a precarious position. It severely restricted their access to trade and consequently left them vulnerable to more attacks. Yet the Alabamas and Coushattas saw an opportunity to reconcile with the French. Earlier in March 1712, on the eve of war with the English, Bienville had met with Alabama, Coushatta, and Abhika leaders, hoping to resolve past hostilities. "The Grand Chief of the Alabamas" (likely a well-known leader named Opoyheatly from the Alabama town of Pakana, which was probably a "white" town of peaceful relations) and his companions took notice as Bienville showed them great respect and "reconciled them with the French allies."[43] Opoyheatly and fellow mikos were impressed that Bienville acknowledged their importance, and that the French were willing to provide them with their needs.[44] Opoyheatly realized that he needed a new strategy—one that would give his people power and status, not weakness.

The Alabamas and Coushattas had considered solidifying their position in the Southeast by inviting the French to build a trading post and fort in the heart of their territory. This was an important decision, for the ramifications would be great. If the French accepted their invitation, the Alabama Nation would have direct access to the interior trade routes and challenge the dominance of English traders at Charles Town, who were now their enemies. More importantly, the Alabamas and Coushattas knew that it would create a center for trade on their own terms. Opoyheatly delivered a message to Lamothe de Cadillac, then governor of Louisiana, requesting a meeting. Opoyheatly, fellow mikos, and their companions traveled to Mobile to discuss an offer with French officials in September 1715. Speaking on behalf of the Alabama Nation, Opoyheatly offered Cadillac peace between their people. He also officially invited the French to build a fort within the Alabama Nation—"the kind that would be suitable for French people."[45] Cadillac willingly agreed to the terms; he knew that such a fort was ideal because of the strategic location of the Alabamas and Coushattas at the junction of three rivers and the abundant game there for the deerskin trade. Cadillac and the Grand Chief sealed the agreement with the calumet ceremony.[46]

By 1717, France completed the construction of Fort Toulouse (named in honor of the Count of Toulouse, Admiral Louis Alexandre de Bourbon) with the assistance of Alabama and Coushatta labor. Commonly known as "Fort des Alibamons," or "aux Alibamons," the structure was "fifty toises square, with quarters for officers and soldiers and a large magazine for munitions and food supplies."[47]

Fort Toulouse was only 150 yards from the Alabama town of Pakana (the residence of the principal chief of the Alabama Nation) and approximately four miles from the Coushatta town of Taskigi. Not surprisingly, this placed Fort Toulouse closer to the Alabamas, in particular to Opoyheatly. Yet the fort was still close to one of the Coushatta towns, but not their main village of Coosada. This is significant when considering the relationship between the Alabamas and Coushattas in the early stages of their coalescence and alliance. The Coushattas' mikos likely had a voice in the decision-making process, but based on the written accounts, their participation in the negotiations with Cadillac was secondary compared to that of the Alabamas under the leadership of Opoyheatly. It seems that the diaspora and resettlement acted as a catalyst for strong, more centralized leadership. Indeed, Opoyheatly's position as the "grand chief" within the Alabama Nation, representing all towns in diplomatic negotiations with the Europeans, was very reminiscent of the positions of his Mississippian predecessors. Like the chiefs in simple chiefdoms, Opoyheatly was the principal negotiator in the diplomatic talks (encouraged by Europeans) and, with the townspeople's support, represented the voice of the Nation. The difference here, however, was that the mikos from other towns likely had more sway in the decision-making process and had more autonomy than under chiefdoms.

The location of the building site was also significant; it was on an ancient mound on the bank of the Coosa River. Mound sites of the Mississippian ancestors of the Alabamas and Coushattas were ceremonial centers where trade symbolized alliances and provided access to goods that were previously unavailable. Thomas J. Pluckhahn has argued that mounds acted as "corporate facilities meant to reinforce kin or community ties."[48] Mounds also represented the overall strength of the community, and the newly built French fort atop the ancient mound demonstrated that the Alabamas and Coushattas had prominence in their country; they were a people to be respected. The Alabamas and Coushattas had persuaded the French to build the structure on a mound central to their towns for a reason: Fort Toulouse would be incorporated into their new center of exchanges and diplomacy, ultimately changing their world. Just as under chiefdoms, the Alabamas and Coushattas understood that land was not just a place to hunt, farm, and find shelter; it had a deeper meaning. Their territory was the space that the townspeople controlled and from which they could profit because of its location. Land had become a source of power and strength, especially when European nations competed for trade and alliances.

Fort Toulouse was, in the perspective of the Alabamas and Coushattas, one of their villages. They helped maintain the fort, and even assisted the French when chaos erupted. For example, on September 19, 1721, the garrison lacked supplies, especially food, and twenty-four soldiers staged a revolt and attacked their commander, Marchand de Courcelles. The ensign escaped and immediately ran to one of the Alabama towns, requesting aid. The Alabamas agreed to apprehend the mutineers who, fearing retribution, had escaped to the Carolinas. The Alabama men caught and killed sixteen rebel soldiers and imprisoned the rest.[49] The Alabamas' participation in the capture of the insubordinate Frenchmen was to maintain law and order within their community, which now included the fort. They refused to condone a rebellion that threatened to destroy their center. The Alabama and Coushatta townspeople had coerced the French garrison to accommodate to their world.

Jesuit Relations

It seems that the French tolerated Alabama and Coushatta control over the fort. To balance the scales, the French diocese sent missionaries to Fort Toulouse in the hopes of converting and thereby managing the local Indian population. The Jesuit and Capuchin priests stationed at the fort, however, had little luck converting members of Alabama and Coushatta towns or monitoring the garrison's behavior and relations with them, much to the chagrin of French officials. The colony of French Louisiana had at least one priest (six in total who all served at different times between 1724 and 1763) stationed at Fort Toulouse. The priests had their work cut out for them. Before European contact, Alabama and Coushatta cosmology focused on order prevailing over chaos, allowing the existence for human life on earth. They revered nature and animals, both of which played a predominant role in their religion.[50]

The Alabamas and Coushattas believed that water covered the entire earth, where only animals lived. One day, a few animals decided to create land from the ocean's floor, but a beaver and frog failed in their attempt. A crawfish volunteered and dove into the water but initially failed because the water was too deep. On the third attempt, the crawfish reached the bottom of the ocean, scooped the soft earth from the primeval sea bottom with its tail, and built a great mud chimney, eventually creating a large mass of land. The animals agreed that the crawfish had performed a good job, but the earth was too flat. A horned owl convinced a buzzard to fly above. When the buzzard's expansive wings swooped down, it etched deep holes and valleys into the earth and made mountains and hills when they swung back up; as the buzzard glided through the air, it made parts of the earth level and flat.[51]

The Alabamas and Coushattas also conceived their universe as having a Lower, Middle, and Upper world; each had beings and creatures that dwelled there. The key was to promote balance and order in nature between the worlds. The Lower World underlay both earth and water where chaotic forces dwelled. It was not considered an evil place, but one where powerful spirits represented creativity, chaos, and fertility. The Middle World, where humans lived, was a four-sided earth surrounded by water where a half-circular sky formed a mass that did not touch land. The Upper World represented purity and perfection where the Life Giver was the supreme cosmic being that represented order and eternity. This being was an impersonal force that was neither good nor evil. The Life Giver's equivalent in the Lower World was the Horned Serpent, or the Alabama *chintoosakcho* (Snake-Crawfish), another ambivalent being.[52]

After contact with missionaries at Fort Toulouse, changes within the Alabama and Coushatta religion occurred. The Life Giver, for example, transformed into the persona Aba Mikko, who compared somewhat to the Christian God, and the Horned Serpent became more malevolent. Another incorporation was the concept of heaven and hell. The Alabamas and Coushattas had no known understanding of duality in the afterlife before encountering Europeans. Deeds done in a lifetime did not necessarily affect one's ability to travel to the spirit world. According to ancient beliefs, when an Alabama or Coushatta died, the soul detached from the body and began its journey to the Upper World. Family members were required to provide grave goods for the deceased; burials often included food, blankets, and weapons to ensure successful passage. Those who took the journey saw a horizontal plane with a dome-like sky where the moon, sun, and stars made their pathways. The dome sky rose and fell against the earth during regular cycles only to leave a small passage where a person passed cautiously to the Upper World. Once there, spirits of the deceased, including humans and animals, lived peacefully in a beautiful, lush land.[53]

By the mid-eighteenth century, however, European mission-aries had made an obvious impact on Alabama and Coushatta cosmology. The Alabamas and Coushattas told French traveler Jean-Bernard Bossu that "if they had not taken someone else's wife, stolen, or killed during their lives, after death they would go to a very fertile land where there would be plenty of women and hunting grounds and where everything would be easy for them." If they had done the opposite or "disrespected the Great Spirit," they would go to a barren, destitute place where thorns and briars grew everywhere, and where neither hunting nor women existed.[54] This may have indicated some adaptation to Christian beliefs of good deeds and the imagery of heaven and hell.

Despite having had some influence over the Alabamas and Coushattas, Jesuit priests had no control over the fort or the Alabama and Coushatta towns. On September 20, 1721, French commissioners ordered the construction of chapels and churches to be built within the territory of the Alabama Nation; they wanted Frenchmen stationed in the Louisiana provinces "to be more regular in fulfilling their duties as Christians than they have been up to the present."[55] Father Alexis Xavier de Guyenne, a Jesuit priest who served the Alabama fort between 1727 and 1729, experienced frustration when he built small chapels in two Alabama villages, only to see them burned down by the townspeople. The Alabamas later invited him back and helped him rebuild the chapels, but Guyenne had relocated to another post before its completion.[56]

This incident proved that the Alabamas wanted to see the chapels erected with their permission first, and only with the townspeople's invitation could Guyenne do so. It also demonstrates that the Alabamas and Coushattas viewed the fort and its people as a part of their own community; by destroying the chapels the townspeople made it clear that the Alabamas and Coushattas controlled their own social and religious matters, and, as it would seem, those of the French fort. The priests, then, had no power over the fort or the Indian population surrounding it. Maintaining the fort was in the hands of the Alabamas and Coushattas, especially as close relationships developed.

Intimate Relations

The transformation of the Alabamas and Coushattas' physical landscape in turn changed their relationship with those in and around their territory. As a diasporic community, the Alabamas and Coushattas created social relationships with their new neighbors. The most common associations were between European men and Indian women. Throughout the early eighteenth century, intermarriage was widespread throughout American Indian communities and, if politically or economically advantageous, encouraged by both European and Indian cultures. Among the Alabamas and Coushattas, frequent interaction with European militiamen and traders led to intimate relationships.

After the construction of Fort Toulouse in 1717, Frenchmen had considerable contact with the Alabamas and Coushattas; the fort was only a short walking distance from most Alabama and Coushatta towns. Moreover, close contact with the French persisted because of the garrison's reliance on American Indian trade for survival. In the early years, the French garrison had great difficulty obtaining provisions; each soldier had to provide his own supplementary food outside of a small portion of rationed grain. The fort, however, had no gristmill, so the soldiers had Alabama and Coushatta women do the work in return for one-third of their rationed grain (soldiers complained that their price was too steep). Members of the garrison soon relied heavily on these women for valuable foodstuffs and pottery.[57]

Such close contact ultimately led to intimate relationships between soldiers and Alabama and Coushatta women; countless numbers became the wives or mistresses to these Frenchmen. Ninety-one private soldiers, forty-four officers, and fifty-eight other men living at the fort sought female companionship among the Alabamas and Coushattas because few French women lived near or at the fort.[58] Most of the Alabama and Coushatta women likely came from the towns of Pakana and Taskigi; they were closest to the fort, enabling frequent meetings.

In Alabama and Coushatta society no stigma was attached to such relations. In fact, women's sexuality was not taboo.

European observers reported that young women who had reached puberty but had not yet married experienced some sexual freedom. Caleb Swan, an eighteenth-century English traveler, noted that the Alabamas and Coushattas allowed women to do with their bodies as they pleased "without secrecy or shame."[59] Many Europeans noted the frequency of premarital sexual activities of women. Such accounts, however, likely exaggerated the occurrence because of their own ethnocentric predispositions toward American Indians, especially as women exposed more of their bodies than did their European counterparts. In Alabama and Coushatta oral tradition, for example, elders forbade premarital sex and inappropriate familiarity between unmarried couples.[60] The truth probably lies somewhere between these accounts.

During the first years of contact with southeastern peoples, the French viewed such intimacy with these communities as advantageous. In 1708, Father La Vente, a Mobile parish priest, commented: "We do not see that the blood of the Indians can do any harm to the blood of the French."[61] La Vente further encouraged the French Crown to sanction intercultural marriages to ensure the legitimacy of children from such unions and that proper catechism followed suit. In order to ensure moral behavior in such relations and Catholic conversion, the French sent Jesuit missionaries to the Alabama post. Father Guyenne first held the position in 1727, but he stayed only three years. After his departure the position was often left vacant, which left the onus upon the Mobile diocese. The mixing of cultures, along with the lack of religious direction, alarmed the French diocese, especially when they learned that many of the women who intermarried had not converted to Catholicism and kept their traditional beliefs. In 1728, the Superior Council of Louisiana, with the support of the Crown, banned French marriages with American Indian women. Church administrators based at the French colonial headquarters in Mobile responded in kind by discouraging Frenchmen from socializing, especially on an intimate level, with the Alabamas and Coushattas. But because the Alabamas and Coushattas were so close to the fort, this was an unrealistic demand.[62]

Both the Indian women and the colonists largely ignored the French ordinances prohibiting mixed marriages. They continued to intermarry, presumably according to Native customs, given the social significance of marriage for Alabama and Coushatta clans. For example, before a marriage between a European and an Alabama or Coushatta woman occurred, certain obligations had to be met. Even a European faced clan approval or disapproval of the match; clan elders could also arrange a suitable man for a woman, who was typically around age fifteen (age twenty for men). Although parents could discourage the marriage, a woman's maternal uncle determined if a man's efforts succeeded. The deciding factors included whether a man was a good hunter, an appropriate provider, and had good character.[63]

Many Alabama and Coushatta marriage ceremonies to European men likely took place without the watchful eyes of the French diocese; traditional Native ceremonies sufficed. Unfortunately, we have no written documentation of these Native ceremonies and they do not appear in parish records, but Alabama and Coushatta oral traditions shed light on what may have transpired. Customary Alabama and Coushatta marriages began when a bridegroom sent a blanket and other articles of clothing to the female relatives of the bride. After her clan accepted the proposal of marriage, a ceremony confirmed that the bride was "bound" to her husband. On the first morning after her marriage, the new bride placed beans on the fire to cook her husband's first meal. The ceremony, known as *asaamachi*, called for the wife to "forget" about the food by going back to sleep, thereby scorching and ruining her husband's first meal—an act that surely astonished European men who were more familiar with patriarchy. This practice, which continued through the twentieth century, indicated a husband's new place in the woman's household and that the wife was critical to the health of the family.[64]

If a Frenchman opted for an official Catholic ceremony, on the other hand, he and his future wife needed to travel to Mobile. Most Frenchmen at Fort Toulouse rarely made the trip; Native ceremonies were simply more convenient. Moreover, priests performed or recorded few Catholic marriages between Frenchmen and Indian women because the French diocese disapproved of such unions.[65] A rare intermarriage was recorded on June 16, 1738, between Mathias Berthelot, a Catholic native of Le Château (a French town on the island of Oléron in the Bay of Biscay), and Margueritte Panyoüâsas, niece of Pierre Panyoüâsas, a miko of the Coushattas. Record details are not extensive, but the Frenchman was likely an officer at Fort Toulouse. Witnesses present included other officers and relatives of the bride.[66]

Marriage between the two cultures was definitely a political and economic opportunity for both the Alabamas and Coushattas and the French: through her marriage Margueritte and her uncle stood to gain access to lucrative trade and an alliance with the French. Margueritte also had an indirect influence over her French husband and his official duties at the fort. Alabama and Coushatta tradition left men dominating political affairs, but women could use tears, ridicule, indifference, anger, and, above all, matrilineal kinship to bridge the gap between the private and political spheres (often with the support and even encouragement of relatives).[67] For instance, Margueritte would have learned most news coming from her husband's superiors and any information regarding the state of the fort; she would have passed it on to her uncle, who was a leader among the Coushattas. This exchange kept communication between the two cultures open and helped the Coushattas manage the French in their territory and at Fort Toulouse.

Indeed, many Alabama and Coushatta women viewed European visitors as symbols of status and wealth and therefore sought their company, and Margueritte was no exception. After all, trade goods (as gifts or exchanges) could be had more easily if Europeans visited the Alabamas and Coushattas on a regular basis or lived among them. Such ties were beneficial to both parties. For example, English trader Jacob Mathew apparently had married an Alabama woman sometime in the 1730s (no record of the marriage exists), and lived among her clan members. Mathew provided easy and guaranteed access to valuable trade items within her community. It is likely that she gained increased status as she probably had influence over how he treated her people; she would have demanded fairness and ensured that no trading abuse occurred. Likewise, Mathew reported to his superiors in 1738 that he was "well assured" the Alabama and Coushatta townspeople would never hurt the English because of his good relations with his wife's people.[68]

Jacob Mathew's confidence in his safety and the preservation of English interests can be explained by the matrilocality of Alabama and Coushatta society. After a woman married, her husband (even if he was a European) moved to his wife's town, where her clan resided. Members of the household lived in a cluster of cabins where close relatives worked, ate, and slept. They included women and their husbands, their unmarried children, married daughters, grandchildren, and elderly or dependent male relatives. Interestingly, women lived independently of their husbands; most wives had their own separate living quarters, a tradition that may have surprised European men. Women very rarely visited their husband's cabin, except to deliver foodstuffs. Women also had complete control over their dwellings, land, and property.[69] If a woman was dissatisfied with her new European husband, she could end her marriage with no shame. She kept her children and all property and could remarry.[70]

Unlike their European counterparts, Alabama and Coushatta women had individual autonomy and depended on their clans, not their husbands, for support. Thus, women who married European men became agents of cultural exchange when they conceived children with them.[71] For example, until grown, children belonged exclusively to their mother's clan and lineage, not to their European father. Thus, the mother's extended family played the most important role in childrearing. Her brothers taught children Native skills, customs, traditions, and discipline. The Coushattas used the term "ugly uncle" to describe the punishment they received from their mother's brother. They also had a "pretty uncle" who indulged them and counterbalanced the other uncle's anger. The uncle also had the responsibility of naming a child based on what he had seen or imagined while in battle.[72] Although the relationship between father and son was meaningful, the two were members of different clans and were not each other's closest male relatives according to the matrilineage.[73]

Even the position of Alabama and Coushatta males in the community depended on the status of their mother's lineage. Unlike Europeans, the Alabamas and Coushattas traced ancestry through the mother, not the father. Therefore, a child of both European and Native blood had an equal chance of high rank or authority within the community. At times, it was even an advantage because of his or her connections and familiarity with both European and Indian cultures. The leader of the united Creek Nation in the late eighteenth century, Alexander McGillivray, had both Coushatta, French, and Scottish ancestry. His grandmother, Sehoy I of the Wind Clan, was from Taskigi, the closest Coushatta town to Fort Toulouse (approximately a half mile from the fort). She married a French officer, Jean Baptiste de Courtel Marchand, and in 1722 gave birth to her daughter, Sehoy II, who later married the Scottish-Indian trader Lachlan McGillivray. Those like McGillivray provided cultural continuity, albeit mixed with French and sometimes British ancestry.[74]

New Commodities

Frequent contact with Europeans in the late seventeenth and eighteenth centuries in their new homeland transformed the world of the Alabamas and Coushattas. Their center at Fort Toulouse fostered economic exchanges that increased their wealth and enhanced their status. When Europeans first introduced new trade goods to southeastern peoples, materials such as metal, beads, and cloth became trade commodities. Men and women incorporated European shirts, wool blankets, and copper and silver into their traditional dress. An eighteenth-century Coushatta warrior, Stimafutchki, wore a European shirt made of limbourg, accentuated with a cloth turban wrapped around his head. Stimafutchki displayed a variety of metals in his ears and nose (note the mustache, a European fashion), as well as a metal gorget around his neck, indicating his status among Europeans. Men also crafted body ornaments from European coins by piercing holes through them and used them for either earrings or necklaces or sewed

Stimafutchki, or Good-Humor-of the Coushattas. An eighteenth-century Coushatta warrior, drawing by John Trumbull. Smithsonian Institution, National Anthropological Archives, Negative 1169 L 3.

them to their clothing. European trade goods such as these were highly valued and became cherished possessions that passed from one generation to the next. For instance, archaeologists excavated an Alabama burial mound in East Texas dating from the 1850s and found among the remains a 1737 French coin that had been pierced and crafted into a necklace. The Alabamas and Coushattas obtained most of these goods in exchange for deerskins, so men consequently spent more time on hunting trips after European contact.[75]

European domesticated animals such as cattle, swine, and horses also became prized possessions in Alabama and Coushatta society beginning in the eighteenth century. Alabama and Coushatta townspeople valued these animals as commodities, and many associated wealth with the number of animals held in reserve. Many even became preoccupied with their care. Gun Merchant of Okchai, for example, purchased cattle from Fort Toulouse and in 1749 avoided a trip to Charles Town because he had not finished building a fence for the animals. He later received six more cattle as gifts from the governor of South Carolina, but was greatly annoyed that the governor refused to provide him with a slave to take care of his new prized possessions.[76]

The value of the animals led to many incidents of thievery on both sides. In February 1772, The Wolf (miko of the Alabama town of Mucclassa) complained to British Indian agent John Stuart that a British trader, John Pigg, had stolen a couple of his prized horses. The Wolf later received two three-gallon kegs of rum for one horse that he lent to James Gray who planned to pick up presents from the governor of British Florida, but never returned with his horse. On the other hand, as the British colonies expanded west, stealing horses and cattle from British plantations became a lucrative operation for many young Alabama and Coushatta men.[77]

In addition to being signs of wealth, cattle offered a new food source. The Mortar, the esteemed miko of the towns of Little Okchai and Okchai, complained to Governor James Wright of Georgia on behalf of his kinsmen in 1763 that British colonists from Virginia had settled on Alabama, Coushatta, Abhika, and Tallapoosa hunting grounds and brought with them their cattle and horses. Consequently, bear and deer that had been the main sources of both food and trade for The Mortar's people were dwindling. Colonists either had killed the woodland animals or had driven them off with their domesticated animals. Moreover, he stressed that his people had no fences to keep the cattle out of their lands. Alabama and Coushatta hunting parties therefore killed any cattle that they found in their territory on the Upper Creek side of the Savannah River above Augusta. This was how The Mortar's people "fill[ed] their Bellies when they [were] hungry[,] having nothing else to do it with."[78] With deer and bear scarce, cattle became a replacement and source for food and hide. The Mortar concluded that Wright ought not to complain to him about the slaughter of the colonists' cattle, but instead should clear the colonists out and tell them that any future conflict over this issue was their, and not his people's, fault.[79]

One of the more notorious items introduced by Europeans was liquor. Like most American Indian experiences, the sale and consumption of rum, brandy, and whiskey created many problems in the Alabama and Coushatta community, especially when corrupt traders provided American Indian men with credit and encouraged them to consume excess alcohol. Consequently, drunkenness became the most frequent cause of community and family disruption. Even upstanding members of American Indian society were susceptible to the temptation. In 1737, Bienville learned that the "chief of the Occhanya Alabamas" (Alabamas from the settlement of Okchaya, whose members included those from Coosada, Little Okchai, and Okchai) died because of thinking "himself stronger than the brandy which killed him."[80] Despite the chief's death from what seems to have been alcohol poisoning, his peers wanted to continue trading brandy. Alabama and Coushatta mikos feared "that they would get brandy no longer" because of this incident, and "begged him not to deprive them of this drink for that, since they never drank [it] before night for fear of the sun's rays, to which they attribute his death."[81] The Alabamas and Coushattas had tried to convince Bienville that the combination of sun exposure and alcohol (suggesting perhaps dehydration), not the alcohol alone, had killed their esteemed leader. They told Bienville that they would be able to handle alcohol's ill effects and would avoid it during the daytime. In reality, these men were avoiding the real issue: alcohol had killed one of their leaders and they could be next. Despite their efforts to curtail abuse, alcoholism unfortunately prevailed. On June 24, 1750, Pierre de Rigaud, marquis de Vaudreuil, the governor of French Louisiana from 1743 to 1752, regretted that many of the Alabamas and Coushattas, Tallapoosas, and Abhikas "are perishing every day because of the illness that is caused them by the trade in liquor, which cannot be suppressed because of the want of merchandise of the qualities [that we have] long asked for without being able to obtain them."[82] Neither their leaders nor their people could deter the consumption of liquor, and it would continue to be a source of disharmony in the Alabama and Coushatta community.

New patterns of material consumption and adaptation also altered the Alabama and Coushatta languages. New words and meanings for trade goods replaced old ones. Before European contact, Coushattas and Alabamas used *bihí* and *bihi*, respectively, to describe a bow used as a primary weapon in hunting and warfare. After Europeans introduced them to muskets, Coushattas replaced the term "bihí" to mean "gun" as muskets began to replace bows. Coushattas then referred to a bow as *ittobihí*, which they translated as "wood (*ittó*) gun." The Alabamas, however, kept the term "bihi" to describe gun, bow, or blowgun.[83] New forms of exchange also led to similar changes. The Alabamas and Coushattas had used stone beads (*cato kona:wa*) as a form of currency before the introduction of European coins. The Coushattas replaced this term with *tokná:wa*, meaning "precious metal" or "money"; there is a noticeable similarity between the two. As silver and gold became a popular medium of currency (and ornamentation), they took the root word of "tokná:wa" and simply added its color to describe silver and gold coins respectively: *toknáwhátka* (*hátka* meaning white) and *toknáwlá:na* (*lá:na* meaning yellow). Alabamas also replicated this change with very slight changes in spelling and pronunciation: *toknaawa hatka* for silver, and *toknaawa laana* for gold coin.[84]

The new words that they incorporated into their respective

languages often described material that was familiar to their world. For example, Coushattas traded for woolen clothing, but they had never seen sheep. They at first may have assumed that wool was a type of rabbit fur. As a result, the Koasati (Coushatta) word for rabbit and sheep was the same: *cokfí*. They used this root word to describe wool, *cokfihíssi*. The Alabama word for wool coat or blanket was *chokfibáana*, which translates as "lots of rabbits"; the Alabama word, *chokfihissi*, meant both "wool" and "rabbit fur." In another example, the Alabama and Koasati word for horse was "big deer," *chichoba* and *cicó:ba*, respectively, as they were unfamiliar with horses until the Spanish encounter. The Alabamas and Coushattas also borrowed some of their new words from another language or association. The word for cattle—*wá:ka* in Koasati and *waaka* in Alabama—closely resembled the Spanish *vaca* (cow). A similar example is the Koasati term for English speakers: *waciná* (*wachina* in Alabama). Phonetically it sounds very similar to "Virginia," and is likely named after the English settlers from Virginia who they had first encountered in the seventeenth century.[85]

Interestingly, older Alabama and Coushatta words are more dissimilar to each other in speech and spelling when compared to the newer words that they had to create based on European contact. The Alabama and Coushatta union after European contact in the sixteenth and seventeenth centuries had obviously made an impact on their respective languages. As allies and kin, both the Alabamas and Coushattas interacted on a frequent basis with each other and with Europeans. As a result, they created words that both could recognize.

The Wolf's Invitation to the British

As trade relations rapidly developed with the French at Fort Toulouse in the early decades of the eighteenth century, some Alabamas and Coushattas wanted the same convenience with British trade. The Wolf (also known as The Wolf King), the influential miko of the Alabama town of Mucclassa, extended the same invitation to the British as had been given to the French earlier. The Wolf had an honorable reputation in his community. The British recognized him as "a Man famous amongst the Indians[,] his Country-men, and firmly attached to the English," and had long desired that the British establish a trading post in Alabama and Coushatta territory.[86]

Britain's presence in the southern interior had been a source of disappointment since the Yamasee War. The disaster forced South Carolina into an economic slump, and by 1729, proprietors handed over the colony to the British Crown. Southeastern peoples recognized by 1730 that South Carolina competed for their trade against French Louisiana.[87] Taking advantage of British interest in the South, The Wolf initially invited a British trader, John Spencer, to trade in Mucclassa. In a report to Britain's Board of Trade, Jonathan Dobell noted in 1745 that Spencer had maintained good relations for some time with the Alabama townspeople and even resided with The Wolf.[88] The Wolf, who likely had kinship ties to Spencer, wanted the Alabama and Coushatta community at large to benefit more directly from British competition with the French at Fort Toulouse. The events that followed indeed accomplished this goal.

Shortly after founding the British colony of Georgia in 1733, Governor James Oglethorpe sought protection for its western boundary. The Alabamas and Coushattas, Tallapoosas, and Abhikas quickly learned that Oglethorpe wanted to build a fort and trading post in their territory to compete with Fort Toulouse and to promote friendship with the British. He had even convinced the South Carolina colony to pay part of the construction and maintenance costs. To help negotiate a deal and to prevent hostilities with neighboring American Indian communities, Oglethorpe commissioned Captain Patrick McKay, a Scotsman, to regulate trade, to distribute presents, and to monitor French and Spanish activities in the region.[89]

In 1734, McKay traveled to the towns of the Abhikas, Tallapoosas, and Alabamas and Coushattas to obtain permission from them to build a British fort. At first he encountered indifference when he met with Alabama leaders, possibly including Opoyheatly. The townspeople were annoyed at McKay's behavior. McKay had caused great offense when he suggested that they burn down Fort Toulouse and expel the French from the region. In the perspective of the Alabamas and Coushattas, this action would destroy not only their center, but also their influence and status among their neighbors; it was simply an absurd idea. McKay also failed to understand their relationship with the French: many Frenchmen had kinship ties to the townspeople. The Alabamas and Coushattas therefore turned down McKay's proposal to establish a post in their territory.[90] McKay had better luck, though, in Okfuskee, a satellite town of the Abhikas, where he persuaded its residents to agree to the British post. Completed and garrisoned in summer of 1734, the fort overlooked the Tallapoosa River. It was ideally located to compete with Fort Toulouse, but it never matched the success of other British forts in the Southeast.[91]

The Wolf knew that the British, despite their construction of Fort Okfuskee, were still vexed by the existence of Fort Toulouse in Alabama and Coushatta territory. As early as 1739, The Wolf had convinced the British that they at least had a trading partnership, albeit informal, with Alabama and Coushatta towns, which "at this Time more especially was of so great Value" considering the rivalry and war between France and Britain.[92] The Wolf wanted to make clear to Governor Oglethorpe that Alabama and Coushatta towns wanted British trade, despite his people's obvious connection with the French at Fort Toulouse. It was a sound economic decision. Ideally, The Wolf and his fellow townspeople would have access to both British and French goods and would be able bargain for the best price in the process. Thus, The Wolf and his "good offices" made repeated attempts to remove Oglethorpe's doubts and fears by visiting him in Savannah and giving him "assurances of friendship."[93]

The Wolf's attempts to persuade the British that he was protecting their interests in Alabama and Coushatta territory caught Oglethorpe's attention. In 1745, The Wolf convinced a group from the Upper Creek town of Wackonkoy (who had previously been living with the French) to establish a new town called Little Wackonkoy, adjacent to his town of Mucclassa. He then pressured James Spencer to work with British commissioners to add Little Wackonkoy to his trading license.[94] The Wolf likely wanted to demonstrate his influence in Alabama and Coushatta territory and neighboring towns by taking these people under his care and direction. More importantly, this action showed British authorities that The Wolf was committed to bringing more British trade to Upper Creek towns, even at the expense of the French.

The Wolf also took full advantage of events in November 1746. Governor James Glen of South Carolina invited all of the neighboring towns' mikos to Charles Town, hoping to establish another British fort and to encourage the friendship of the Alabama and Coushatta, Abhika, and Tallapoosa towns. Most of the towns' representatives attended, including Malatchi, miko of Coweta (a Lower Creek town). Here The Wolf had his opportunity. Glen, pleasantly surprised, reported that The Wolf "not only gave us leave and their Lands to built it [a fort] upon, but also promis'd to defend our men with all their force, in case they should be attacked by the French."[95] The Wolf's motives were clear: if the British built a fort in the Alabama town of Mucclassa (fewer than eight miles from Fort Toulouse), the Alabamas and Coushattas would profit from both British and French competition and have access to more trade goods, of which the French were having difficulty providing. One can also speculate that The Wolf sought to upstage the leaders from the Alabama town of Pakana, who traditionally had the most influence among Europeans. Indeed, another fort within the center of Alabama and Coushatta territory would only add to The Wolf's and Mucclassa's political status and power within the Alabama Nation.[96]

After The Wolf's speech, Malatchi of Coweta, possibly threatened by The Wolf's power grab, spoke out against the invitation. Malatchi threatened Glen by declaring that "as long as he lived he would neither permit us [the British] to take that Fort [Toulouse] or to build one of our own there, if he could prevent it."[97] Representing Coweta and his Upper Creek and French kinsmen, Malatchi's voice echoed throughout Alabama and Coushatta territory. The townspeople who supported Malatchi probably felt threatened by the idea of two forts and French and British soldiers stationed within such a close proximity. Warfare between France and England was ongoing, and two rival garrisons in their towns was potentially a powder keg waiting to explode. If the townspeople were pressed to choose a side—an ominous predicament—which one would they choose, and would their decision cause a rift within the Alabama and Coushatta community?

The Wolf tried to reason with Malatchi and his kinsmen who failed to see his viewpoint. But The Wolf could not garner enough support among Alabama and Coushatta townspeople, so Glen declined his offer. It seems that The Wolf had overstepped his leadership within the Alabama Nation. Even if he had the support of the townspeople from Mucclassa, the failure of his plans demonstrates that one decision affected the entire Alabama Nation. One Alabama town at this point could not act alone: they needed the backing of the entire Nation. Despite The Wolf's failure to bring another fort into Alabama and Coushatta territory, his actions made it clear that he was intent on keeping his people in the center and in direct access to trade routes. In the end, even the presence of Fort Okfuskee in Upper Creek country worked to The Wolf's advantage. Because of Fort Okfuskee's close proximity to Alabama and Coushatta towns, British traders often visited the towns and either stayed or traded with townspeople on a more regular basis. The Wolf had understood that encouraging competition between the British and the French was the key to power.

Fanning Rivalry

During the first half of the eighteenth century, the Alabamas and Coushattas no doubt had benefited from inviting the French to establish a post in the midst of their territory. Fort Toulouse became a passageway leading to and from Carolina, where both the French and the Alabamas and Coushattas could regulate trade in the southern interior and receive good bargains. Townspeople effectively gained a direct market for deerskins, eschewing Carolina middlemen. The Alabama Nation was at the center of European trade.

Indeed, the French recognized the extreme importance of their relationship with the Alabamas and Coushattas. Lieutenant-General de la Tour Vitral's orders from Bienville stated that he was to "keep himself on good terms with the Alibamons."[98] The French valued the Alabamas and Coushattas, a peo-

ple they had "so much interest in treating with consideration."[99] Fort Toulouse was equally important to the French, and
this recognition worked in favor of the Alabamas and Coushattas throughout the eighteenth century. Bienville noted that
the post "advanced in the direction of Carolina and [was]
very important in preventing the English from entering Louisiana."[100] The Alabama fort, described by the French as the
"key to the country," formed the easternmost boundary of
French Louisiana.[101] The fort was one of the nine parts that
divided the colony, and the French officially named the district
"Alibamons." In fact, both the French and the British referred to
Fort Toulouse as the "Fort des Alibamons" or "the Alabama
fort."[102] The Alabamas and Coushattas dominated the territory,
and the French and the British acknowledged this.

French recognition of Alabama and Coushatta power also
extended to trade agreements. On September 20, 1721, French
commissioners ordered that French merchandise shipped to
Fort Toulouse should only sell at a 50 percent profit. This was a
reasonable deal for Alabama and Coushatta townspeople if
compared to the other rates at French forts: the Natchez and
Yazoo rate was 70 percent; the Natchitoches and Arkansas was
80 percent; and the Illinois was 100 percent.[103] The Alabamas
and Coushattas demanded such price breaks and quickly realized that competition helped them receive better discounts.

The Alabama and Coushatta townspeople cashed in on their
collective importance to the French and demanded persistently that they charge the same prices for their goods as did the
British in Carolina. As early as 1720, Alabama men complained
to Bienville that the French "were not buying their rabbit skins
at a price equal to the English of Carolina," and that French
merchandise was more expensive than what the English offered.[104] This complaint was one of many that erupted from
Alabama and Coushatta towns, and the quality and quantity of
French goods exacerbated the problems at Fort Toulouse.

In the first half of the eighteenth century, the Alabamas and
Coushattas learned that French and British traders sold goods
of different quality. The British limbourg cloth, for example,
was more durable than what the French had to offer. British
traders also had great quantities of ribbons, earrings, mirrors,

buckles, belts, shoes, coats of fine materials, and decorated shirts—all of which "appeal to their tastes." The French, on the other hand, had powder and lead—items that the Alabamas, Coushattas, and their neighbors "obtain with great difficulty from the English."[105] From 1720 to 1750, the quantity of munitions and goods flowing from France to the Louisiana colony also declined, leading to shortages and colonial inability to supply southeastern peoples with trade goods. Quantities of supplies including powder and lead declined drastically during wartime. France had engaged in a series of continental wars, including the War of the Spanish Succession (1702–13) against Spain, and the War of the Austrian Succession (1744–48), known as King George's War in the colonies, against Britain. British superiority at sea prevented many French colonies from receiving supplies during these wars, exacerbating shortages of trade goods. Considered a frontier post, Fort Toulouse's interior location made it even more difficult to deliver supplies there. The French also suffered from mutinies at sea that disrupted their supply line, including one incident in October 1722 in which the crew and a group of prisoners seized a freighter full of critical supplies headed for Fort Toulouse.[106]

French troubles caused great frustration among the Alabamas and Coushattas: they could not get the best bargain for something that was not readily available. Although most Alabama towns remained closely tied to the French as they remained within their territory, anti-French sentiments arose among a small faction of Alabamas who were unhappy with the French traders' inability to provide them with necessary trade goods during the last year of King George's War. On October 25, 1748, a group of young men called on their kinsmen to "storm the fort and kill the garrison."[107] The faction had the power to severely hurt the garrison, and the French were worried. The men never convinced others to act on their anti-French feelings, but they stirred up dissention within the Alabama and Coushatta community. Soon after the event, mikos from each town assured the French that they would promote peace among their kinsmen.[108]

To make matters worse, in 1744 Vaudreuil reported that the scarcity of French merchandise made the Alabamas and Coushattas, Creeks, Choctaws, and other peoples dependent on English trade goods. The inferiority of French goods was also a problem. Vaudreuil reported that shipments of muskets and bullets repeatedly arrived damaged. Many Alabama and Coushatta townspeople were disillusioned by the French failure to provide their towns with sufficient high-quality trade goods from Fort Toulouse and therefore sought better opportunities with the British.[109]

British traders frequently courted mikos of Alabama and Coushatta towns, hoping to negotiate trading alliances. In all of their dealings with the French and the British, The Wolf, Opoyheatly, and others realized their people had control over the central lands at the juncture of the Alabama, Tallapoosa, and Coosa rivers. The Alabamas and Coushattas took full advantage of the rivalry and, indeed, helped fuel the fire. The Alabamas, for example, informed Bienville that they made no objection when British traders visited their towns because the latter sold their wares more cheaply than French traders. They suggested that if the French offered the same prices, they would have no need to see the British. The Alabamas and Coushattas also noticed that the French had difficulty matching cheaper English prices on credit terms. In 1743, French traders offered only two livres per deerskin, whereas British buyers would pay the equivalent of five livres for each skin. In Alabama and Coushatta terms, a trade item could be bought from the French for five deerskins or could be had from the English for only two. French officials noted with frustration that Alabama and Coushatta men and women "do not restrict themselves to commerce with the English and that they do not abandon the French entirely."[110] The townspeople therefore had enough leverage to demand an equal exchange rate from the French.

Many Alabamas and Coushattas like The Wolf agreed that they should give the British a chance to compete for their trade. Yet most Alabama and Coushatta mikos continued to claim friendship with the French, or at least agreed to remain in between the two rivals. The Wolf, who had invited the British, and Opoyheatly, who had invited the French, agreed on one issue: British traders could provide essential trade goods that the

French often could not. According to British records, the Alabamas and Coushattas received most of their supplies and clothing from neighboring British traders, despite the lack of a treaty with the British colonial government.[111] Avoiding an official trade agreement with the British gave the Alabamas and Coushattas more leverage. As long as they received trade goods, the townspeople reconciled their differences with both British and French traders.

When the Alabamas and Coushattas demanded better prices and quality goods after dealing with British traders, the French realized that they had little recourse. In 1735, an officer at Fort Toulouse, sieur Benoît, wrote to Bienville, who remained the governor of Louisiana until 1743, that "if we continue to refuse them [the Alabamas] this request, it is to be feared that these Indians may become alienated from our interests."[112] Bienville heeded the advice and informed his men that the French should consent to the demands of the Alabamas and Coushattas. According to Bienville, the French had secured the southern interior "except in the direction of the Alabamas where our establishment [Fort Toulouse] which is situated on the frontier can exist only as long as we keep the Indians in this region in our interests."[113] The French needed the Alabama Nation, and Bienville depended entirely on the cooperation of Opoyheatly, the Wolf, and others to protect Fort Toulouse and its occupants.

The French had many reasons for concern. Bienville complained constantly that British agents like McKay "schemed" to turn southeastern peoples against the French, and The Wolf's actions toward both governors Oglethorpe and Glen confirmed his fears. Alabama and Coushatta townspeople had realized that French supplies would continue to be limited and low in quality compared to what the British offered. Vaudreuil understood the townspeople's predicament: "Supposing even that our goods were of better quality, the fact that there was a difference in price would be enough to give the preference to the English."[114] The Alabamas and Coushattas consequently accepted British bargains and set aside their trading relationship with the French at Fort Toulouse, despite its convenient location in the center of their territory. The Alabamas and Coushattas proved that they could manage their relationship with both empires and even profit from them.

These examples demonstrate how the Alabamas and Coushattas actively pursued trading opportunities and bargains, especially as Franco-British rivalry intensified in the 1740s and 1750s. In the Alabama and Coushatta worldview, trade agreements, like political or military alliances, were not guaranteed. Opoyheatly and The Wolf sought the upper hand in trade relations as a way to ensure the interests of their people; until the mid-1750s, it mattered little with whom agreements were made. Thus, as new markets opened so did economic opportunities. Interestingly, trading with both the French and British kept the Alabamas and Coushattas at the center of the local economic system. From this perspective, the scantly populated European settlements were, in fact, on the periphery.

The Alabamas and Coushattas had built a prosperous diasporic community that quickly established new trade networks by the start of the eighteenth century. Valuable incentives had promoted their involvement in the Indian slave and the deerskin trades, and Alabama and Coushatta participation in such ventures was to a large degree inevitable. Yet they quickly discovered that trade relationships were complicated and often led to intense rivalry and violent disputes with their European and Indian neighbors. After warring with the Chickasaws, Choctaws, Mobilians, and France and England in the first decade of the eighteenth century, the Alabamas and Coushattas invited both French and English emissaries to build forts in the heart of their territory. This preserved their location in the middle of the imperial rivalry and allowed them to obtain power over their neighbors. Although they persuaded the French to establish only one fort, the Alabamas and Coushattas gained new opportunities for trade and personal relationships that proved equally important in diplomatic negotiations during war between foreign powers.

A consequence of establishing trading networks with Europeans was the gradual transformation of Alabama and Coushatta ethos, language, and, most predominantly, kinship. There is no doubt that the Alabama and Coushatta worldview had altered with European contact, but there was still continuity that recalled their Mississippian roots. Most importantly, the union between the Alabamas and Coushattas remained intact. The Alabamas and Coushattas had created a new world with Europeans in their midst, yet they also were constructing a new space where they would be at the center with both American Indian communities and European nations.

3

Leverage Gained, Leverage Lost

The oral tradition, "How Fire Came to the Alabamas and Coushattas," tells the story of how bears were the keepers of Fire. They protected and carried Fire wherever they traveled, and were also careful not to let any other animal or those outside the Bear Clan use or sit close to it. Despite the Bears' caution, one day they haphazardly left Fire on the ground while they ate acorns nearby. The Bear guardians lingered as they ate, and their neglect of Fire caused it to become very weak, so weak that it called for help. A group of Alabamas and Coushattas heard the cries, and rushed to Fire's aid. They collected sticks from the surrounding woods and placed on Fire a stick from the north, west, south, and finally the east, representing the four world-quarters or cardinal points that were sacred to their people. When the Alabamas and Coushattas had finished placing all four sticks on Fire, it grew strong and burned for a long time. According to Alabama and Coushatta storytellers, this was how Fire left the care of the Bears and came to stay with them.[1]

This story reflects how the Alabamas and Coushattas worked together to obtain fire, one of the most important elements of endurance and power. Their gathering of the four sticks and methodical placement of each in its sacred direction suggests their coalescence through kinship and the formation of social and political bonds. They took great care to build such a union—a slow and deliberate process not too dissimilar from starting a bonfire from dry kindling—not only to help them combat enemies in the wake of their diaspora, but also to thrive in their new landscape. Fire left in the care of the Alabamas and Coushattas also provides a metaphor for their creation and continued construction of a diplomatic center where power rested, like the earthen mounds of their ancient ancestors. The critical task was to keep the fire burning. They learned that maintaining internal cohesion as well as cooperation with their American Indian and European neighbors was absolutely necessary; war could destroy everything. The Alabamas and Coushattas were now responsible for fire, which could only be maintained with solidarity.

Cooperation was vital because their sacred center lay along the junction of the Alabama River, between imperial rivalries, and the Alabamas and Coushattas would soon witness a battle for control over the southern interior in the mid-eighteenth century. Inviting the French to build a fort in their territory had increased Alabama and Coushatta influence not only in trade, but also in politics and diplomacy. When rivalries and regional disputes erupted, the Alabamas and Coushattas promoted peace and neutrality between American Indian and European communities. The goal of the Alabamas and Coushattas in the long run was to maintain their center in this chaotic zone. As the contest erupted and eventually led to brutal wars in the last half of the eighteenth century, the Alabamas and Coushattas discovered that developing relationships with their neighbors and holding the balance of power promoted their sovereignty and survival. Yet just as fire eventually dies out, the Alabama and Coushatta center could not last forever. The Alabamas and Coushattas would be forced to make a difficult decision whether to stay or find a new homeland in the western hinterlands.

Diplomatic Brokers: Captain Pakana's Mission

In October 1737, the principal war chief of the Alabamas, Captain Pakana (from the Alabama town of Pakana), presented French commander Diron d'Artaguette with two maps drawn on an albino deerskin, "a present as an unexampled rarity."[2] One map, created by Captain Pakana, depicted Chickasaw country based on his visit to the town of Oyoula Tchitoka and the diplomatic talks that followed. The second map, drafted by Chickasaw headman Mingo Ouma with the help of Captain Pakana, depicted a series of circles, each representing American Indian nations of the Southeast and their respective boundaries. The Chickasaws' territory was painted white on the map, yet was surrounded by an outer red circle that represented the red warpaths of their enemies, such as the Choctaws, whom the French aided. Although drawn from the Chickasaws' perspective, Gregory Waselkov has noted that American Indian maps not only identify the spatial relationship between peoples, but also political and social ones.[3]

From the Alabama and Coushatta perspective, the Chickasaw map recognized their territorial boundaries as a united nation. It identified white (or peaceful) paths, trade routes, and hunting grounds as finger-like extensions. The Alabama River connected the Alabama Nation (which included the Coushattas) to the French in Mobile; according to the map, no other direct path to Mobile existed. Everything near the Alabama Nation designated the sacred space that their people had created after their diaspora. The location of the Alabama Nation appeared separately from surrounding Creek towns and groups: the Cowetas, Cussitas, Yuchis, and Okfuskees. The white paths drawn to these towns indicated that they were peaceful. Mingo Ouma and Captain Pakana also noted the locations of their English and French neighbors with circles, though these were quite small compared to the circles identifying the locations of the Chickasaws and the Choctaws. The European nations were not in the center, but mere players off to the far ends of the map. The most important feature of the Chickasaw map was the central position of the Alabama Nation. White paths led directly to each town in the Alabama Nation's territory or to French and British forts.

The Chickasaw map clearly indicated that the Alabamas and Coushattas claimed land that was at the center of the Franco-British imperial rivalry. It was a dynamic zone where territorial claims overlapped and peoples collided. Captain Pakana used the center to broker relationships with neighboring peoples. His efforts promoted the territory of the Alabama Nation as a place of refuge where neighbors, even former enemies the Chickasaws and the Choctaws, sought council and reprieve.

One source of local conflict was the heightened aggression between the Choctaws and Chickasaws that lasted throughout the early to mid-eighteenth century. French emissaries had repeatedly encouraged the Choctaws to destroy the Chickasaws, whom the British had supported and armed for decades. The Choctaws had allied with the French in the early 1700s after they experienced repeated Chickasaw slave raids against their towns. The Chickasaws' infamous reputation as one of the most successful slaving groups in the South was deserved. They sold most prisoners to Carolina traders in exchange for European goods. The Choctaws often reciprocated the Chickasaw attacks and with French encouragement hunted them down for their scalps, which they delivered to Mobile in exchange for a lucrative bounty. French commander Artaguette noted that "they often bring us scalps, but considering what it costs in war expenses they are expensive scalps."[4] After years of warfare between the Chickasaws and the French-allied Choctaws, Mingo Ouma, an esteemed Chickasaw war chief, and Choctaw headman Shulush Houma (Red Shoe) desired a temporary truce.

The Alabamas and Coushattas, having "the reputation among all the nations of being people of intelligence and of good council," intervened and attempted to negotiate an end to the vicious war.[5] After Shulush Houma gave indication of wanting peace (despite disagreement within his nation), in April 1735 Captain Pakana and fellow Alabama and Coushatta mikos allowed four Chickasaw chiefs and thirty warriors to visit the Alabama Nation. Captain Pakana advised Mingo Ouma to seek peace with the Choctaws. After much discussion, Mingo

Ouma agreed that many French and Choctaw raids against the Chickasaws had caused too much instability and death. Captain Pakana insisted that he and six of his fellow headmen of the Alabama Nation go to Mobile to negotiate a peace on behalf of the Chickasaws. According to the governor of Louisiana, Jean-Baptiste Le Moyne de Bienville, "the Alabama chiefs whom I had with me, caused me to permit them [the Chickasaws] to come to see me."[6] Captain Pakana served as a mediator and helped broker a temporary armistice between the Chickasaws and the French.

Upon Captain Pakana's request, Choctaw ambassadors including Shulush Houma visited the Alabama Nation to discuss relations with the Chickasaws. Shortly after attending several assemblies with Captain Pakana, the Choctaws agreed to a temporary peace, despite their long-standing rivalry with the Chickasaws. Shulush Houma, like Mingo Ouma, realized that an armistice made his people a stronger force, helped to maintain autonomy, and provided added stability in the southern interior.[7] While peace between the two tribes was not completely successful in the end, Captain Pakana had demonstrated his power and wisdom in diplomacy. Like principal chief Opoyheatly, Captain Pakana's reputation as a great leader grew in the Alabama Nation and neighboring communities: his leadership resembled that of ancient Mississippian chiefs. It is ironic that the Alabamas and Coushattas, once hunted down by Chickasaw and Choctaw war parties, were now the keepers of the realm because of Captain Pakana's leadership and skills in finding the middle ground.

Years later, Captain Pakana continued his role as an ambassador and led another series of diplomatic negotiations, this time between the French and the Chickasaws. Acting on behalf of Bienville, Captain Pakana brokered another deal with the Chickasaws. In February 1737 the Captain and Mingo Ouma arranged a prisoner of war exchange: two Frenchmen for a Chickasaw headman named Courcerac. Mingo Ouma agreed to the trade only if it was conducted by Captain Pakana of the Alabama Nation.[8]

On June 26, the Captain traveled to Chickasaw country with five other headmen, including the Coushatta war leader Tamatlé Mingo and twenty-five Alabama and Coushatta warriors. Arriving on July 16, Captain Pakana was surprised to learn that the British had arrived earlier and broken the agreement by exchanging the imprisoned French officer Claude Drouet de Richardville; the British did this without considering the repercussions. The other French soldier meant for the exchange, a man named Gamot, had escaped en route to Georgia. The Chickasaws' imprisoned headman, Courcerac, had already been released and escorted home as a part of the bargain. Courcerac's sister expressed to Captain Pakana that she deeply regretted her people's failure to live up to their end of the prisoner exchange. Captain Pakana, insulted by this blatant show of disrespect, responded by making the Chickasaws "ashamed by telling them how little faith they had in him."[9]

Through fault or design, the Chickasaws had quashed Captain Pakana's efforts to act as a broker between them and the French. Despite the debacle, Captain Pakana used the situation to his advantage. In diplomatic talks with Captain Pakana, Mingo Ouma related his people's affairs: "What do the French think they are doing and of what use are our scalps to pay them for it that they try to persuade all the nations to dip their hands in our blood? Do they find treasures in our heads [which make them] return to our lands?" After a long conference with Captain Pakana, who encouraged the Chickasaws to pursue peace, Mingo Ouma told him that his people "would hope that the French would become their friends."[10] Captain Pakana had become not only a broker of peace, but also a confidant to Chickasaw chiefs; he empathized with their distress over the war with the French and influenced their decisions to end it.

Captain Pakana's honorable interactions with Mingo Ouma gained another ally, the "Great Chief of the Chickasaws," Ymaiatabé Leborgne. Ymaiatabé viewed the Alabama Nation as a place of refuge where Captain Pakana maintained peaceful relations with neighboring peoples. Ymaiatabé complained that the continual conflict with the Choctaws left them so weak that "they cannot enjoy a moment's rest" and requested that Captain Pakana allow a group of his people to settle among the Alabamas.[11] Ymaiatabé's plea also stemmed from his poor relationship with British Indian agents. During one event, Ymaiatabé told a British agent to cease making hostile remarks while Captain Pakana spoke to Chickasaw townspeople. According to Captain Pakana, the Englishman "reprimanded him with a blow of the fist and made this poor one-eyed man stop speaking." Ymaiatabé wanted out.[12]

When Mingo Ouma heard Ymaiatabé's request, he announced, "Those who had such plans ought to be regarded as women, since they are abandoning their country at a time when it needed them." Despite the remarks, Ymaiatabé planned to escape with his followers to the Alabama Nation that autumn.[13] It is unclear if Ymaiatabé's people settled among the Alabamas, but it is understandable why Captain Pakana would have considered his request. First, if a group of Chickasaws became part of the Alabama Nation, it would increase the number of warriors, thereby adding to the strength of the Nation. Second, and more importantly, this act would demonstrate to outsiders that the Alabama Nation welcomed those who sought refuge. The Alabamas and Coushattas probably understood the difficulties of finding safe ground in such a chaotic zone.

Captain Pakana and his kinsmen stayed with the Chickasaws for two weeks. He participated in a general assembly of all the Chickasaws and performed the calumet ceremony of peace with them. On August 14, 1737, Captain Pakana returned to his town of Pakana "in ceremony holding up a calumet that the Chickasaws had given him on receiving him as a great chief of their nation."[14] Captain Pakana and Tamatlé Mingo of the Coushattas (likely under the direction of the Captain) related to Artaguette his affairs with Mingo Ouma, and gave him the two deerskin maps described earlier. Captain Pakana assured Artaguette that because of his efforts the French would be able to travel safely via the Mississippi River.[15] Captain Pakana seemed to have everything under control.

Later that year, however, Captain Pakana threatened retaliation if the Chickasaws staged any attack against Fort Toulouse, which he likely viewed as part of his town, or molested any Frenchmen near the Mississippi River. The Captain sent word to Mingo Ouma that they needed to keep the paths white—that is, to allow peaceful commerce and travel along the rivers and other trade routes. The Alabamas and Coushattas wished to see no more French blood spilled on their ground. Moreover, Captain Pakana guaranteed that any attack on the French would spark a full-scale war between the Alabama Nation and the Chickasaws. Although this threat was a risk, the Chickasaws, who had already fought many costly wars, heeded Captain Pakana's advice and expressed their wish to maintain peaceful relations with both the Alabama Nation and the French at Fort Toulouse.[16]

By brokering peace, Captain Pakana demonstrated the Alabama Nation's central role in this process. The Captain had commanded respect within his own community and from others, and Bienville needed his assistance. Captain Pakana promoted harmony between his neighbors and the French for three reasons. First, Captain Pakana and his people had sought to protect their French kinsmen; townspeople closest to Fort Toulouse, such as his town of Pakana, had the most intimate relations with the French garrison. Though we know few details about the Captain, he probably had French kin, which could have helped motivate his efforts. Second, if Captain Pakana brokered peace agreements between the French and their American Indian enemies, the demand for military supplies would be alleviated and trading paths would be better protected from enemy raids. If the plan worked, a regular supply of trade goods and European arms and munitions would flow into Alabama and Coushatta towns. Last, and most importantly, Opoyheatly had invited the French to build Fort Toulouse in their territory on the sacred mound, and both he and the Captain wanted to help ensure its safety. The townspeople considered Alabama and Coushatta lands, including Fort Toulouse, as the center of their world: a balance to the existing order was necessary for its survival. The area outside their sacred space was chaotic and dynamic, where peoples collided and competed for status, wealth, and land. Captain Pakana's actions demonstrate that the Alabamas and Coushattas held sacred the stability and balance within and around their center, just as their Mississippian ancestors.

The Creek Alliance

The Alabamas and Coushattas had learned in their earlier encounters with Europeans that alliances with neighboring towns were a necessity when living in territory claimed by many. Diaspora communities in the Southeast were especially vulnerable when Spain, France, and Britain competed for alliances with larger peoples such as the Chickasaws, Choctaws, and Cherokees. European imperial machinations compelled smaller, diasporic groups like the Alabamas and Coushattas to band together. Maintaining successful alliances with their like-minded neighbors could be advantageous; it provided protection against their more numerous enemies and increased their power among foreign emissaries. The Alabamas and Coushattas were among these groups to join a broad alliance with neighboring diasporic peoples that shared similar Mississippian roots: they were known collectively as the Creek Indians. Details describing the original creation of the Creek alliance (often referred to as the Creek Confederacy) are unclear and are still debated among historians, but most agree that it existed by the mid-eighteenth century.[17]

According to oral tradition, the Creeks consisted of around thirty-three separate communities. Satellite towns of the main ethnic groups may have numbered up to one hundred. Europeans divided the peoples they called Creeks into two regions—upper and lower. The Abhikas, Tallapoosas, Alabamas, and Coushattas were included in the upper towns (often referred to as the Upper Creeks by Europeans). The lower towns included the Cowetas, Cussitas, and Apalachicolas. The upper towns were located along the Coosa, Tallapoosa, and Alabama rivers, while the lower towns were situated along the Flint, Chattahoochee, and Ocmulgee rivers. The combined peoples occupied over five hundred square miles of territory stretching from East Florida to the Appalachian Mountains, from the area east and west of the Savannah River to the Mobile River and its tributaries. The Upper Creeks encompassed more than 10,000 people during the first decade of the eighteenth century.[18]

As Europeans fought for hegemony over the Southeast in the eighteenth century, representatives of the Alabamas and Coushattas met often with their closest neighbors, the Tallapoosas and Abhikas, to discuss foreign policy. These conferences usually assembled when mikos sent scouts to neighboring villages; the sticks in the messenger's bundle represented the number of days before the meeting began. Each town had special envoys that communicated information. Conch-shell heralds announced meetings, the arrival of town leaders, and the departure of envoys. They also gathered for one of the most important seasonal events that dated back to the days of Mississippian chiefdoms, the Green Corn Ceremony (*buskida*). During late summer or early fall, men and women from Creek towns celebrated the harvest of their crops during a four- to eight-day ritual cycle. It was a time of renewal and purification as they rebuilt a sacred fire that burned year-round. The post-contact world altered the ceremony by focusing more on community bonds, but the meaning remained the same. This tradition brought towns together and provided opportunities to renew their alliances.[19]

When towns gathered for meetings, attending representatives probably spoke the Mobilian trade language that most southeastern peoples understood. Finding a common language was necessary in order to communicate with peoples like the Alabamas and Coushattas, whose languages many found unintelligible. Sharing the Muskogean language helped unite the Creek towns, but each group had different dialects. The Alabamas and Coushattas, for instance, were not true Muskogean speakers; their languages, Alabama and Koasati, respectively, were in the same family, but different (true Muskogean speakers were from the towns of Coweta, Cussita, Coosa, and Abhika). Consequently, their Creek neighbors treated the Alabamas and Coushattas as outsiders, using the term "stinkards."[20]

Despite these differences, in 1743 Father Morand, a Jesuit who resided at Fort Toulouse, reported to Governor Vaudreuil that the Abhikas, Cowetas, and Tallapoosas formed "a single nation with the Alabamas [and Coushattas]."[21] French visitor Jean-Bernard Bossu made a similar remark when he noted that in these meetings the mikos advised young men "to face adversity courageously and to sacrifice everything for the love of nation and liberty."[22] These observations demonstrate the townspeople's close ties to each other, which were sometimes established through kinship. However, both Morand and Bossu lacked the understanding of each group's sovereignty: to the chagrin of the Europeans, these towns did not act as a single nation.

The Creek alliance was complicated and often fleeting. It was by no means a static entity; political schisms were common, if not frequent. As historian Steven Hahn has suggested, the Creeks did not act as a confederacy, but rather "an allied yet individually provincial group."[23] Fluid relationships predominated and were typical of diasporic communities. The structure of the Creek alliance allowed diversity of opinion and town sovereignty. Heterogeneity persisted and when pressed, each group sought its interests at the expense of the Creek alliance. For example, the Lower towns (with the exception of Coweta) had frequent access to British traders in South Carolina and pro-British factions often dominated politics. The Upper towns of the Alabama Nation, on the other hand, traditionally favored the French because of the close proximity of Fort Toulouse.

Based on regional geopolitical interests, the Upper Creek towns often formed external alliances that excluded Lower Creek towns, and the Lower Creeks responded in kind. Small disputes among clans in the various Creek towns developed, but warfare rarely erupted between these communities; it was not in their best interests to fight each other when rivals surrounded them. The union, then, offered added security in the midst of warfare and slave raids from their enemies. Membership also gave the allies additional opportunities and legitimacy when dealing with European emissaries. The Alabamas and Coushattas recognized that the Creek alliance enhanced their negotiating hand vis-à-vis the European powers.

Diplomatic Maneuvers

As they formed alliances with their neighbors and acted as brokers in diplomatic negotiations, the Alabamas and Coushattas knew that they were at the center of Anglo-French rivalry. Alabama and Coushatta townspeople particularly enjoyed high status with the French, who were desperate to preserve peace in order to protect their colony from British incursion into Louisiana. Leaders like Captain Pakana realized that taking the middle ground was critical if they were to benefit from European imperial competition. For the most part, then, Alabama and Coushatta leaders pursued a diplomatic course of peace in order to maintain their power while foreign emissaries vied for American Indian allegiances during conflicts and wars.

One incident that tested the Alabama and Coushatta balance involved a meeting with Bienville, governor of Louisiana. In April 1735, vexed by British competition, he invited Captain Pakana, Opoyheatly, and five other leaders from Alabama and Coushatta towns to Mobile. When Bienville questioned them about their relations with the British, they announced that the Alabamas and Coushattas "would observe an exact neutrality between the whites," and they would do everything in their power to keep their neighbors in the same sentiments.[24] Captain Pakana and Opoyheatly had obligations to the townspeople to avoid involvement in European disputes. Moreover, based on their experiences, they both knew that British traders had valuable trade goods that the French could not necessarily provide, especially during war.

Their test continued during King George's War (1744–48). The French tried desperately to convince Upper Creek towns to make war on the British despite Creek declarations of neutrality. Nevertheless, according to Vaudreuil, the Alabamas "still preserve a precise neutrality" between the French and the British; it best served their interests.[25] The Wolf of Mucclassa followed Captain Pakana's lead by also practicing this strategy during the war. According to British trader Jonathan Spencer (who lived with The Wolf's kinspeople), the Alabama Nation was "in strict Amity with the Creeks" who remained largely neutral.[26] Captain Pakana and The Wolf had talks with their Abhika and Tallapoosa neighbors and, according to The Wolf, had resolved that "whatever the White Men might do, it should make no matter of Disturbance to them: that no Red Men's Blood should be spilt, but that they would continue just as they were."[27] The Wolf pursued neutrality between the British and the French despite his attachments to Spencer. Thus, the Alabamas and Coushattas kept two fires burning, one for the French and one for the English.

The determination of the Alabamas and Coushattas to stay out of European conflicts was much easier when paltry disputes and harmless competition erupted in the Southeast, but their strategy proved more difficult during the French and Indian War (1754–63). The war began as a border conflict between Great Britain and France near Fort Duquesne in Pennsylvania and quickly triggered what Europeans labeled the Seven Years' War. Each country battled for control over its colonial possessions. The strategy of King Louis XV of France was to lure British troops into North America to facilitate an attack on the exposed German state of Hanover. The French Crown consequently reserved its troops for Europe, and it sent very few to Louisiana or Canada.[28] The shortage of French soldiers in the colonies made alliances with American Indians vital to a French victory. Southeastern peoples witnessed little or no battles because soldiers contained most of the fighting to the north. Yet the Alabamas and Coushattas and their neighbors discovered that this war was different from other colonial skirmishes between Great Britain and France: gaining American Indian alliances seemed much more important to agents in a war where the winner would take all.

When news of the war spread, the Alabamas and Coushattas openly declared their neutrality, as they did in previous disputes. Noninolvement in this war was important to them. There is no doubt that the Alabamas and Coushattas actively encouraged the ongoing rivalry between the two empires; it benefited the Alabama Nation, especially when it came to trade and gift giving. Actual warfare, however, was not necessarily a benefit: it would disrupt trade routes, potentially reduce gift distribution as resources dried up, and risk the lives of their warriors. More importantly, the natural order and balance of their center would be in danger.

Initially the Alabamas and Coushattas made the most of European courtship by receiving agents and their gifts of friendship. French and British emissaries traveled frequently to various towns in an effort to gain the allegiance of southeastern peoples. Both the British and the French acknowledged the importance of sealing an alliance with the Alabama Nation because of its strategically central position. Located between the Alabama, Coosa, and Tallapoosa rivers, Alabama and Coushatta territory ran through primary trading routes to the Upper and Lower Creeks and the Choctaw Nation. If the French or English won the favor of the Alabama Nation, agents would be able to travel safely in the quest to obtain American Indian alliances during the war. Moreover, British superintendent of southeastern Indian affairs Edmond Atkin noted that in addition to their command over some 475 warriors, the Alabama Nation had maintained an alliance with the Abhikas and the Tallapoosas, which would equal even more potential allies.[29]

The Alabamas and Coushattas' refusal to take sides vexed Atkin. According to his report in 1755, "the Policy of the Creeks leads them to live in Peace with all their Neighbours; but above all to preserve a good Understanding with all white People, English, French, and Spaniards; with each of whom they have Intercourse." Even Atkin appreciated the shrewd diplomacy of the Alabamas, Coushattas, and their neighbors; their neutrality provided them with the upper hand. Atkin commented that "they take part against neither, but are Courted by them Severally, and receive Presents from each."[30] Alabama and Coushatta leaders saw an opportunity dangling in front of them and made the most of it. Situated between empires, they played each off the other and initially received favorable trade and gifts from both.

Their strategy was a clever one, yet when the sacred center of the Alabama Nation was threatened or perceived to be in danger, the Alabamas and Coushattas were hard pressed to decide their next move. One such incident occurred when Atkin attempted to obtain alliances with the Abhikas, Tallapoosas, and the Alabamas and Coushattas in 1759. He understood that since 1716 the Alabamas and Coushattas had "the most intimate connection with the French and been particularly serviceable to them many ways more than other Indians."[31] Members of Alabama and Coushatta towns at times swayed to the French cause when pushed, or at least remained on friendly terms. Members of Pakana and Taskigi had close ties to the French; after all, Fort Toulouse was within a short walking distance from their towns. Despite this knowledge, Atkin was unprepared when a group of young Coushatta (and possibly Alabama) warriors described as "renegades" from Taskigi and Coosada, discovered his party traveling through the Alabama Nation on September 7, 1759, and attempted to kill them all.[32]

So what provoked these men to attack Atkin and his entourage, especially considering the benefits of maintaining neutrality? A possible reason was the threat of attack on Fort Toulouse by the British. It is unclear whether the invasion was merely a rumor propagated by the French, but, according to Atkin, the possibility sent some townspeople to aid the French garrison. Such actions were understandable considering that the fort was in the heart of their territory; the Alabamas and Coushattas drew both power and trade from it. To attack the fort was a direct assault on the Alabama Nation. Maintaining their community center was critical to their position in the Southeast. Also, kinship ties to the French should not be ignored as another reason; family loyalty could sway members to cross the line drawn by the British.

Warriors from other Alabama and Coushatta towns joined the resistance against the British. Atkin reported that the townspeople added to the hostility by propagating "lies to incense and create Jealousies among the Creeks," further impeding the British Crown's aim to obtain alliances.[33] The Alabamas and Coushattas' warnings to other communities about British terrorization had delayed Atkin's goal of obtaining friendship with members of neighboring towns. A group of warriors made repeated threats against him, and Atkin suspected that the townspeople had arranged many of these plots at Fort Toulouse. In grand irony, Atkin noted that the Alabamas and Coushattas had regularly supported the French by obtaining goods from British traders, from which they had no official agreement with the British Crown. Bemused, he believed that if not for British supplies from the Alabama Nation, Fort Toulouse would be unable to maintain its garrison.

Punishment for the Alabamas and Couhattas' attack was swift. On September 7, 1759, Atkin banned all British trade with the Alabama Nation and to all other peoples thought to reside in its towns. Opoyheatly and other town leaders took the injunction seriously. The Alabamas and Coushattas had relied on British trade goods when the French came up short. Whereas some townspeople discussed a possible solution to Atkin's order, others responded violently. On September 28, 1759, Atkin addressed Creek leaders in Tuckabatchee. He told the leaders that they had been too friendly with the French, going so far as to call them Frenchmen. He was so dissatisfied that he refused to shake their hands, which was a show of extreme disrespect. An Alabama headman named Tobacco-Eater responded to Atkin's impudence by telling the Abhika and Tallapoosa representatives how much he despised the British agent. Enraged, Tobacco-Eater then threw his hatchet directly at Atkin's head, but just missed him, striking the board above him instead. Tobacco-Eater attempted to repeat the attack with a mortal blow, but another warrior held him back and prevented further injury. Atkin was lucky to survive; he later learned that Tobacco-Eater's attack was part of a plot to murder him and expel the British from their territory. Although Tobacco-Eater's assassination attempt failed, his actions reflected the Alabamas' bitterness toward Atkin's injunction and his attempt to convince neighboring Creek towns to side with the British. He was effectively destroying the Alabama Nation's center, and Tobacco-Eater wanted him dead.[34]

To the Alabamas and Coushattas' detriment, the trade embargo proved effective. Just as Atkin suspected, the French at Fort Toulouse struggled to supply their own garrison, and Alabama and Coushatta townspeople faced the unpleasant prospect of doing without trade goods, especially much-needed muskets, powder, and shot. Opoyheatly called a meeting of his council and town mikos. Shortly after Atkin's injunction, six leaders from Okchai, Little Okchai, Coosada, Taskigi, Wetumpka, and Pakana, traveled to the neutral ground of Tuckabatchee to meet with Atkin on October 9, 1759, in the hope of resolving the dispute. Speaking for the "General Voice of those towns," they offered him a "Token of Friendship by putting clean white dressed Deer Skins on his [Atkin's] seat under him and also others under his feet." Opoyheatly described his people's "Great Distress" because they lacked needed British goods. He explained that the French were "utterly unable to supply their wants." According to Atkin, Opoyheatly and the others "humbly request[ed] to be looked upon and treated as well as the Creeks by having the same Trade allowed to them professing equal Friendship and promising to have in perfect Peace with his Majesty's Subjects." They stressed that the Alabamas and Coushattas had sent them based on common agreement and had authorized them to agree to the terms necessary to reopen trade.[35]

After Opoyheatly's demonstration of friendship, Atkin agreed to discuss terms of peace. He would allow the Alabamas and Coushattas to purchase trade goods from licensed British traders at the same rates as other southeastern towns, such as Little Tallassee on the Coosa River. Opoyheatly and the others had to agree, of course, to a long list of stipulations. First, all peoples from Alabama and Coushatta towns could buy British goods for their use only; they could not donate or sell any items to the French. Second, they had to refrain from interrupting trade with the Choctaws or with any other traders passing through Alabama or Coushatta territory. Third, they had to cease acting as couriers to the French by delivering their messages to Mobile or Fort Tombecbé; Atkin stressed that the French should be responsible for this task, not the Alabamas and Coushattas. Fourth, Alabama and Coushatta men and women had to terminate all relations with the French, which included trade and any other personal visits. Fifth, they had to deny trade from any British subject without direct permission of Atkin himself. Sixth, they had to pay a rightful penalty if they caused any physical or monetary injury to any British subject. Finally, they had to make a public declaration of their loyalty to the British Crown by flying the British colors in each town square during all public occasions. The Alabamas and Coushattas had to "faithfully observe and comply" with all of Atkin's terms in order for the treaty to be valid. If the townspeople broke any of these agreements, Atkin threatened to halt all trade in their towns.[36]

The full implications of the treaty were quite severe. The Alabamas and Coushattas had to recognize the authority of the

British Crown and, more importantly, had to deny their French kinsmen entrance into their towns. Opoyheatly and his men discussed the stipulations at great length, and finally agreed to accept Atkin's terms. On October 10, 1759, after Atkin distributed much needed gifts among the men, Topoye (representative and chief warrior of Coosada), Eefamico (representative and chief warrior of Taskigi), Emahthlyhahgio (miko of Little Okchai), and Eefahgio, (a representative of Wetumpka, possibly affiliated with the town of Coosada), signed the Treaty of Friendship and Commerce with the British. Opoyheatly, however, waited seven long days before signing the document (it was the last document with Opoyheatly's mark).[37] His delay made it obvious that he struggled over the treaty's stipulations; he was apparently very reluctant to sever ties with the French. Opoyheatly, after all, had invited them into their territory, and Pakana had close and intimate contact with the French.

By signing the treaty, Alabama and Coushatta townspeople, at least in theory, proclaimed their friendship to the British. Interestingly, the treaty was not an alliance to the British Crown, but an agreement that recognized British hegemony over trade. Yet the mikos and their kinspeople probably did not intend to abide to Atkin's long list of stipulations. In fact, they openly evaded the treaty's provisions. Atkin's restrictions were ridiculous if one considers that Fort Toulouse was in the middle of their territory. How could they avoid the French and prohibit visits with them? Moreover, many of the Alabamas and Coushattas had French kin and could not simply end all contact. Atkin, though disgruntled with the townspeople's continued commitment to the French, could not enforce the treaty. Opoyheatly and other mikos knew Atkin had bigger problems than their ignoring his rules: the British had a full-scale war to fight with the Cherokees and their Creek allies.

The Mortar's War: The Creek-Cherokee War Party

Despite the agreements made under the Treaty of Friendship and Commerce, hostilities between the British and the Alabama Nation intensified under the leadership of the war chief Yahatastonake, commonly known as The Mortar, or The Great

Mortar. The Mortar lived in Little Okchai, but also had kinship connections to Okchai (his brother-in-law was the head warrior, Gun Merchant). It seems that The Mortar had filled the space left by Captain Pakana (presumably the Captain died earlier, though records provide no details). Unlike the Captain, however, The Mortar was uninterested in brokering peaceful relations; Little Okchai was likely a red town, which may help explain his commitment to war. The Mortar traded often at Fort Toulouse and was largely pro-French, especially after dealing with Atkin at the infamous Creek council in 1759 at Tuckabatchee. Before Tobacco-Eater struck Atkin with his hatchet, as described earlier, the British officer had refused to let The Mortar take the peace pipe that the rest of the men had passed around to smoke. Atkin had accused The Mortar of being tied to the French and therefore had no right to engage in the calumet ceremony. Atkin's reproach deeply offended The Mortar and caused great resentment toward the British agent and his cause.[38]

Considering his grudge toward Atkin, it is clear why The Mortar joined the Cherokees in a war against the British (1760–62). The Cherokees' main target was South Carolina and British traders in Charles Town. The Cherokees, along with many other southeastern peoples, despised corrupt British trading practices, especially as they relied heavily on liquor for trade. Without a doubt, liquor had been a sore subject among many American Indian communities for decades. Even the French recognized the abuse. According to French commander Louboey, it was "the main thing in all negotiations with the red men."[39] French Governor Vaudreuil noted earlier that Englishmen often took advantage of intoxicated men, when after "seeing that they have spent everything in drink, [the trader] gives them credit in order to attract them better."[40] This practice often led to a vicious cycle of debt, and Cherokee and Creek leaders believed that Atkin did little to prevent such abuse.

The Mortar's role in the war began in June 1760 when he and fellow warriors attacked and killed eleven British traders. The Mortar traveled to the Cherokee Nation in an effort to help organize allies in a full-scale war against the British. Fort Toulouse became a safe haven for those wanting to fight the

British, and some warriors from Alabama and Coushatta towns joined the faction. According to Louis Billouart de Kerlérec, then governor of Louisiana, the war party numbered 8,000 men. The Mortar assured Kerlérec that they destroyed all but thirty of a British army of 3,000 men sent to destroy the Cherokees (Kerlérec, however, believed that the numbers they cited were too high). They also made a series of successful raids on English settlements. At a meeting with Kerlérec in Mobile, The Mortar requested that the French provide warriors with trade goods; he and his men had quit the British and could no longer obtain their goods.[41]

Increasing pro-French sentiments and lack of British trade within the Alabama Nation led some of its warriors to participate in the Cherokee war against the British. Moreover, many Alabama and Coushatta warriors, like The Mortar, opposed Atkin's display of power, which directly challenged their own. Atkin's orders suspending trade cut down the Alabama Nation's superiority and dominance in the area. Trade from the French was scarce during the war, and Alabama and Coushatta townspeople likely felt abandoned. After Atkin was finished with them, many feared that they would have very little opportunity or power left. In response, a faction of Alabama and Coushatta warriors abandoned any hope of neutrality in an attempt to destroy the British presence in the Southeast.

Yet one problem remained. The Mortar's faction needed weapons and supplies to fight the war. The French, while willing to support them, lacked goods to distribute. French officials warned the governor that they needed to maintain a steady flow of presents and weapons to support this faction. Kerlérec argued that "if we continue to be in the state of destitution in which we have been left for such a long time, we must not doubt that the same nations [Alabamas and Cherokees] will turn their weapons against us after having made their peace with the English, and this colony is by no means in a position to resist them."[42] Cherokee, Creek, and Alabama and Coushatta warriors warned that if the French failed to send them assistance and goods, they would be forced to abandon the French cause. The French therefore tried to distribute presents and provisions from their limited supply.[43]

Like those fighting alongside the Cherokees, some towns-people within the Alabama Nation gave their loyalty to the French and consequently forbade British enemies from entering their towns. In 1761, the combined Alabama and Coushatta towns of Pakana, Coosada, and Taskigi prevented British traders from selling goods among their people. Little Okchai, on the other hand, permitted Englishmen John Rae and William Trewin to trade with the townspeople. Ironically, these traders entered the town even though The Mortar (who had led the townspeople of Little Okchai) had organized a war party that killed many Englishmen.[44]

These examples demonstrate the varying responses to the British during the war. Many Alabamas and Coushattas had refused to submit to British authority, despite Atkin's threats to cut off trade. His injunction had initially worked, but the townspeople did as they pleased, seeking their own needs. They continued to battle with the British, yet traded with them in order to obtain essential goods that the French could no longer provide; many townspeople were simply trying to survive the war.[45] The downside of this individual town autonomy and self-interest during the war was the division it created within the Alabama and Coushatta community as a whole, which threatened balance and order.

The Mortar's actions against the British despite The Wolf's previous friendship with them also demonstrated that complete agreement on foreign diplomacy was difficult. Each had different motivations for assisting either the French or the British. Leadership and decision making at the town level predominated, especially during war. The Mortar and The Wolf were looking after the interests of their town, instead of those of the Alabama Nation. Yet these leaders would not purposely harm the health and stability of the Alabama Nation; their main concern would always be the Nation's security. It is important to note that such disagreements in diplomatic strategies did not equate a breakdown of the Alabama and Coushatta alliance or connection to each other. It was simply a natural consequence of bringing people together with different interests in the wake of imperial rivalry.

Lost Leverage

Shortly after the French suffered many losses, including Quebec in 1759 and Montreal in 1760, France ceded their colony of Louisiana (including New Orleans) in November 1762 to Spain by the Treaty of Fontainebleau. Although the French hoped that this transaction would be temporary, Spain took control of the Mississippi Valley by 1766. The subsequent 1763 Treaty of Paris, which officially ended the Seven Years' War in Europe, forced France to cede to the British Crown all territory east of the Mississippi River and north of Lake Pontchartrain and to evacuate the North American continent immediately.[46] The Treaty of Paris affected all southeastern peoples as the British laid claim on their lands. Both French and British representatives quickly called the southeastern peoples together in order to discuss the peace agreements.

In the spring of 1763, Georgia governor James Wright invited the mikos of the Upper and Lower Creek towns to Savannah to discuss terms of the British victory. The Mortar, The Wolf, and fellow Upper Creek leaders thought carefully about Wright's talk. Wright argued that the Alabamas, Coushattas, and their neighbors were vulnerable because of the French defeat stating, "You know you cannot do well without us, but we can do without you." Wright further recognized that "you have tried the French and you know they can not supply your Wants." This harsh statement was a truth that the Alabamas and Coushattas knew too well. Yet Wright assured them that "if you will cast your Eyes round you[,] you will see that no Indians are so happy or so well supplied as those in Friendship with the English." He warned that those who were inclined to leave British territory for lands west near the Mississippi were in danger of being mistreated by the Spanish: "Witness the Chacktaws [*sic*] and many other Nations on the Mississippi, they are more like Slaves than a free People." Instead, Wright suggested that if the Alabamas and Coushattas, Abhikas, and Tallapoosas made peace with the English, "we should live like Brothers and have but one fire; and we can pour in Goods upon you like the Floods of a great River when it overflows; We bestow our favours on our Friends heartily and without Reserve." Wright's concern, however, was that the mikos had not controlled their "bad young men," and that they needed to correct such rebellious behavior. Wright threatened that if they "use the English ill," he would send British troops to invade their towns and annihilate their people.[47]

The Mortar and other Alabama and Coushatta mikos realized their predicament: they were no longer able to live in the world they had created on their terms. Throughout the first half of the eighteenth century, the Alabamas and Coushattas had profited from their juxtaposition in between two imperial powers. Wright's metaphor of "one fire" was an agonizing one: they could no longer burn two fires like those that they had in the past between the French and the British. In fact, the world that once had offered them status and influence with emissaries and their neighbors now had them trapped. They had to submit to the British or leave.

In November 1765, the governor of Louisiana, Jean-Jacques-Blaise D'Abbadie, and Robert Farmar, the acting governor of the Britannic Majesty's Florida colony, held a series of meetings in Mobile with southeastern peoples. D'Abbadie, with Farmar present, delivered a lengthy speech announcing that the kings of both France and England "have felt horror at seeing the earth reddened by so much bloodshed," and that "they have made their peace and have arranged their lands so that they will no longer be at war." He suggested that the Choctaws and the Alabama Nation were "on the side of the English, who promise to provide for all your needs and for those of your old men, of your wives, and of your children, but this will only be to the extent to which your conduct is good and (you are grateful for all the words that they bring you)."[48] D'Abbadie assured the mikos that the British wanted peace and would allow them to remain on their lands.[49] In later talks, British agents stressed to the Abhikas, Tallapoosas, Alabamas, and Coushattas that "it is strictly the command of the Great King, that we shall not presume to possess any Lands belonging to Indians except such as shall be ceded with their own Consent, So that you are the entire Masters on that Subject."[50]

Despite all of these assurances, many southeastern peoples hesitated to believe in British offers of peace and secure boundaries. French agents spread rumors that the British intended to enslave or annihilate them and populate their lands with Anglo settlers. Word from other groups about British duplicity confirmed their fears. Perruquier, a Choctaw chief, made many allegations against the British in a speech to D'Abbadie: "My father, the British have always corrupted the ways among all the tribes." He argued that his people were sick with the alcohol that English traders had always given them too readily, leading to many of their deaths. Perruquier remembered, "When I learned that they would come to our lands, I said: 'They will put us to death: kill them!' I well know that you had forbidden it. But, as I know in my heart that they would enslave us, I could not refrain from attacking them."[51] These suspicions were valid when southeastern peoples lost their opportunity and position between two imperial rivals after the war. The British claimed control over the Southeast owing to their victory, and the issue of land ownership was on the minds of many.

Indeed, the British colonists placed great value on land in the Southeast, just as the Alabamas and Coushattas had. The Mortar eloquently expressed his people's connection to the land in 1763, shortly after the war: "[We] love our lands a great deal. . . . The Wood is our fire, and the Grass is our Bed, and our Physic when we are sick. . . . He [The Mortar] and his Family are Masters of all the Land, and they own no Masters but the Master of their Breath." He added that the Alabamas and Coushattas were concerned that the "White People intend to stop all their Breaths by their settling all round them."[52] Alabama and Coushatta land was their sacred space and, more importantly, it was their life and existence.

The Mortar's message also indicated that the Alabamas and Coushattas associated the lands they occupied with preserving their sovereignty. Only through the consent of the townspeople could Europeans enter Alabama and Coushatta territory. When colonists abused this understanding and encroached onto their land in July 1763, The Mortar complained immediately to Georgia governor James Wright. He apprised Wright of the unlawful colonial settlements and of his hearing that the British refused to recognize Alabama and Coushatta sovereignty and claims to land. The Mortar stressed that the Alabama Nation had not "lent" or "granted" the colonists this land; he was also "surprized [*sic*] how People can give away Land that does not belong to them."[53] His use of these terms suggested that Alabamas and Coushattas completely understood territorial boundaries; it was their homeland and they wanted the colonists removed. As a war chief, The Mortar was also suspicious of British intentions. He believed that "white People intend to take all their Lands, and throw away the old Talks intirely [*sic*]: that it make[s] their Hearts cross to see their Lands taken without their Liberty."[54] The Mortar's use of "liberty" in its association with land demonstrated that without his people's permission, British settlers could not settle or take the Alabamas and Coushattas' land. The Alabama Nation was a sovereign entity, and members expected outsiders to respect their territorial boundaries.

Such protests were nothing new. A kinsman of The Mortar had lodged a similar complaint earlier in 1759 when he requested that then Georgia governor Henry Ellis issue a decree to all colonists to withdraw immediately from Upper Creek hunting grounds. More importantly, he and fellow mikos "strenuously urged" Ellis to "have a Paper given Us to show those People [the British colonists] that it must be done."[55] A piece of paper proving that the Alabamas and Coushattas were the lawful possessors of their territory meant nothing to them until Europeans started encroaching onto their lands. The Alabamas and Coushattas had understood natural markers as territorial boundaries, but now they physically had to prove their claim with objects that Europeans recognized: walls, fences, gates, and, above all, paper indicating ownership of land. The Alabamas and Coushattas would later equate this type of property protection to a "title" to their lands, which their future generations would fight desperately to obtain.

The Mortar's concerns for the welfare of his people intensified when in early 1764, D'Abbadie and his troops evacuated Fort Toulouse. Those living at the fort packed up their belongings, headed first for Mobile, and then settled in Spanish Louisiana. British major James Farmar sent James Germany, a trader and interpreter, to stay at the abandoned fort in an attempt to mollify the Alabamas and Coushattas. A faction of Alabamas, however, rebelled against British authority shortly after the French left. In March 1764, an Alabama war party (possibly led by The Mortar) killed fourteen British traders; the remaining traders in Alabama territory fled for their lives.[56] These actions demonstrated the Alabamas' difficulty coming to terms with separation and loss. They obviously resented the British takeover. Their center—created and recognized as a source of power—had been destroyed.

Despite the expanding British control over the Southeast, the Alabamas and Coushattas did not intend to abandon their sovereignty. Thomas Campbell witnessed the resistance when he traveled to Abhika, Tallapoosa, and Alabama and Coushatta territory in November of 1764. He observed while among these once powerful groups that they were "jealous of our [Britain's] growing power from the quick increase of inhabitants in our settlements and the cultivation of their neighbouring lands."[57] Campbell's observations were accurate. The Alabamas and Coushattas, along with their Upper Creek brethren, prepared themselves for another war against the British. The British, however, had no desire to fight a costly campaign, so ambassadors scheduled various conferences and meetings in 1765 and 1766 to persuade the Upper Creeks to maintain peaceful relations with the British people.

Creek leaders met with John Stuart at the Congress of Pensacola in May 1765. The Mortar, who still had considerable influence in the Alabama Nation, spoke on its behalf and offered peace: "This is the Land of the Red people and but very poor; These white Wings are Emblems of Peace, which I now Present you, untainted and Spotless, as Marks of my really Good and friendly intentions; and henceforward you shall hear of no Act of mine, which does not tend to promote friendship and Harmony." He looked to his warriors who had removed their hatchets and other weapons that were "now all buried in Oblivion" in favor of "White Talks." The Mortar told Stuart that he was the "Voice of my People," and was "determined that the Path shall not only be made white and streight [*sic*] here but everywhere."[58] The Mortar then presented a belt of wampum and directed Stuart to hold the opposite end to mark their friendship and peace.

The Mortar and his rebel faction finally had come to terms with the British victory, despite his earlier Nativist sentiments to expel them from the Southeast forever. The Mortar's decision to agree to a "Long and Lasting Peace" was because of the Alabama Nation's reliance on European goods that only British traders could provide after the French departure.[59] In his last recorded speech, The Mortar lamented this dependence: "In former times we were entirely unacquainted with the Customs of the White People, but since they have come among us, we have been Cloathed as they are, and accustomed to their Ways, which makes it at this day absolutely necessary, that we should be suppl[i]ed with the goods in the Nation."[60] The Alabamas and Coushattas had once claimed vast hunting grounds, but Anglo-American intrusions left them searching for game beyond the Cherokee River, especially "as Deer skins are become Scarce."[61] The Mortar realized that they had no more opportunities and were dependent on the white man.

Leaders of the Alabama Nation knew that they had to accommodate to British hegemony; they needed to establish new trade relations in order to continue the flow of goods into their towns and villages. In June 1766, Topoye, miko of Coosada, traveled to the former French stronghold of Mobile and discussed trade with Stuart. Topoye told Stuart that his people desired "to be neuter." This expression in Topoye's mind meant that the Alabamas and Coushattas wanted to be connected to everyone and at peace with the British; it was the ideal situation that the Alabama Nation tried to preserve before the French and Indian War. He promised Stuart that they would "live in peace and under the Colours of the English" and "hold fast the Words of the English."[62] Topoye addressed Stuart as "father" (a role not associated with power in the Coushattas' matrilineal society if one considers the more important role of the maternal uncle), and requested that Stuart send supplies immediately because "my young men are poor for guns and ammunition, and our Women are very poor."[63] Topoye revealed that if the British refused to give his people gifts and needed goods, they would be forced to find trade elsewhere and leave the British behind.

Added to Topoye's dilemma, French agents tried to persuade Alabama and Coushatta townspeople to travel west with them. Though tempting, Topoye told the French that he "loved his own Ground."[64] At that point, he would be willing to face separation from his French kinsmen rather than leave the land that his people had claimed for so long. It was their sacred space—their homeland—and Topoye made it clear that he and his people could not abandon it so easily. Yet they had to make critical decisions. Considering their predicament, the Alabamas and Coushattas realized that they would lose a part of their old world.

The Second Migration

In April 1764, the first group of Alabamas and Coushattas quit the British and migrated west shortly after the French evacuation of Fort Toulouse. Eighty townspeople (probably clan groups) from Pakana and Coosada—the two main towns of both the Alabamas and Coushattas—left for Mobile and requested from Governor D'Abbadie a place to settle in Spanish Louisiana. Considering the close proximity of the two towns to the fort, they probably refused to submit to British authority and left because of their kinship ties to the French. One can also speculate that the Alabamas and Coushattas quit their homelands in search of a new space where they could regain their sovereignty, something they risked losing if they stayed behind. Led by Coosada's war chief Tamatlé Mingo, they settled temporarily on the east bank of the Mississippi River, south of Manchac (a profitable trading center), and north of New Orleans.[65] Tamatlé Mingo's position as leader of both Coushattas and Alabamas signified that he filled a power vacuum left by former Alabama chiefs Opoyheatly and Captain Pakana, who were likely deceased, and The Wolf and The Mortar, who stayed behind.

After Tamatlé Mingo's group arrived in Manchac, they sought revenge against the British in August 1765. Tamatlé Mingo and his warriors joined a party of Houmas and attacked Fort Bute (in British West Florida), on which the British had just begun construction. In a grand show of force, fifty warriors had Ensign Archibald Robertson and his soldiers at their mercy. The Englishmen locked themselves behind closed doors, and for two days the war party confiscated supplies, slaughtered livestock, and, in an act of true protest and reprisal, threw British artillery into the Mississippi River.[66] The Alabamas and Coushattas' actions clearly demonstrated their anger toward the British for destroying their center, along with their status and influence in the southern interior.

Two years later, a second group of two hundred Alabamas left their homeland and temporarily settled on the banks of Santa Rosa Bay, near the town of Valparaiso (presently the town of Shalimar on Four Mile Point, Florida) before heading to Louisiana. According to George Gauld, a surveyor and cartographer of the Gulf Coast, they departed "on account of the present war between the Choctaws and the Upper Creeks, being unwilling to take part with either."[67] The townspeople apparently refused to be in the middle of a war between their neighbors. Unfortunately, we know little else of this group and from which towns they came. They likely had communication with their kinspeople in Spanish Louisiana, who provided information about the new land, settlements, trade, and quality of life and subsequently convinced them to leave.

Another group of sixty-four Alabama warriors along with their families migrated west in December 1771 and settled along the banks of the Mississippi River, a few leagues down from the Iberville River. Here they raised crops and engaged in trade at New Orleans, which was the hub of economic activity in the Mississippi Valley. Feeling the pressure of Anglo-American settlement, despite British attempts to contain westward expansion, the Alabamas asked English superintendent John Thomas to prohibit Anglo-American residences closer than one league from their newly constructed village. British agents made an honorable effort, but the Alabamas soon found it difficult to maintain a comfortable existence. Sometime after 1773, forty Alabama men and their families moved farther west and made a permanent settlement near a small creek in the Opelousas District of Louisiana. Another thirty Alabama men moved with their families nearby to the Red River and established a village sixteen miles above Bayou

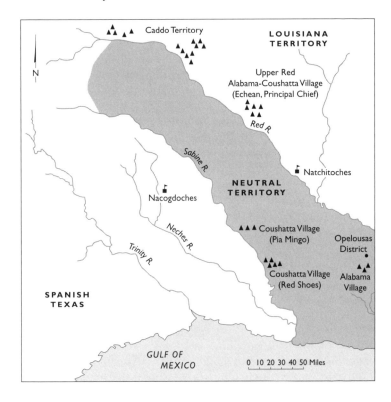

Alabama and Coushatta village locations in western Louisiana and eastern Texas, 1805–1809

Rapide. By 1804, this group had migrated farther up the Red, finally settling in Caddo Territory.[68]

Despite the temporary separation, the majority of Alabamas and Coushattas reunited in Spanish Louisiana after the American colonies expelled the British from what became the southern United States. By the end of the eighteenth century, many of the remaining Alabama and Coushatta townspeople migrated west when their Coushatta leader, Red Shoes, reportedly opposed an ongoing war with the Chickasaws. Another motive for leaving their Alabama homeland was the increased hostilities with Anglo-Americans who encroached on their territory; in 1793, Red Shoes reported to Spanish officials that his men had engaged in a war with Americans apparently because of land disputes.[69] Red Shoes's group first established a village on Bayou Chico in the Opelousas District around 1795. Then, in 1801, approximately two hundred men and their families moved to the east bank of the Sabine River, eighty miles southwest of the American trading post at Natchitoches. A few Coushatta families who had remained on the Bayou Chico soon joined the Alabama village on the Red River in Caddo territory, further integrating the Alabamas and Coushattas. Another Coushatta village of approximately 450 men (not including their families) led by Pia Mingo relocated from Mississippi Territory to the Sabine River and lived in detached settlements near Red Shoes's village. In 1805, the Alabama and Coushatta population in Spanish Louisiana numbered 1,650.[70]

The Stayers

As is often the case with other diasporas, a faction—albeit a small one—remained in the ancestral Alabama homeland, residing among the Upper Creeks. Those that stayed behind faced uncertainty and in the end faired poorly. After the United States secured its independence, the new government claimed the territory east of the Mississippi River. The indigenous peoples of the Southeast were stunned by a series of treaties made between 1783 and 1786; their leaders ceded to the new American Confederation varying quantities of land for future sale to Anglo-Americans.[71]

At the start of the nineteenth century, these groups witnessed a rapid expansion of American settlement onto their lands. Angered by Anglo-American encroachment, trading abuses, and fraudulent treaties upheld by the U.S. government, a pan-tribal movement spread throughout the North and South. Inspired by the Shawnee leader Tecumseh, the resistance stressed unification, common ownership of land, traditional living, and noncooperation with whites. According to Benjamin Hawkins, U.S. agent for Indian Affairs south of the Ohio River, a group of Alabama and Coushatta stayers incited hostilities against Anglo-Americans and threatened to destroy towns and to kill any chief loyal to the American government. Hawkins noted that they were ready for the whites "whom they had the power to destroy by an earthquake which would swallow them up in soft and miry ground."[72] This group apparently played an active role in a faction known as the "Red Sticks" during the Creek wars. Led by Chief Menawa, these anti-American Upper Creeks gained momentum after Tecumseh's death at the Battle of the Thames in 1813. Andrew Jackson led several thousand soldiers of the Tennessee militia along with many Cherokee warriors to victory against the Red Sticks at the Battle of Horseshoe Bend in March of 1814. Their movement met the same fate as Tecumseh's attempt at pan-tribal unification. Those who survived eventually amalgamated into other Creek groups. Yet those individuals experienced extreme hardship when the U.S. government removed them to Indian Territory in the 1830s.[73]

The scattering of town- and clan-level migrations between 1765 and 1804 led to a somewhat weakened solidarity within the Alabama Nation. Unlike past settlement onto territory claimed exclusively by the Alabamas and Coushattas, greater distance between towns and villages in Spanish Louisiana and British-controlled Alabama meant longer travel time and made intervillage contact and communication less frequent. After the French and Indian War ended in 1763, groups of Alabamas and Coushattas split apart temporarily. Those who supported the French migrated to Spanish Louisiana; others remained in central Alabama and preserved a twenty-year peace with the British Empire. The ability of the Alabamas and Coushattas to relocate and to leave both their kinspeople and ancestral homelands behind was possible because of the autonomy of each town; townspeople left at different times for different reasons. The overwhelming factor in their decision making, however, was Anglo-American encroachment and growing physical separation from their kinspeople. Despite this second Alabama and Coushatta diaspora, it is important to note that the stayers in Alabama kept in contact with their migrating kinspeople in the west.

Although the majority of the Alabamas and Coushattas eventually reunited in Spanish Louisiana by 1805, an interesting development had occurred because of their temporary separation. Throughout the eighteenth century, many outsiders simply referred to both Alabamas and Coushattas as members of the Alabama Nation, or focused on their specific town affiliation. American accounts at the turn of the nineteenth century, however, recognized more clearly both the Alabamas and Coushattas as two entities united by kinship. Moreover, after their break with the Creek alliance, identity to a specific Alabama or Coushatta town became less important. Based on American and Spanish reports, it seems that they stressed their identity as Alabamas and Coushattas instead of their town affiliation (e.g., Pakana or Taskigi).[74]

Political changes also made an impact on the relationship between the Alabamas and Coushattas. Coushatta chiefs Tamatlé Mingo and Red Shoes, who led the migrations west, filled the void left by Alabama chiefs who had either died or remained in Alabama. This development likely increased the status of the Coushattas, and it seems that when they migrated west, they left behind their secondary status that had been predominant in the early eighteenth century under the Alabama Nation. The Coushattas provided effective leadership for both Alabamas and Coushattas. More importantly, further integration of both Alabama and Coushatta men and women also occurred as a result of their diaspora when many Alabama and Coushatta towns combined in their new homeland in Louisiana.

Prior to the French and Indian War, the Alabamas and Coushattas sued for peace with their neighbors and pursued diplomatic neutrality as British and French powers struggled for control over their colonial possessions in the Southeast. The Alabamas and Coushattas had profited from relationships with their Creek neighbors, especially when French and British agents vied for their allegiance during the contest for empire. Yet when the French and Indian War threatened to destroy the Alabama and Coushatta center, many townspeople broke their attempts to remain neutral with the Creeks and instead supported the French. Many Alabamas and Coushattas (despite their treaty of friendship and commerce with the British) provided the French assistance and supplies, ironically acquired from British traders. The Alabamas and Coushattas' kinship ties to the French and the proximity of Fort Toulouse in fact prevented long-term neutrality. Other Alabama and Coushatta townspeople, however, continued to allow British agents in their towns for trade. In the end, individual towns made decisions based on their own self-interest rather than those of the neighboring alliance or the Alabama Nation.

The eventual cessation of hostilities between the French and British empires ultimately destroyed Alabama and Coushatta diplomatic strategies. They were no longer able to exist in the middle between larger entities. Moreover, the Creek alliance was no longer useful to the Alabamas and Coushattas, so they broke their ties and began to seek a new center. By the close of the eighteenth century, the majority of Alabama and Coushatta towns had separated themselves from the Abhikas, Tallapoosas, Cowetas, and others by migrating west. Such ephemeral alliances with neighboring communities were typical among diasporic groups focusing on survival. The Alabamas and Coushattas had built alliances to regain control of their physical space yet left them when it was no longer in their community's best interests. They avoided such long-term commitments because additional crises could force them to leave again.

The break with other southeastern peoples and associated migrations westward constituted the second collective diaspora of Alabama and Coushatta men and women. They hoped for a better life in the west, where the Spanish promised to protect them and help establish a new center for settlement and trade. The Alabamas and Coushattas transformed themselves from diplomatic brokers and members of an alliance of like-minded neighboring Creek towns to groups of autonomous villages dispersed throughout Louisiana. The decision of the Alabamas and Coushattas to leave their ancestral homeland on the Alabama River ultimately preserved their identity as a sovereign, coalescent people. Indeed, after the end of the eighteenth century, outsiders no longer associated them with either Creeks or Upper Creeks. Outsiders would refer to them as the Alabamas and Coushattas from the start of the nineteenth century to the present day. The world that their ancestors created had been destroyed, but like the migration of their Mississippian predecessors, the second Alabama and Coushatta diaspora would provide a new starting point.

« »

4

Creating a New Center

Alabama and Coushatta oral tradition recalls the ancient story of six brothers who were the best hunters in their village. One day, the youngest brother ventured out on a hunting trip a great distance from his home. The first night he came across a campfire, and slept. The next morning, two strangers who had made the fire appeared and invited the young hunter to eat with them. Grateful for the meal, the hunter offered to watch over the camp while his new friends hunted. The young man decided to prepare a meal while he waited for their return. He tapped his fingers against a clay pot and it grew larger, big enough to cook plenty of food for the three of them. When they returned, they looked at the meal and unhappily told the young man that they were spirits and could not eat boiled food. To resolve the problem, they left together to hunt for more meat. After following a trail for four days, the young hunter discovered two red kernels that the strangers called corn. Encouraged by the spirits, he followed the trail, picking up kernels as he walked, and ended up at a large field of ripe corn. The strangers then taught him how to grow it and build corncribs. They also gave him a tobacco seed and instructed him to plant it and smoke the leaves after harvest. He was lost in thought for a moment while he contemplated these friendly gifts. When the young hunter looked back, the spirits had already disappeared.[1]

The hunter traveled a great distance and eventually found valuable sustenance in the end. The Alabamas and Coushattas likewise journeyed to a faraway place in order to restore their homeland, and they found fertile lands in Louisiana. The Alabamas and Coushattas' migration took them to territory that other indigenous groups had occupied, lands symbolic of the campsite already built. Just as the young hunter relied on the aid of strangers to cultivate the land and find game, the Alabamas and Coushattas learned much from the Native inhabitants. They settled where their crops could be grown in abundance and where large game roamed. This story may echo the Alabamas and Coushattas' cooperation with neighboring peoples who were strangers to them initially, but who proved to be critical to their survival in the end.

Just like those of their Mississippian ancestors, the most important goal of the Alabamas and Coushattas in the wake of their second migration was to find suitable land, political allies, and trade networks. The Alabamas and Coushattas began a new life in Spanish Louisiana, yet they continued to keep alive the memory of their ancestral homeland through oral tradition and ancient practices. Men and women adapted to their new surroundings and looked for political opportunities that resembled those in the past. As they began to build a new center, they recognized that the lands they claimed constituted another dynamic geopolitical zone similar to that in their old homeland.

Maintaining Traditions

By the first decade of the nineteenth century, the Alabamas and Coushattas had cleared the land and had built villages along the Red and Sabine rivers. They chose the locations that would replicate their old world, and the vast prairies and scattered timberland near the rivers provided them with ample resources. Despite the disruption of migration and resettle-

ment, the Alabamas and Coushattas kept their lifestyle of farming and hunting; men and women cultivated corn and raised
domesticated animals, such as horses, hogs, and cattle, and
hunted game, just as they did in the past.[2]

Like their Mississippian ancestors, they took advantage of
their environment: their diets included roasted and boiled venison, fish, turtles, eggs, peaches, persimmons, plums, grapes,
chestnuts, honey, and acorn bread. Outside of corn, women
cultivated an abundance of sweet potatoes, maize, wild rice,
melons, and sorghum to supplement their diet.[3] Women continued their ancient practices of making baskets, pots, bowls,
and other pottery vessels with the raw materials available.[4]
According to one ceramic tradition, women used the "coil
method," then smoothed red or yellow clay with their hands.
They applied decoration only around the outer edge of pots,
bowls, and cups, making designs from a turkey feather in one-
inch zigzags. They dried out the finished pots in the sun, and to
prevent holes they placed them into the fire until they turned
black. Women also fashioned small to large gourds into cups
and jugs, and buckets for carrying water; they also wove baskets from pine needles or grass (a practice that exists today)
and used them as carrying and storage devices.[5]

Their migration west endangered such traditional practices,
but archaeological evidence has showed that the Alabamas
and Coushattas retained their ceramic technology. European
and American wares were readily available, but traditional-
ists within the community must have shunned these foreign
items in favor of Native pottery. Archaeologists who completed
excavations at the Alabama and Coushatta villages on the
Red River unearthed iron arrowheads and tools, copper, glass
beads, peach pits, carbonized oak and hickory nut fragments,
and Native pottery sherds with polishing stones. The archaeological evidence suggests that while they adapted to some
Euro-American items, women manufactured stoneware and
rendered oils from plants and nuts—a preserved culinary practice.[6] Written records confirm this maintenance of tradition in
the Alabama village at Opelousas. Families here were close to
self-sufficient; they concentrated on farming and raising cattle
and horses and largely avoided reliance on American trade

Log habitation, 1791. An eighteenth-century Alabama and Coushatta dwelling, drawing by J. C. Tidball. Smithsonian Institution, National Anthropological Archives, Negative 1169 A.

goods. According to American accounts, they rarely traded for American goods. Other Alabama and Coushatta villages, however, conducted some trade at the American trading post at Natchitoches, or the Spanish post at Nacogdoches.[7]

The Alabamas and Coushattas also had increased opportunities to hunt large game for trade in their new land. On hunting trips, they formed small parties of around fifteen people and tracked animals on the prairies. With the onset of winter, great herds of bison descended from the Ozarks into the southern regions of Louisiana. According to one hunter, "bison blacken the whole surface of the earth, and continue passing, without intermission, for weeks together, so that the whole surface of the country is, for miles in breadth, trodden like a large road."[8] Women accompanied them on the hunt and methodically prepared and smoked the meat.[9] From the sixteenth to the nineteenth centuries, women also fashioned hides (most often from white-tailed deer) and other furs into clothing, blankets, and moccasins, which was a complicated process that required great skill and time.[10]

Many Alabamas and Coushattas—excluding those in Opelousas—relied on the income from hunting these and other large game animals, including bear. During one year alone, a Coushatta party killed at least 118 bears, each yielding eight to twelve gallons of oil, which never sold for less than one dollar a gallon. Hunters earned another dollar or more for the hides. They used the money to purchase trade goods at Nacogdoches, which was approximately forty miles from the Coushatta villages. The Alabamas and Coushattas had successfully reestablished a trade network for goods that they had depended on for almost a century. They were re-creating their world once again.[11]

The Caddo Alliance

The Alabama and Coushatta migration to Spanish Louisiana left them vulnerable to potential warfare with Native inhabitants. They realized that territorial claims overlapped with the new space in which they had chosen to settle. To avoid a potential conflict, the Alabamas and Coushattas sought alliances with existing American Indian residents. They likely chose this path based on the experiences in Alabama with their former Creek allies. They had learned that pan-Indian unions were necessary not only to obtain information about their territory, but also to maintain influence in dealing with their enemies and foreign nations.

In Spanish Louisiana, a powerful union had already existed among the Caddos. The Caddo Confederacy, as many knew it, originated in the early nineteenth century when Dehahuit, the leader of the Kadohadacho chiefdom, united his people. Dehahuit, son of the great "Peacemaker," Tinhiouen, was no more than forty years of age in 1806 and held great influence among all of the neighboring peoples of the Southwest. The Confederacy claimed territory that stretched from the Red to the

Sabine rivers. His long-term goal was to establish a pan-Indian alliance with migrating peoples who had left the East, including the Alabamas and Coushattas, Choctaws, Shawnees, Delawares, Kickapoos, Pascagoulas, and western Cherokees. He would even allow some of them, including the Alabamas and Coushattas, to live on Caddo lands. His leadership of various groups over a wide distance was reminiscent of the power of his precursors, the paramount chiefs of the Mississippian era. Dehahuit favored close relationships with other peoples to increase the Caddos' power and his own, especially when dealing with foreign nations who fought for control over Caddo territory in Louisiana.[12]

The Alabamas and Coushattas had common links with the Caddos: they had similar backgrounds of movement, agricultural lifestyles and traditions, and, most importantly, interests of maintaining sovereignty. According to Robin Cohen, diasporic communities have "an inescapable link with their past migration history and a sense of co-ethnicity with others of a similar background."[13] It is not hard to see, then, why the Alabamas and Coushattas joined the Caddos: like the Creek alliance their ancestors had forged, the Caddo alliance enhanced their power and offered protection. Red Shoes and Pia Mingo, both Coushatta chiefs, and Echean, chief of the Alabamas on the Red River, welcomed the relationship with open arms. They, after all, were in a new land, and had to rebuild their social and political networks and, more importantly, a new center. The only potential danger the leaders faced was to lose their own autonomy or, even worse, their identity under the leadership of Dehahuit. Past Alabama and Coushatta alliances with outsiders, however, were ephemeral, and the benefits outweighed the risks. Indeed, the union proved critical when the various emigrant peoples encountered Spanish and Anglo-American encroachment onto their lands.

At the Center

Although the Alabamas and Coushattas maintained a stable existence while allied with the Caddo Confederacy, they faced an uncertain future when the United States purchased Louisiana from France in 1803. Unbeknownst to the peoples residing within the Louisiana borders, Alabama, Coushatta, and Caddo territories (among others) became part of the United States according to the European-American exchange. President Thomas Jefferson debated which path to take toward the estimated 2,000 American Indians in what later became the state of Louisiana. Jefferson sent agents to assure Indian leaders that the United States had no intention to remove any American Indians from their lands. He declared, however, that they should abandon hunting in favor of farming and raising livestock, like his ideal southern yeomen; it was his way to assimilate the American Indians. To tempt them, he planned to increase the number of trading houses in the territory that made available American trade goods at fair prices, easing their transition to "civilized" life while securing friendship with the United States. His opponents, however, argued that his plan was only a tool used to provide "moral justification" for the purchase of Indian lands so they could be sold later to white settlers—exactly what American Indians feared.[14]

To implement his American Indian policy in the South, Jefferson appointed the former governor of Mississippi Territory, William C. C. Claiborne, as governor of Louisiana and Dr. John Sibley as the Indian agent for part of the Territory of Orleans and territory west of the Mississippi River. Sibley's duties were to relay important information, to promote trade, to distribute presents and annuities, and to maintain peaceful relations with American Indians.[15] Sibley's occupation of the post at Natchitoches along the Red River was a diplomatic strategy to compete with Spanish trade at Nacogdoches.

It was at this point in 1804 when the Alabamas and Coushattas understood that their territory once again lay at the center of imperial competition. Jefferson's aggressive policy fanned an intense rivalry between the United States and Spain, especially after each debated the boundaries of Louisiana. Jefferson believed that French Louisiana had included Texas, and stretched as far west as the Rio Grande and even to the Pacific. The Spanish Crown, however, insisted that they had colonized Texas in the eighteenth century and was therefore under Spanish control. Both countries appealed to Napoleon to clarify the boundary to no avail. Jefferson then offered to resolve the dilemma by creating neutral territory between the Sabine and Red rivers directly between Alabama and Coushatta villages in exchange for West Florida. The Spanish Crown considered his solution outrageous, nothing but a grand imperialistic scheme. Jefferson's organization of an expedition to explore the western territories seemed to confirm Spain's suspicions. Before he dispatched the party, however, the Royal Council of Spain decreed that the international boundary of Louisiana was "north to the vicinity of Natchitoches as far as the Red River."[16] Spain stipulated that Americans could not cross any areas west of the boundary, but Jefferson ignored them and sent explorers to the Red, Arkansas, and St. Francis rivers to begin negotiating with American Indian nations there, including the Alabamas and Coushattas.

Manuel Salcedo, the last Spanish governor of Louisiana, was most worried that the American expedition parties would "with study and with cautious skill . . . separate [the Indians] from our friendship" and "attract and conciliate the Indian nations to them [the United States]."[17] Salcedo knew only too well that Jefferson's American Indian policy involved courting small and large tribes with presents and promises of trade and turning them against the Spaniards. If the Americans were successful in this venture, Spain's plan to rebuild an empire in Louisiana would fail. Salcedo's fears were confirmed with American Indian agent John Sibley, who was "endeavoring to lead away from our obedience the Indians that live on the frontier." Fearing Sibley's actions, the Spanish governor requested that the Crown "not spare any means to have our traders inform the chiefs and other members of the said tribes that their real interest lies in remaining loyal to this government."[18] And it was going to take considerable courting to convince them.

The conflict between Spain and the United States played into the favor of the Alabamas and Coushattas. From rumors spreading throughout the territory and increased contact with Indian agents, Red Shoes, Pia Mingo, and Echean realized that Spain dared not risk alienating any of the American Indians east or west of the Sabine River. They had even heard that the United States planned to invade Spanish Texas, and both would likely need the friendship and alliance with the Caddo Confederacy and its allied peoples to guarantee expansion and settlement in the area.[19] The Alabamas and Coushattas, who lived within this newly contested territory and were members of the Caddo alliance, sought to advance their own agenda by playing the two rival powers against one another as they had in the mid-eighteenth century. The Alabamas and Coushattas invited emissaries from both countries into their territory, and each in turn vied for their allegiance. Ultimately, Red Shoes, Pia Mingo, and Echean used their diplomatic skills and brokered a relationship with the Caddo Confederacy to enhance their own status among European and American agents. This diplomacy again provided them with gifts, favorable trade, and protection.

The Coushattas were the first to openly welcome emissaries. They received an initial offer of allegiance from Spain on May 29, 1806, when José Maria Guadiana, sent by Don Francisco Viana, the adjutant inspector in the Provincias Internas of New Spain, visited their villages on the Sabine. Guadiana planned to enlist one hundred warriors to join his force against Thomas Freeman and his team, who Jefferson sent to explore the Red River. Yet Pia Mingo and Red Shoes refused to support the plan. They had learned from past Alabama and Coushatta leaders that maintaining neutrality enhanced their status with the two contending nations. Nevertheless, the chiefs willingly accepted both nations' gifts of friendship. Foreshadowing future events, seven Coushatta warriors ignored their leaders' neutrality and aided Guadiana in his effort to intercept the Americans near Caddo Village.[20] Red Shoes and Pia Mingo, like their predecessors, could chastise the young men for their actions that clashed with the collective good. Yet they also lacked dictatorial power and could not prevent their kinsmen from seeking their own interests and personal gain.

The upper Red River village, consisting of Alabama and some Coushatta families, adopted a similar diplomatic strategy when Freeman and his men reached their territory. Upon their arrival, Freeman learned from Talapoon, a Caddo messenger, that three hundred Spanish dragoons with an estimated five hundred horses and mules had established camp near the neighboring Caddo Village. Dehahuit warned Freeman in the message that he did not know the Spaniards' intentions, but based on his talks with the Spanish commander, Juan Ignacio Ramón de Burga, he assumed that they planned to intercept the American party. Angered at the possibility of the powerful Caddos, Alabamas, and Coushattas supporting the Americans in their bid to explore the West, Ramón had asked Dehahuit if he "loved" the Americans. Dehahuit, who spoke on behalf of his people and his allies, responded cautiously: "He loved all men; if the Spaniards came to fight, they must not spill blood on his land, as it was the command of his forefathers, that white blood should not be spilled on their land."[21] As the Caddos and their Alabama and Coushatta neighbors expressed their willingness to stay out of the conflict, Alabama chief Echean invited Dehahuit and Freeman's party to meet at his upper Red River village.

Echean knew quite well the power of diplomacy. It is unknown which Alabama town he came from prior to the migration, but one can speculate that he was from Pakana, especially considering his leadership over the majority of the resettled Alabamas; Pakana had been a white town that had done well in peace talks and produced the principal chiefs of the Alabamas. Echean must have known about the esteemed former Alabama leaders such as Opoyheatly and Captain Pakana who had brokered diplomatic negotiations in the past. Echean's village now was at the center of peace talks between representatives of two powerful nations, the Caddo Confederacy and the United States. Similar to the location of the Alabama village of Pakana and Fort Toulouse, the upper Red River village stood on the north side on a sandstone bluff about thirty feet high. Its layout consisted of a square on the high bluff surrounded by individual rectangular lodges made of logs with cypress or cedar frames.[22] Though the sandstone bluff was not an ancient Mississippian earthen mound, the village was equally situated in a strategic location, and the Alabamas must have chosen it for its resemblance to their ancient homeland.

While U.S. agent Freeman waited for Dehahuit's arrival at the village, Echean decisively planned to fly a Spanish flag in the chief's honor. The Spaniards had visited Echean's village earlier and had given him the flag. Echean had welcomed the Spaniards and accepted their gifts of friendship. Yet he openly received the Americans as well, albeit with even more gratitude. By openly displaying the Spanish gifts and by presenting the Spanish flag, Echean showed the Americans that they had competition; his tactic succeeded. When Freeman discovered the Spanish flag, he distributed lavish presents and, predictably, an American flag. He requested that they fly the flag over the village, to which Echean agreed.[23] Echean's actions proved that the Alabamas and Coushattas were masters of the game and that they had successfully re-created a new center of exchange and relationships despite their migration and resettlement.

During the meeting between Dehahuit, Echean, and Freeman, an interpreter explained the United States' mission and dispute with Spain. Freeman added that because the United States claimed Caddo and Alabama-Coushatta territory, the Americans were their fathers and friends and would "protect them and supply their wants."[24] Dehahuit, with Echean's support, tactfully reminded the American agents that the Spaniards had treated his people and his neighbors well, and he expected the same quality of treatment from the United States. Dehahuit also announced that he and Echean would allow the Americans to become his fathers, brothers, and friends, and to provide for the "wants" of both the Caddos and the Alabamas and Coushattas.[25] Their motives were clear: they both agreed that as long as the Americans provided their people with supplies and gifts, they would remain neutral—a strategy that had proven successful in the past.

In the last week of August 1806, Spanish forces confronted the members of the Red River Expedition at Nanatsoho Bluff and forced the Americans to retreat to their post at Natchitoches. At Dehahuit's village, Spanish soldiers aggressively cut down the American flag in the town square. The battle over Louisiana territory had begun, and all-out war seemed possible.[26] After a series of diplomatic exchanges, however, the Spanish Crown accepted the Neutral Ground Agreement of 1806 in order to avoid a costly war with the United States. The easternmost boundary crossed the Arroyo Hondo to the thirty-second parallel (bordering the Red and Sabine rivers), forming the western boundaries.[27]

Although the agreement settled the border dispute, diplomats failed to resolve whether the United States controlled the Red River. Hence, all four Alabama and Coushatta villages continued to be in the middle of international conflict. The upper Red River Alabama and Coushatta village in Caddo country lay east of the Red River (unofficially designating it as United States territory), and the two Coushatta villages on the Sabine River and the Alabama village in the Opelousas District fell within the newly designated "Neutral Territory." Their claim to land along the Red and Sabine rivers located in a critical geographical center of imperial rivalry ultimately led both Spain and the United States to continue to court their villages. Spanish officials wanted the Alabamas and the Coushattas to move west into uncontested Spanish territory, thereby creating a buffer zone against American encroachment. The Americans, on the other hand, simply hoped to maintain peaceful relations with both the Caddo Confederacy and its allies. Similar to their position in the eighteenth century, the Alabamas and Coushattas placed themselves between rival nations, made alliances with neighboring peoples, and reaped the rewards in government-sponsored gifts.

Murder and Clan Law

Not surprisingly, the strategy of Echean, Red Shoes, and Pia Mingo failed to last. They could not keep two fires burning long: conflict was inevitable. Events in 1807 changed their world, and uncontrollable circumstances forced the Alabamas and the Coushattas to make a difficult decision once again. It began on February 13, 1807, when Captain John Burnett informed U.S. Indian agent John Sibley that an Anglo-American named Samuel Watson murdered a Coushatta at the salt works near Natchitoches. According to Burnett's report, Watson had no choice in the matter because the Coushatta man attempted to kill him. Watson, however, suspiciously left the scene of the crime before the sheriff could question him, and he escaped from local officials without a trace. Sibley knew this episode

endangered their good relations with the Alabamas and Coushattas and requested that Governor Claiborne issue a warrant
for Watson's arrest.[28]

One month later, Red Shoes (the principal leader of the Coushatta village on the Sabine River) and his uncle, Pia Mingo,
visited Sibley at Natchitoches. They told Sibley that Tom, the
murdered man, was Red Shoes' brother. Sibley had no idea
what the ramifications would be in such an event. Clan retaliation or revenge of a member's death (whether accidental
or not) was a long-standing social institution inherited from
their Mississippian ancestors. Alabama and Coushatta clan
members in these circumstances would seek out the offender.
Based on ancient customs, upon the offender's capture, they
would tie the prisoner to the pole in the chunkey yard in the
village square ground and would encourage him to sing his
war song while clan members tortured him. After the prisoner
expired, his captors would remove his scalp and cut it into
pieces. Then they would tie the pieces to pine twigs and lay
them atop the roof of the house of the murdered person, whose
blood they had avenged. They believed this act appeased their
clan member's soul. Kinsmen then celebrated for three days
and three nights.[29]

The Coushattas obviously wanted retribution for Tom's death
and demanded that Sibley help find the murderer. Sibley took
great care in explaining to Red Shoes that as soon as American
agents caught Watson, he would stand trial. Seeking equal justice, Sibley stressed that if found guilty, Watson would be punished for his crime as if he had killed a white man. Red Shoes,
who was hardly convinced, received gifts and provisions to
assuage his loss.[30]

A month later Red Shoes and Pia Mingo returned with thirty-
three Coushatta warriors. The group made a show of force,
telling Sibley that they were incensed that Watson still evaded
capture. Red Shoes demanded satisfaction for his brother's
murder. Sibley nervously explained that authorities had worked
hard to capture Watson but remained empty handed. The third
time the two chiefs returned to Natchitoches, Red Shoes demanded gifts for the loss of his brother because he "could not
think of losing his Brother for nothing."[31] Red Shoes received a

hat and a regimental blue coat—gifts that obviously were not equal to his great loss. Sibley failed to understand the implications of Red Shoes's dissatisfaction and clan obligations. Because Watson had eluded capture, Red Shoes had failed in his responsibilities as a leader and as a clan member to avenge his brother's death and faced disgrace in the eyes of his kinsmen.[32]

In May 1807 Pia Mingo traveled to Echean's village on the upper Red River and attempted to convince the Alabamas and Coushattas there to abandon their lands and join the Coushattas in their westward migration. Pia Mingo apprised Echean of the Coushattas' confrontation with Sibley and how the Americans failed to keep their promise to arrest Tom's murderer. Moreover, Pia Mingo stressed that Texas governor Manuel Antonio Cordero y Bustamente offered an advantageous alliance if the Alabamas and Coushattas settled in Spanish territory. Pia Mingo and Red Shoes knew that the Alabamas and Coushattas would no longer profit after the United States and Spain settled on a peace, so Spain's offer seemed like a good one. Pia Mingo apparently believed that their center was in the process of collapsing, and his nephew's murder was an ominous sign of the events to come. He also warned Echean of another reason to evacuate: the Red River continued to rise above normal, hindering cultivation. Pia Mingo suggested that remaining on the Red River would only lead to hardship on many fronts. Echean, on the other hand, disagreed and refused to leave.[33]

Shortly after Pia Mingo's visit, Siache, a young Coushatta warrior, killed an Anglo-American man near Bayou Cossachie, located forty miles from Natchitoches. White Meat, a Choctaw, reported to Sibley that he and his friend, Tombolin, had visited the Coushatta village on the Sabine when Siache confessed to the murder. Siache admitted that while with Pia Mingo and Red Shoes at Natchitoches, he wanted to kill a white man after witnessing Sibley humiliate Red Shoes with his stingy offer of gifts, but the two chiefs forbade him to do so. A few days later, Siache confronted an Anglo trader named O'Neil coming back from Natchitoches. After a brief encounter, Siache fought with O'Neil and killed him, against the advice of White Meat's son-in-law, Charles, who had advised Siache to keep the trading path white and free of bloodshed.[34]

Pia Mingo's War

On June 9, 1807, Sibley sent a search party to find O'Neil's body. Before they found the corpse, the Coushattas from both villages on the Sabine hastily cut down their corn, packed their belongings, and headed west for Spanish territory. Without their Alabama kinsmen, the Coushattas trekked through the rolling grasslands, crossing clear streams and banks covered with thick, overgrown white cane. Their destination was the Trinity River, a region abounding with game and rich soil, surrounded by hilly prairies and forested plains. Upon their arrival in Spanish territory, Pia Mingo and Red Shoes sent word to the neighboring Apalachees and Pascagoulas to join them in their war against the Americans. The Coushattas held "war talks" to persuade the tribes in western Texas and those still on the Louisiana-Texas border to create an anti-American, pan-Indian union.[35]

Pia Mingo, his subchiefs, Payxacho, Usacho, and Canasagi Mingo, and seventeen warriors met Spanish governor Cordero at Bexar on October 13, 1807. They expressed their loyalty to the Spanish Crown and spoke of the "disdain with which they look upon the seduction of the American government."[36] Pia Mingo requested that Cordero establish a trading house near their settlement on the Atascosito, which would enable them to trade pelts for necessary items "without having to depend upon or trade with any citizen of the United States, whose name and government they hate."[37] Pia Mingo had exacted political retribution for Sibley's mistakes and incompetence and he and Red Shoes continued war talks with their new neighbors in order to punish the United States.

The Coushattas stayed with Cordero for two weeks, and he generously entertained them each day. He agreed to submit a petition to his superior regarding the trading house near the Coushatta villages. To keep them in good relations with Spain, Cordero had the Coushatta chiefs eat with him at his table. Cordero described them as "the most civilized I have ever known among these Indian tribes"—according to his own European standards, of course. Pia Mingo and others expected such treatment from foreign emissaries, but this was a rare

event. Yet the Spaniard's willingness to dine with them probably helped convince Pia Mingo and Red Shoes that they had
made the proper decision. According to the governor, "they
went away very happy."[38]

Cordero needed to maintain the Coushattas' allegiance;
he wanted to create a buffer against the unrelenting U.S. expansion into Spanish Texas. Rumors of an Anglo-American invasion designed to conquer all of Spanish America had spread
throughout the Provincias Internas, and Spain took great pre-
cautions to protect the Louisiana-Texas border. Keeping with
the policies of their predecessors, Spanish agents lavishly
courted neighboring tribes, including the Caddos and the Alabamas and Coushattas, providing presents and obstructing
the political maneuverings of the United States. Between 1808
and 1810, violent rebellions erupted east and west of New
Orleans. Louisiana became a "hotbed of conspiracies," and
war between the United States and Spain once again seemed
inevitable.[39]

Despite the Coushatta departure, Echean and his kinspeople
in Louisiana still had some advantages, namely with John Sibley. Concerned with Coushatta and Spanish propaganda, Sibley held a Grand Council meeting with tribal leaders residing
in U.S. territory, and presented gifts in token of the United
States' "good will." Sibley ensured advantageous trade between the Indian nations and suggested that they ignore other
American Indians making war with the United States. Echean,
however, did not attend, through fault or design. In November
1807, Echean traveled to Natchitoches to trade animal hides for
provisions. He told Sibley that he had heard nothing from his
Coushatta kinsmen after they had failed to persuade his people to move with them into Spanish territory. According to
Sibley, Echean believed that these Coushattas were "fools" to
ally with the Spanish when they knew that the United States
offered them benefits if they stayed.[40]

Echean's statement is a significant one. Did he resent Pia
Mingo, Red Shoes, and his Coushatta kinsmen for migrating
west, or was it just a statement for the benefit of Sibley? The
answer likely lies somewhere in between the two, but one can
speculate that Echean may have considered the Coushatta

chiefs' decision as one made in haste, without careful consideration of the interests of the collective body of Alabamas and Coushattas. Echean was no principal chief like Opoyheatly, but he probably expected Pia Mingo and Red Shoes to heed his advice and remain in their territory. Echean believed that peace with the Americans was a better course, expressing frustration with the Coushatta decision. Rather than moving away from their newly established center that Echean had taken such great care to develop (at least in his mind), he still believed that there were many opportunities remaining in Louisiana. Echean therefore resisted yet another migration that may have endangered his position as a great leader among both the Alabamas and Coushattas, especially considering his close relations with the powerful Dehahuit. By remaining in Louisiana, the Alabamas and remaining Coushattas in the upper Red River village still had power by brokering their relationship with the Caddo Confederacy. Described by Sibley as "war-like people with Spanish predilections," the Caddos had five hundred or more warriors, and Sibley continued to court them and their allies.[41]

Indeed, Echean's kinspeople continued to profit from their status by choosing to remain in U.S. territory; he hoped to maintain good relations with both the American and Spanish governments. Echean and his Alabama and Coushatta kinspeople on the upper Red River had enjoyed relative stability. They farmed near the riverbanks and infrequently traded at Natchitoches for blankets and provisions.[42] It is understandable, then, why they chose to stay behind: life farther west was too unpredictable and they likely feared leaving their new homeland so soon after their diaspora.

In the perspective of Pia Mingo and Red Shoes, on the other hand, the Coushattas' decision to ally with Spain was a difficult one, but Sibley's handling of Tom's murder broke the neutrality. Moreover, Sibley demanded that they surrender Siache, adding to the chiefs' anger. Although they hardly praised Siache's actions, they refused to deliver him to the local American authorities. His fate, after all, was certain death. Moreover, Governor Cordero met earlier with the Coushattas and courted them by offering presents, promises of trade, and protection as he did for other western tribes such as the Hietans and the Taovaya-

Wichitas. Migrating west offered the Coushattas better opportunities as long as foreign nations continued to dispute territory on the Texas-Louisiana border.[43] Thus, the majority of the Coushattas had voluntarily left the Anglos and their Alabama kinsmen behind and migrated west, initiating yet another diaspora.

Murder in Opelousas

The small group of Alabamas living in the Opelousas District near the lower Red River also decided to remain in U.S. territory after the majority of Coushattas relocated west in 1807. Yet they, too, experienced their share of conflict with the encroaching Anglos. Shortly after the Coushatta migration, a confrontation between an Alabama and an Anglo-American from Opelousas ended in murder. The details about the murder are unclear, but the death was probably the result of a dispute over land. Local authorities arrested five Alabamas and charged them with the murder. Oddly, village leaders delivered the accused men to American authorities.[44] It seems that the Alabamas wanted to avoid further confrontation with the United States and to remain in Opelousas, so they sacrificed a few for the whole community.

In July 1808, the authorities granted the suspects a trial before the Superior Court of the Opelousas District. To no surprise, the jury found four Alabamas guilty of murder, and American citizens of Opelousas demanded their immediate execution. When Governor William Claiborne of Louisiana pardoned two of the Alabamas, the Anglo community became alarmed and citizens protested the pardon. Claiborne noted regretfully that a few citizens "manifested so sanguinary a Spirit" and spoke and acted "as their passions dictate[d]," calling for the massacre of the pardoned Alabamas. Claiborne ordered a militia escort to attend the execution of the two condemned men and to protect the pardoned Alabamas.[45]

The Alabamas' relationship with neighboring Indian communities had persuaded Claiborne to be more generous despite the Americans' hostility toward them. Claiborne admitted that he had pardoned the two Alabamas to prevent further hostilities with their kinspeople and their neighboring Choctaw allies, whom Americans considered a threat to white settlement. Tensions with the Choctaws had peaked after the murder of one of their kinsmen earlier that year, so Claiborne believed that the pardon would demonstrate how the U.S. government was "merciful and just towards [the tribes]."[46] If he lost the Alabamas, the Choctaws, and other allies of the Caddo Confederacy to Spain (as Sibley had with the majority of the Coushattas), the Spaniards could gain yet more allies in any war over Louisiana territory. Like their brethren along the upper Red River, the extraordinary situation allowed the Alabamas in Opelousas to benefit from their friendship with another larger tribe, the Choctaws. The relationship provided the Alabamas in Opelousas with a source of power they lacked on their own.

Such alliances were critical if they wanted to remain in Louisiana. When American encroachment on their lands became a constant menace, the Alabamas in Opelousas requested that the U.S. government issue them an official land grant suitable for farming. According to a report sent to Governor Claiborne, the Alabamas complained in "great distress" that they had no claim to their lands in Louisiana. Unlike the majority of their Alabama kinsmen living on the upper Red River with the Caddos under the leadership of Echean, the group of Alabamas in Opelousas had more white settlers among them. They told Claiborne that they felt cheated as their people had settled and improved the land for many years, but now whites claimed their territory. Anglo-American squatters, on the other hand, told Claiborne that it was necessary to remove the Alabamas from their lands and settle them elsewhere. The Alabamas responded by reminding Claiborne that the majority of their men and women had lived there for approximately forty years and that they had peacefully interacted with the white community by taking jobs as cattlemen, boatmen, and cotton pickers, all to help support their economy.[47] Over the decades, the growing number of white settlements surrounding the Alabamas and Coushattas had made an impact on their livelihood and increased their ties to the community.

Consequently, the Alabamas in Opelousas believed that they had a guaranteed right to land, even among white settlers.

They refused to leave the Opelousas District as their Anglo-American neighbors demanded, regardless of the execution of their two men. Instead, they requested that the United States allow them to establish a small settlement near their former village in Opelousas that had been claimed by American trespassers. In addition, the Alabamas requested that the government give them a land grant "which [they] may expect will be permanent."[48] The Alabamas' demand marked a complete transition in their concept about claims or "titles" to land, a change that had occurred as early as 1759 with the Upper Creeks' protest to the Georgia governor regarding white encroachment. Alabama and Coushatta ancestors, after all, had marked their territorial boundaries with only posts or natural barriers, such as rocks, rivers, or outcroppings, and not with written land deeds.[49] The Alabamas' appeal to President Jefferson for a permanent land grant indicates their complete comprehension that they needed these titles to preserve their territory and protect it from the inevitable American expansion and settlement.

The Alabamas' bid for a land grant harmonized with their strategy of gaining profitable returns by capitalizing on their influence in Louisiana. The Alabamas had maintained their elevated status by brokering relations with their kinsmen on the upper Red River who lived among the Caddos, as well as their Choctaw neighbors. President Jefferson therefore gave them land to keep the Alabamas (those in Opelousas and on the upper Red River) out of hostilities. In a message to Congress on December 30, 1808, Jefferson requested that the United States issue the Alabamas a land grant. Two months later, on February 28, 1809, Congress approved a grant of 2,500 acres for fifty years.[50] The Alabamas in Opelousas gained a secure tract of land, yet their influence abruptly ended because they had pledged loyalty to the United States.

Reunion in East Texas

During the Alabamas' struggle in Opelousas, their Coushatta kinsmen were following the great bison herds through the vast East Texas plains near the Neches and Trinity rivers. By 1809, the Coushattas had established a permanent village over the eastern boundary of the Trinity River, ninety miles, or thirty leagues, below the town of Salcedo.[51] They primarily lived as hunters and traders and supplemented these activities with some farming—and occasional cattle rustling. According to a complaint written by an American settler to Spanish agents in 1809, some young Coushattas had regularly stolen cattle from him. This crime, common among both whites and American Indians, may have been a result of deeply embedded hostilities toward Anglo ranchers who had taken control of their former lands. Moreover, cattle theft obviously provided additional monetary gains.[52]

The Alabamas and Coushattas again had struggled with separation as their people settled in the United States and Spanish territory, respectively. They had irregular contact with each other, and relations deteriorated somewhat. Some Alabamas resented the Coushattas for abandoning their center in Louisiana. In November 1807, Echean had threatened to "disown" his Coushatta kinsmen and to "have no connection with them" if Red Shoes failed to surrender Siache to American authorities.[53] This threat was likely an empty one, made merely to demonstrate his proposed loyalty to the Americans in order to gain favor with Indian agents. But Echean's threat could have led to irreparable consequences: he risked dividing his own people by placing a barrier between them.

Reminiscent of their past separation in the 1780s, it was not long before the Alabamas and Coushattas again reunited. By 1810, the Alabamas and Coushattas' world had changed. After the United States purchased the Louisiana Territory, western expansion was inevitable. American settlers populated these lands at an alarming rate. The remaining Alabamas and Coushattas in Louisiana had a choice: they could stay and attempt to avoid detection and conflict with white settlers, or they could migrate farther west and re-create another center. The majority of their people decided on the latter. It was a difficult decision, but their experience with past diasporas made the adjustment easier. Their connection to the land and people in Louisiana was more ephemeral than it had been in Alabama, so when the crises occurred, they moved on.

The majority of the Caddos also migrated farther west in the early decades of the nineteenth century and resettled near the banks of the Sabine River.[54] The power of the Caddo Confederacy had declined after a series of epidemics reduced their population, crippling their community. The Caddos' loss of status helped compel Echean and his people to terminate their alliance with them. In April 1809, Governor Salcedo reported that 200 Alabama men and their families (which included Coushattas), probably led by Echean, abandoned their claim to land in the United States and established a permanent settlement on the Neches River, twenty-four miles above Nacogdoches, where they continued to farm and trade. Likewise, the group of Alabamas in Opelousas left after 1813 when Louisiana land commissioners denied the official land grants issued to American Indians; this governmental rejection of their territorial claims was a bad omen. The Alabamas began their journey after receiving word from their Coushatta kinsmen that East Texas had a sparse Anglo population and vast expanses of fertile land.[55]

Despite the Alabama and Coushatta migration to East Texas, a small group of Coushattas who had not migrated with Pia Mingo and Red Shoes remained near Caddo territory above Lake Bodeau, 510 miles above its mouth and established Indian Village. Little is known about this group and why they initially stayed behind, but it is likely that they had been under the protection of the Caddos. In 1822, these stayers numbered approximately 350. By 1850, however, encroaching Anglo settlement forced many of them to join their Alabama and Coushatta kinspeople in East Texas. The few families that stayed behind escaped detection. These Coushattas maintained frequent contact with their brethren in Texas by traveling the Coushatta and Alabama traces, open paths that connected Alabama and Coushatta villages between Louisiana and Texas. Intermarriage between the groups continued, as it does today. The Coushattas' Indian Village remains to this day in the southwestern Louisiana town of Elton. Only until the late nineteenth and twentieth centuries did this community again flourish.[56]

During the Alabamas and Coushattas' stay in Louisiana during the first decade of the nineteenth century, leaders such as

Echean, Pia Mingo, and Red Shoes effectively re-created a new center by establishing an alliance with neighboring peoples—namely the Caddo Confederacy. They subsequently brokered this relationship as they had with others in the past in order to increase their leverage with Spanish and American emissaries who vied for their allegiance and friendship. They received gifts, trade concessions, and protection from both sides during times of imperial rivalry.

This strategy proved successful until events such as the Coushatta murder made it necessary for each village to make a separate decision based on its own best interests rather than those of the entire Alabama and Coushatta community. The Coushattas were the first to leave Louisiana and broke their alliance with the Caddos because it was no longer useful. Their previous migration from their homeland in Alabama—also disjointed and made separately—had left the Alabamas and Coushattas more decentralized. The actions taken by Pia Mingo and Red Shoes demonstrated that the Coushattas had considerably more autonomy and independence than they did under the Alabama Nation in the early eighteenth century. Some internal strife was a consequence of such actions, and it led to another episode of short-term separation with their kinspeople. Decisions based on self-interest can lead to permanent division in any group, but two very important factors kept the Alabamas and Coushattas united: kinship ties and a shared history as a coalescent and diasporic people. This connection between the Alabamas and Coushattas proved stronger than the external pressures that might have separated them. As they journeyed west, they re-created a new center once more.

« »

5
Finding New Ground

Alabama and Coushatta storytellers passed down through generations the tale of a rabbit who outwitted the buffalo. It began one day when Rabbit made an arduous journey through the forest. Rabbit spotted a buffalo, and although everyone had said that the buffalo was strong, Rabbit believed he was stronger despite his small size. Rabbit challenged the buffalo to a test of strength to see who could pull the other over a mark atop a hill with a long grapevine. When the buffalo agreed, Rabbit took the vine to the hill, found another buffalo, and made the same challenge. Rabbit gave one end of the vine to one buffalo, and the second end to the other beast on the other side of the hill. Rabbit hid in the middle and yanked the vine to start the contest. Each buffalo jerked back and forth, as the animals were equally matched. Indeed, they were shocked that Rabbit had so much power. The two buffalo wanted to see how Rabbit was succeeding, so they slowly walked up the hill. When they reached the top they saw each other instead of Rabbit, who, aware that he could no longer play the two against each other, ran away.[1]

The buffalo agreed that they should punish Rabbit, so they prevented him from drinking any water, which they controlled. When Rabbit tried to drink, the buffalo ordered him off the land. Yet clever Rabbit had one last trick: he found a fawn's skin, placed it over him, ran to the water, and cried. When the buffalo asked him why he was distressed, the disguised rabbit told him that the buffalo had forbidden all animals to drink. The buffalo responded: "It is only Rabbit who cannot drink any more. You can always get all the water you want." Rabbit, still disguised as a deer, then happily drank the water, and later told everyone how he had fooled the buffalo.[2]

The story of the rabbit, one of the most loved heroes in tribal lore, can be seen as symbolic of the Alabama and Coushatta experience in the first half of the nineteenth century. Many perceived the Alabamas and Coushattas as weak because they were not as numerous as other peoples or nations. The rabbit's contrived contest between two buffalo can be a metaphor of the Alabamas and Coushattas' ability to play off two nations that were gaining strength in East Texas: Mexico and the United States. Instead of fighting them directly, the Alabamas and Coushattas stayed in the middle and watched them struggle against each other, as their ancestors had done with other powers in the past. They would engage the empires in their newly created center for as long as they could. Through guile and cunning, the Alabamas and Coushattas would emerge from the imperial contest with their main objectives in sight: sovereignty and title to their lands.

Beginning the Contest

Throughout the first two decades of the nineteenth century, the world of the Alabamas and Coushattas gradually shifted westward. By 1820, the communities of Alabamas and Coushattas, who previously lived in Alabama, West Florida, and Spanish Louisiana, had migrated to East Texas in order to find new ground once again and re-create their homeland. The memory of their ancestor's journey west described this change; it was a decision that they had to make in order to preserve their sovereignty in the wake of Anglo-American expansion.

Once they arrived, they constructed new villages near the Trinity and Neches rivers and forged new relationships and alliances with other diasporic communities from the East.

Around the same time the Alabamas and Coushattas had migrated west, diasporic groups of Shawnees, Delawares, and Kickapoos also arrived in East Texas, having crossed the Mississippi River in search of better trade and hunting grounds. These communities previously had lived in New Jersey, Ohio, and Pennsylvania, but Anglo-American settlement pushed them out and left their people fragmented. They migrated west to the Red and Angelina rivers in the first decade of the nineteenth century, then south to the west banks of the Red and Sabine rivers, just north of Nacogdoches. Like the Alabamas and Coushattas, they migrated in small groups, occupying areas that were claimed by many.[3]

Similarly, in the 1770s an eastern faction of Cherokees led by principal chief Duwali (known as Colonel Bowles by Americans), settled near the White, St. Francis, and Arkansas rivers in Spanish Louisiana. Duwali, who was sixty-two in 1822, was the "white chief" or *uku* among his people; it was an honorary title given to the most respected men in his community. As their numbers increased to 2,000, Spanish and American officials recognized them as the "Western Cherokees." Under pressure from American encroachment in present-day Arkansas, Duwali led his tribe in the winter of 1810 into East Texas, which then belonged to the province of Coahuila and Texas in the viceroyalty of New Spain. They, like the Shawnees, Delawares, and Kickapoos, also settled near the Spanish trading post of Nacogdoches.[4]

As these movements took place, new challenges quickly arose. Not surprisingly, these emigrant peoples clashed with western tribes when they resumed hunting trips into regions inhabited by the Comanches, Wacos, Wichitas, Lipan Apaches, Tawakonies, and Taovays. This conflict was a consequence of diasporic groups settling into new territory, unwelcome by host communities. As they moved west, the Alabamas and Coushattas had encroached on other peoples' territory. Life in East Texas became very unpredictable and often dangerous because western tribes were formidable. Their combined population numbered an estimated 3,000 warriors in 1822. They raided horses and cattle and challenged the Alabamas and Coushattas and other emigrant peoples over hunting grounds.[5]

In the face of such confrontations, Alabama and Coushatta leaders again sought alliances with other neighboring peoples that shared their interests. The Western Cherokees, repeatedly at war with the Comanches and the Lipan Apaches, were interested. The origin of the enmity between the Cherokees and Comanches was competition for game and territory. Comanches conducted raids near central Texas, an area that the Cherokees used for hunting. Many Cherokee warriors had been killed in Comanche raids, and clan law obliged them to avenge their deaths; as a result, the warfare escalated. In March 1824, Richard Fields, the Cherokees' diplomatic chief, invited the other emigrant peoples in East Texas to join a pan-Indian union.[6] Demographics help explain the origins of the proposed alliance. Juan Antonio Padilla, secretary to the commandant general of the eastern Provincias Internas, estimated in 1830 that only 2,000 emigrant Indians lived in Texas compared to 4,700 Comanches and their western compatriots.[7] The emigrants had a smaller population than their western neighbors, so an Indian alliance offered them valuable protection. For diasporic communities, unity always created strength.

In an attempt to secure their hunting rights, to defend their property, and to prevent further encroachment, the Alabamas and Coushattas, Shawnees, Delawares, and Kickapoos (all located near the Neches, Trinity, and Angelina rivers) formed a pan-tribal union with the Western Cherokees and organized to deter any further raiding by western tribes.[8] The Western Cherokee Union was an alliance of like-minded peoples. The immigrant tribes cultivated the land, hunted to supplement their diets, and exchanged foodstuffs and game for trade goods. They also shared in common their diasporas from eastern homelands and migrations to East Texas. The Comanche-related tribes, on the other hand, originated in the western plains of east Colorado, New Mexico, and western Kansas. By 1821, they controlled lands east of the Rocky Mountains between the Arkansas River and the Rio Grande and lived mostly by hunting large game, especially buffalo. Historian

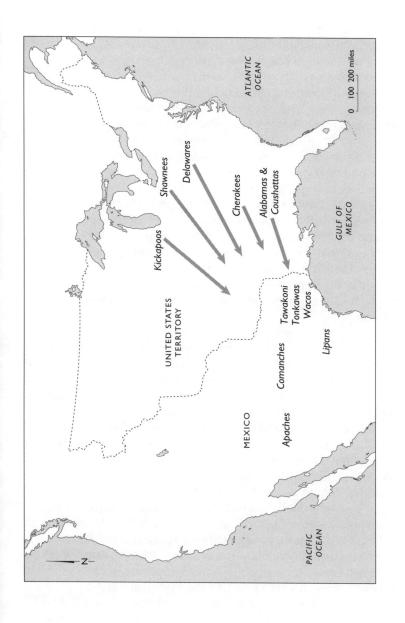

American Indian diasporas, 1763–1820

David La Vere has argued that the conflict between the Comanches and the eastern tribes was a true culture clash. Whereas the settled, agricultural peoples from the East saw the Plains Indians as "savage," the western tribes saw the emigrants as invaders.[9] Conflict was therefore inevitable.

Similar to the Creek alliance in the eighteenth century and the Caddo alliance that followed, the Western Cherokee Union was an informal alliance; each group maintained its identity and cultural heritage and often based its decisions on calculations of its own interests rather than those of the Union. Although details of communication among the members are sparse, we know that leaders and their representatives met occasionally to recruit war parties and to discuss intertribal affairs. The Union began as a defensive expedient. On the assumption that the enemy of my enemy is my friend, the enemies of the Comanches were natural allies. In time, however, the Union brought the unexpected advantage of strengthening its members' hands in dealing with Mexicans and Anglo-Americans.

Life in East Texas

Despite the fighting between the Western Cherokee Union and its rivals, the Alabamas and Coushattas thrived in East Texas. They claimed a prime settlement location with vast prairies and gently rolling hills interspersed with timber, numerous rivers, clear-running streams, and rich black soil. The herds of buffalo that grazed the prairie lands to the west supplied them with an additional source of food.[10]

As the Alabamas and Coushattas made the transition to hunting larger game on the open plains, they likely spent more time training in order to improve their skills. Like their Mississippian ancestors, Alabama and Coushatta men played chunkey, which involved a disc carved out of elmwood or stone (*hassapolohkí*) that one tossed onto open ground. Whichever man shot his arrow or threw a stick closest to the disc won the game; this activity strengthened the warriors' coordination and aim.[11] Alabama and Coushatta men also trained young boys to endure hardships and learn practices that made them stronger warriors, which was vital if they were to succeed in battle against their new formidable enemies the Comanches. Boys learned to swim in cold weather and built their stamina through exercise. Coushatta elders also practiced scratching (a tradition that lasted through the twentieth century) as a rite of passage for fit young men. They cut the skin with either broken glass or garfish teeth and then washed off the blood with cold water; leaving the scratches to dry was a method of punishment as it was quite painful. Rituals like these would prove important as Alabama and Coushatta warriors had to combat their enemies in a place that turned increasingly chaotic and dangerous.[12]

Like their eastern allies, the Alabamas and Coushattas cultivated the land. As they had practiced in the early eighteenth century, men first girdled trees and after they died, then burned them and prepared the soil for planting using metal hoes they had obtained from trade with the Americans. Women next planted seeds in rows and covered the holes with their feet, an ancient practice known as *mastonkayapka*. Men also assisted with planting tobacco, which was usually only done by women in most southeastern tribes.[13] Culinary traditions also remained intact despite their diasporas. Practiced by earlier generations (perhaps as early as the Mississippian period), women processed their corn harvests by placing dry kernels (sometimes roasted) into a pottery vessel with water and a cup of wood-ash lye and soaked it overnight.[14] After they drained the corn into a sifting basket, women ground it in a mortar and made it into a thick porridge soup, often referred to as "sofkey," a mainstay of their diet.[15]

The Alabamas and Coushattas produced enough corn, peas, pumpkins, and other vegetables for their own use and a surplus to take to market and barter for other goods. They sold harvest surpluses at the Spanish trading post at Nacogdoches in exchange for clothing, blankets, tools, and alcohol.[16] To supplement their income and diets, they hunted in the bleak winter months for buffalo, bear, and venison. In a variety of ways, the Alabamas and Coushattas were dependent on the land for survival.[17]

According to an April 1831 report by Francisco Madero, the commissioner of the state of Coahuila and Texas, the Alabamas had established three villages on the west bank of the Neches River. They had constructed sixty-nine log houses to shelter a combined population of 103 families, 100 single men, and 64 single women. Madero's report estimated the Alabama population at 370 (excluding children). Their principal town was "Fenced-in Village," suggesting the demarcation of physical space. The name "fenced-in" illustrated the Alabamas' methods of identifying their land to outsiders and protecting their crops from unwanted invaders. Their own collection of domesticated animals (originally introduced by Europeans) could be destructive to crops, and over generations, the Alabamas learned how to manage them.[18]

In Fenced-in Village, principal chief Antone and two subchiefs, Tallustah and Oppaya, handled tribal affairs with the assistance of the council of elders. Chief Antone, born in Louisiana around 1780, was a powerful figure among his people. Gustav Dresel, a traveler and German consul for a group of immigrants nearby, visited the village in 1839 and noted that the Alabamas regarded Antone as an "absolute monarch," a description that was similar to positions held by the Alabamas' ancient Mississippian chieftains. Antone had a large cabin, an elaborate, two-story storage house, and a summer house. According to Dresel, "between these castle buildings there was a court where several Indian women sat," likely Antone's entourage.[19] The probability of Antone having dictatorial power is unlikely, despite his great wealth and status. Yet Dresel's comments suggest that Antone had similar power compared to his Alabama ancestor, Opoyheatly. Although he lacked command over his Coushatta kinsmen as Opoyheatly had under the Alabama Nation, it seems that Antone represented the Alabamas' desire for strong leadership. One might suggest that this centralization among the Alabamas was the result of their repeated migrations west, especially as unification and collective interests became more important in such chaotic and unpredictable times.[20]

The Coushattas lived forty miles away from Fenced-in Village —close enough for regular contact—in two villages along the east bank of the Trinity River. One contained between thirty and forty wood cabins housing fifty-six families, a total of fifty-seven single men and sixty-four single women; the other had twenty-five cabins where sixty-four families lived, including thirty-one single men and forty single women. According to Madero's report, the Coushattas numbered 426 led by a principal chief, Long King, and, like the Alabamas, two subchiefs, Colita and Nekima. Sometime around the latter half of the 1830s, Colita succeeded Long King as principal chief and provided centralized leadership for the Coushattas (just as Antone had for the Alabamas) as they established their homes in East Texas.[21]

Based on these descriptions, the Alabamas and Coushattas had left behind the political structure of the eighteenth-century *talwas* (towns) and the individual mikos that led them and had returned to their ancient traditions, favoring a system of centralized leadership that was reminiscent of the Mississippian chiefdoms. These political changes not only kept the Alabamas and Coushattas closer together within their own groups, but also helped maintain their identity as a coalescent people, especially as they increasingly depended on each other in the nineteenth century.

Territorial Claims

Not long after the Alabamas and Coushattas settled in East Texas, Mexico gained its independence from Spain in 1821. Mexican independence had a direct impact on western migrations: American settlers from the East began to close the gap between East Texas and the western boundary of the United States along the Sabine, Red, and Arkansas rivers. At the time Anglo-Americans were developing an interest in Texas, Mexico was undergoing a series of political transformations. In February 1821, Augustín de Iturbide, a former military commander of Guanajuato and Michoacán, supported a revolutionary movement fighting for independence from Spain. Later in September, he marched his troops into Mexico City, and on May 19, 1822, his military proclaimed him Emperor Augustín I of Mexico. On January 3, 1823, Iturbide's congress passed the Imperial Colonization Law that invited Catholic settlers to Mexico and authorized the employment of *empresarios*, or land agents, who would settle up to two hundred families in Texas in return for large land grants. The law initially benefited American entrepreneurs such as Stephen Austin, who had applied for a land grant in 1821 to establish a colony in East Texas along the Brazos River.[22] The increase in Anglo-American immigration that followed Mexican independence posed a challenge to American Indians who had immigrated first. The Alabamas and Coushattas seemed to be running into the same problem they had moved west to escape.

Mexico's liberal immigration policy continued despite political chaos. On March 19, 1823, Iturbide voluntarily abdicated his throne after receiving great opposition from regional leaders, such as Antonio López de Santa Anna, who were in favor of abolishing the monarchy and replacing it with a republic. The empowered Mexican Congress took leadership by enacting the Federal (National) Colonization Law on August 18, 1824. This law, and the state law of Coahuila and Texas of March 25, 1825, exempted new settlers from taxes and allotted them land in "quantities varying with the occupation and the wants of emigrants, on a scale of liberality undoubtedly not equaled in the Colonization of any other country."[23] Thus, Mexico opened Texas to settlement by all nationalities including the Anglo-Americans who settled East Texas, in the hopes of building the state's infrastructure, developing its commerce, and creating a buffer against the Comanches and Lipan Apaches who raided Mexican settlements farther to the south. Article 19 of the law stipulated that American Indians (albeit those who were considered "civilized") could also apply for land grants, provided they agreed to abide by Mexico's laws.[24]

Informally, the government viewed some American Indian settlement—especially by tribes who migrated from the Southeast—as an advantageous buffer between hostile tribes on its borders. This allowance gave the Alabamas and Coushattas, who had survived by riding the shifting political currents in Texas, the opportunity to stabilize their community. They would first use their alliance networks and build good relations with the local government and then apply for their title to land. They had no choice but appeasement and collaboration, that is, to recognize the laws enacted and try to take advantage of them.

When Anglo-Americans clashed with American Indians over land claims, fighting broke out because the emigrant tribes, who had arrived and settled first, were determined to keep their land. Once disputes over land titles began, membership in the Western Cherokee Union became more beneficial to the Alabamas and Coushattas. It gave them legitimacy and strength when dealing with the Mexican government; as a smaller diasporic group, the Alabamas and Coushattas needed to be connected with a larger power if they were to be taken seriously. They clearly understood, along with other emigrant tribes, that legal title to land was critical to prevent further Anglo-American encroachment.

In a bid to obtain the Mexican government's support against the Anglo-American squatters, the Western Cherokee Union offered to send troops against the western tribes who raided Mexican and Indian settlements. Stephen Austin, who had settled 300 farmers and ranchers, was alarmed when the Taovayas, Tawankonis, and Wacos joined the Comanches in raiding his colony. On May 24, 1824, he advised the *alcalde* (mayor) of Nacogdoches, Anthony Clarke, to "cultivate the most friendly understanding" with the Cherokees, Alabamas and Coushattas, and other members of the alliance.[25]

Austin worried that if the Mexican government did not take the Union's offer, warriors would attack his colony, which bordered land settled by the Cherokees. On April 30, 1826, he advised Lieutenant Colonel Mateo Ahumada, the principal military commander in Coahuila and Texas, that it was "highly important that your lordship and the Military Commander should write to the Cherokees, Alabamas, and Cushates [*sic*], and to the Alcaldes and Captains of the Militia of Nacogdoches and the Trinity, to join us in the contemplated war."[26] In response, Cherokee chief Duwali, who saw the opportunity to win the favor of government officials, sent Richard Fields to offer Austin and the Mexican government support from Cherokee warriors and their allies. He aimed to present the Union as willing allies of Mexico while at the same time gaining advantage over his enemies.[27]

The plan worked. The Western Cherokee Union would have proved useful if needed in wars against western tribes, so after a series of Texas inspections in 1828 by the commandant general of the eastern Provincias Internas, General Manuel de Mier y Terán, the government decided to grant the Union's members legal title to their lands. The decision derived partly from Terán's report that Anglo-American squatters were illegally encroaching on Mexican territory where they caused resentment not only among the emigrant Texas tribes, but also among longer-term residents of Nacogdoches who already had land claims. In order to halt further intrusions, Mexico passed a law on April 6, 1830, that canceled all empresario contracts except for those covering established colonies, appointed a commissioner of colonization (Terán became the first) to oversee settlement in Texas, and prohibited further U.S. immigration.[28]

The law, which was bound to have provoked a conflict with Anglo-Americans, proved beneficial in the short term for the Alabamas and Coushattas and their allies. In the summer of 1831, Terán helped the Union's members to apply for legal title to the land they claimed between the Neches and Trinity rivers. This process proved time consuming and expensive as the government expected the tribes to pay an attorney to put forward their claims under the colonization laws. The political chief of the Department of Bexar, Ramon Musquiz, reported on behalf of the Alabamas and Coushattas and Cherokees in September that they did not have "the means to pay the fees to the Commissioner and to the Surveyor, nor the amount for the Stamppaper, necessary for issuing them their titles, nor the Land Dues to the State."[29] Such bureaucracy was foreign to the Alabamas and Coushattas, especially considering their past traditions of marking claims to territory with natural borders. Despite the Alabamas and Coushattas lack of experience in such matters, administrative routine deferred to political need. In order to create a line of defense along the Texas borders and to promote "good order on this frontier," in March 1832 the governor of Coahuila and Texas, José Maria Letona, appointed Colonel Don José de Las Piedras to represent the tribes and waived the fees for their titles.[30]

The "title" came with certain guarantees. Mexican officials told chiefs Colita and Long King of the Coushattas and Chief Antone of the Alabamas that they would not allow settlers to challenge their claims to the land they had occupied and cultivated. In March 1832, the government declared that the Alabamas and Coushattas and their allies should "not be disturbed in the lands which they now occupy."[31] Similarly, in February 1833 the town council (*ayuntamiento*) of the Municipality of Liberty exempted these "settled tribes" from all duties and the requirement to place stock on their lands as proof of occupation.[32] Mexico declared its intention of giving peaceful Indians of all nations, especially the southeastern emigrant tribes, the same privileges it had given to Anglo-Americans in the hope that American Indian settlement would both promote trade and act as a protective buffer.

The grants and concessions given to the Alabamas and Coushattas led them to conclude that Mexico recognized their claim to the land; they were "lawful possessors of the soil which they inhabited."[33] Looking back to the early eighteenth century, Alabama and Coushatta worldviews did not embrace the need to obtain foreign government "titles" to the land they had occupied and hunted. The Alabamas and Coushattas gradually adopted Western understandings of documented proof of land ownership to prevent further losses. This change even appeared in their language: the Alabama word *támbatka* translates as "holding title to land" (and "to be grabbing").[34] Chiefs Colita and Antone clearly knew that they needed titles to stay in Texas and to fight off intruders, or "land grabbers." Land had always been what they needed to prosper—even more so in the 1830s as they sought stability given the past decades of movement.

Despite guarantees from the Mexican government and the prohibition of Anglo-American immigration, in 1835 the Alabamas and Coushattas encountered speculators surveying their lands and building homesteads. Colita and others immediately protested to the military commander of Anahuac, Antonio Tenorio, that the settlers were trespassers and added that they expected the government, with whom they had maintained a "faithful friendship," to remove them and to prohibit future incursions. Tenorio advised the military commander of Coahuila and Texas, Martín Perfecto de Cos, to prevent "any persons from depriving these natives of the right they have acquired to their lands by their constant labor."[35] He explained on April 9, 1835, that Mexico had to appease the Alabamas and Coushattas and their allies in the Western Cherokee Union because the army might need their help in the near future to defend Texas, which Mexico was "in imminent danger of losing." Given the Alabamas and Coushattas' close ties with the Cherokees, the capabilities of the Union's military leaders, and its combined force of 3,300 men, Tenorio stressed that it was "absolutely necessary to maintain peace" with the Union.[36] The combined emigrant tribes had some bargaining power, especially when war erupted in Texas.

The Texas Revolution

The Alabamas and Coushattas were in a difficult situation once the Mexican government experienced political turmoil. Antonio López de Santa Anna, a former governor of Yucatán and Veracruz, usurped the presidency on March 30, 1833, scrapped the constitution a year later, and installed a dictatorship. Colita and others had no idea if Santa Anna would revoke their titles or permit them to remain in Texas. Santa Anna's actions ultimately led to rebellion in California and Coahuila and Texas. By the time Santa Anna's troops arrived in October 1836 to put down the insurrection in Texas, it was too late. Texas had set up its own provisional independent government the previous November, with Henry Smith of Nacogdoches as governor and Sam Houston as commander of the army. Santa Anna had a full-scale war on his hands.[37]

Similar to other wars in the past, the Alabamas and Coushattas needed to ride out the conflict and stay neutral. Chiefs Colita and Antone understood that the rebellion in Texas made it necessary to remain connected to both governments if their kinspeople were to keep their lands. Union members stood together and made no immediate commitment to either government. Despite their decision, in March 1835, the military commander at Bexar, Colonel Domingo de Ugartechea, suggested to Colita that the Union should attack Comanches who were raiding Mexican settlements. The Mexican government would supply the ammunition and, in return for the Union's help, allow it to keep all the plunder it could take.[38]

Colita and Antone both refused Ugartechea's offer; it was too risky. When declining, Colita warned that if Mexico proved unwilling to recognize their title to their lands or treated them unjustly, they would join the rebel Texans and convince the Western Cherokee Union to do likewise, despite their preference for neutrality. In May 1835, the military commandant of the department of Nacogdoches, Pedro Ellis Bean, warned Ugartechea not to ignore the threat because rebels in the Nacogdoches District had announced their goal of inciting rebellion and forming an alliance with the Western Cherokee Union to aid their cause.[39]

Ugartechea, worried about Colita's threat, advised the government to prevent Anglo-American immigrants who squatted on lands the Coushattas had occupied for thirty years. Bean immediately received instructions to expel Americans. At the same time, Perfecto de Cos sent additional troops to protect the Coushattas' lands and to buttress the government's authority in East Texas. Even though defeating the rebels took precedence, the government recognized that in order to keep its hold on Texas, it had to keep peace with members of the Western Cherokee Union. Moreover, internal pressures compelled Mexican officials to avoid provoking them.[40]

The rebels were as interested as the Mexican government in the Union's stance. After receiving intelligence that the Cherokees and some of their allies had agreed to aid the Mexican government, in December of 1835 the rebel provisional government appointed Sam Houston, John Forbes, and John Cameron to try to negotiate a treaty of friendship with Union members. Smith directed them to "take all necessary measures in their power for the accomplishment of that end," which left the commissioners under the impression that they had been given the powers plenipotentiary of diplomats.[41] Furthermore, the provisional government had decided to suspend all land grants and surveys in or near Union members' territory.[42] These directives gave the Alabamas and Coushattas the opportunity to obtain from the Texas government official recognition of title to their lands while also relying on the Mexican title they already possessed.

After Cameron resigned because of poor health and Forbes postponed his departure, Houston went ahead by himself, leaving Forbes to follow. Houston had great experience with Indian affairs. Estranged from his own family in Tennessee when only sixteen, he ran away and lived among the Cherokees, eventually creating kinship ties with them. In 1830, they granted him all the rights and liberties of a Cherokee after he had published a series of articles in the *Arkansas Gazette* under his Cherokee name, Tah-Lohn-Tus-Ky, which exposed the long-standing ill treatment of Cherokees by the United States and its Indian agents. Thus, Western Cherokee Union members believed his word was good.[43]

When Houston met with members of the Western Cherokee Union, Duwali and Colita told him that they planned to remain neutral. Neutrality was a careful choice with a particular meaning: rather than keeping their distance from both sides, they hoped to obtain recognition from both without having to pay for it. If they made the mistake of backing the losing side in the war, they risked destroying their way of life; the victors likely would expel them from their lands and force them to move west into an unfamiliar environment and enemy territory. Nonetheless, even though they saw the Texas Revolution as a white man's war not worth the spilling of their warriors' blood, they understood their stake in the outcome: they would have to come to terms with the victor. Thus, Union leaders tried to convince both sides that any unjust action against them—violence or squatting on their lands—would provoke them to counterattack or to choose an alliance with the other side. Their stance left both the Mexican government and the rebels apprehensive, and both took preventive measures to try to forestall hostilities.

Choosing Sides

On February 23, 1836, after Forbes had caught up with Houston, the two offered the Cherokee alliance a treaty of friendship that would officially recognize its members' claims to land in East Texas. Chiefs Antone and Colita agreed to the terms

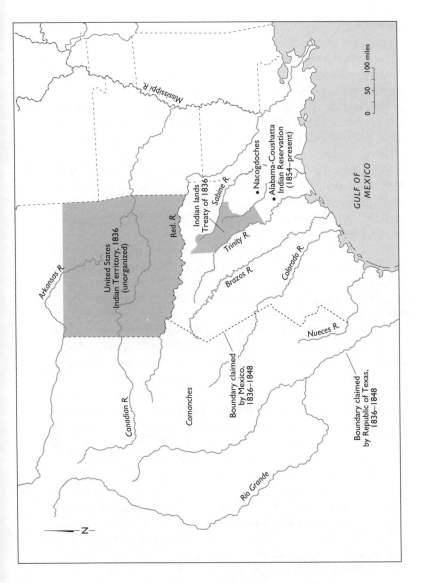

Texas settlement

even though they were likely to suffer if either Texas or Mexico won a decisive victory. The treaty bound the Cherokees, Alabamas and Coushattas, Shawnees, Delawares, Kickapoos—all members of the Western Cherokee Union—and other tribes including the Quapaws, Choctaws, Biluxies, Iowanies, Caddos of the Neches, Tahoocattakes, and Unataquous, to a "firm and lasting peace forever," and stipulated that "friendly intercourse shall be preserved" between these tribes and the government of Texas.[44]

The second article declared that, in return, the tribes "shall have and possess the lands within the following bounds," which included territory west of San Antonio road where it crossed the Angelina and Neches rivers.[45] The treaty failed to include all the lands occupied by the tribes; Union members ceded to the would-be government any additional western lands they claimed. An Indian agency would administer the allocated territory as a reservation and would keep order, regulate trade, and prevent encroachment by Anglo-American squatters. Yet the tribes would live under their own laws. For example, any property stolen from them by Texans would be restored and the accused tried under tribal law. Article 5 stipulated that these lands "shall never be sold or alienated to any person or persons, power or Government," and that both Sam Houston and John Forbes, acting as commissioners for the Texas Republic, "bind themselves, to prevent in the future all persons from intruding within the said bounds."[46] Thus, even though the Union's members surrendered some of the territory they had claimed in 1831 and 1833, they settled for what they took to be the guarantee of permanent legal title to the remainder by the Texas Republic.

The only flaw for the Alabamas and Coushattas in an otherwise advantageous treaty was the stipulation that they should move northeast toward the Angelina River. However, the area was equally fertile, away from the Anglo-American squatters, and far preferable to journeying farther west, where they would have had to give up arable farming and take up hunting on lands claimed by their enemies. Thus, despite the inconvenience of having to rebuild some of the villages, the treaty provided the opportunity for permanent prosperity by granting the Alabamas and Coushattas self-determination, title to their land, and a guarantee that encroachment would be punished —provided only that Texas succeeded in obtaining its independence from Mexico.

After Houston held discussions separately with each tribe, delegates from the Western Cherokees led by Duwali signed the treaty on February 23, 1836. It is not known whether he did so in the presence of what the treaty identified as the Cherokees' "Associate Bands." Although no other known chief signed or made his mark, for reasons also unknown, the treaty bound every member of the Cherokee alliance.[47] Perhaps the others, including the Alabamas and Coushattas, allowed Duwali to represent them to show the Texans a united front. Duwali was in some ways acting like a paramount chief—one who led a number of different groups over a large distance. It was parallel to Dehahuit's leadership of the Caddo Confederacy and its allies. The Alabamas and Coushattas, then, would not have been alarmed at Duwali's actions; they had profited in the past by brokering their relations with such powerful and influential chiefs while still maintaining their sovereignty and identity.

The treaty should not be interpreted as the Western Cherokee Union's preference for Texas rather than Mexico. In the event that the Mexican government suppressed the revolt and reestablished its control over Texas, the Alabamas and Coushattas would have rested their claim to land on the authority of the ayuntamiento issued by the Municipality of Liberty. The treaty denotes the success of the Union's strategy of trying to keep in favor with both sides: irrespective of who claimed victory, the Alabamas and Coushattas expected to receive title to the land they occupied.

Pending the outcome of the war, Chief Antone decided to ensure his people's safety by temporarily relocating to their old ground in Louisiana; according to Alabama and Coushatta recollections, he followed a suggestion from Houston.[48] He may have been trying to avoid demands to choose sides, and the move may illustrate the Alabamas' confidence that, whatever the outcome, they would be able to return and remain in East Texas. They probably lived among a small community of

Coushatta stayers who had settled in 1812 along the banks of the Calcasieu River, in present-day Elton, Louisiana. The number that left for Louisiana is unknown, but they may have been mostly women and children seeking protection from the devastating war ahead. When the revolution was over, they would return home and claim their land.

Most of the Coushattas, together with some Alabama warriors, remained at their villages near the Trinity River for the duration of the war. Both Mexico and Texas courted them, offering spoils of the war in return for support.[49] The majority of the Alabamas and Coushattas remained neutral, but some individual warriors seized their opportunities. Many Texans who had joined the army left their homesteads unprotected, and roaming warriors raided these settlements for valuable items or provisions. Some Coushattas, who knew the landscape well, hired themselves out as guides to invading Mexican armies in return for a portion of the plunder.[50] Although aiding the Mexican government contravened the treaty with the Texas rebels, these individual Coushattas reaped rich rewards. Chiefs Colita and Antone, despite their centralized authority, could not prevent them from doing so. Anglo-Americans, looking from a Western perspective, assumed that the treaty bound everyone, but the nature of Alabama and Coushatta society prohibited chiefs from determining an individual's choices.

Other Alabamas and Coushattas assisted the Texans. The most notable incident, which later became part of their oral tradition, occurred when Chief Colita's village slaughtered some of its own cattle to feed starving Texan women and children in flight (known as the "Runaway Scrape") from Santa Anna's army as it approached San Jacinto.[51] An Alabama and Coushatta recollection described the morning of April 18, 1836, when a scout warned the Texans of Santa Anna's approaching Mexican army. The Texans living near the Brazos River fled from their settlements to avoid the conflict. The refugees had hoped to find safety once they reached the Trinity River but discovered that the ferryboat was gone, and the once calm stream had grown to a dangerous rapid and prevented them from crossing. At once, "a lone Indian reined his horse down the bank of the water, hesitated, and then plunged in. . . .

Halfway across the muddy, rolling water, the rider held forth his hand and boomed a greeting. It was Colita, chief of the friendly Coushattas." The Texans were at first speechless, then they "rang with their shouts of rejoicing" that Colita would save them.[52]

After the Texan refugees told him that they were trying to escape Mexican forces, Colita had his warriors cut down trees to make a raft for the Texans. He and his men succeeded in escorting the Texans across the Trinity River. Coushatta women from Long King Village prepared food for the starving Texans. They ate and "warmed their hearts in this new-found hospitality." Suddenly, however, a Texan woman who was caring for her nine children screamed: she had left her baby asleep in a wagon on the other side of the river. Colita "caught her almost incoherent words" and with his horse crossed the dangerous river once again. He safely returned and gave the baby back to the distressed mother. Colita had "relieved the anxiety of the whites," and the Texans continued on their journey.[53]

Four days later, Colita caught up to the Texans and told them of the victory at San Jacinto. The war was over. According to oral tradition, Colita became a hero and friend to the Texans from then on.[54] Chief Colita's actions in this heroic and legendary description demonstrated the authority he commanded over his people and the respect he had among the white community—a difficult feat considering nineteenth-century racist attitudes toward American Indians. His leadership in this dramatic event was significant: it confirmed to Texan leaders that the Coushattas and his kinspeople were loyal to the Republic and that they deserved to remain in Texas.

The Betrayal

At the battle of San Jacinto in April 1836, rebel forces captured Santa Anna, and the Republic of Texas won its independence from Mexico. The decisiveness of the victory adversely affected the Western Cherokee Union. Colita and others could no longer expect to reap benefits from remaining neutral between Anglos and Mexicans who no longer vied for the Union's allegiance. The Alabamas and Coushattas had a treaty with the victors, but their decline in power left them vulnerable. The steady stream of Anglo-American settlers threatened their homeland. Mexico's commissioner of colonization, Juan Almonte, had reported in May 1834 that the non-Indian population of the department of Nacogdoches (the territory east of the Trinity River) had risen to 9,000, twice the number of the Indian population of 4,500.[55] When they faced such a crisis in the past, they simply began a new diaspora; migrating west always had solved their problems. Yet, the Alabamas and Coushattas could not move to the western plains—to do so would destroy their livelihood as settled agriculturalists and possibly decimate their people. They had to rely on Houston's promise that the treaty would secure the titles to their lands in East Texas.

At first, the omens seemed good. Upon Sam Houston's election as the first president of the Republic of Texas on October 22, 1836, he addressed the "Indian question" at his inauguration. He stated that the treaties of friendship and "the maintenance of good faith with the Indians" were vital. He called for an end to the unlawful seizure of their lands and advised the Texans to "establish commerce with the different tribes, supply their useful and necessary wants, [and] maintain even-handed justice with them."[56] Nonetheless, when Houston submitted the treaty for ratification on November 12, 1836, the Senate refused it because the Texas government had not authorized Houston and Forbes to make what they viewed as "extravagant promises."[57] The senators claimed that the treaty "was based on promises that did not exist and that the operation of it would not only be detrimental to the interests of the Republick [sic] but would also be a violation of the vested rights of many Citizens."[58] They argued that Houston and Forbes had no right to recognize the tribes' titles to their lands. The Republic had no obligation to honor the treaty and had good reason not to: some Texans had already settled on and sought title to territory that the treaty promised to the tribes, and the senators supported the Texans' claims rather than those of American Indians.[59]

Texas senators made it clear that they sought to promote and protect Anglo-American settlement in East Texas. Such attitudes were anticipated. The majority of Texans were former residents of the United States who searched for new land, and they brought their ethnocentric beliefs with them. Most Americans agreed that removal was the most realistic and appropriate solution to the "Indian problem." American leaders blindly professed the virtue and humanitarianism of Indian removal. Many emphasized the white man's duty to remove and to seclude American Indians from areas of Anglo "civilization." They reasoned that removal would "save the Indian race" and that Anglos would use the land more efficiently than had the Indians. Many had rejected Thomas Jefferson's ideal of gradual integration of the two cultures and replaced it with Andrew Jackson's harsh Indian policy.[60] Prompted by Jackson in 1830, the U.S. Congress had passed the Indian Removal Act and had appropriated money to finance the negotiation and purchase of land from tribes still living in the Southeast—the Cherokees, Creeks, Chickasaws, Choctaws, and Seminoles. Tribal leaders eventually signed treaties that sold their remaining territory east of the Mississippi River in exchange for federal annuities and land, or reservations, in Indian Territory (present-day Oklahoma). Tribal factions protested the decision and rejected the treaties their leaders had signed, so Jackson sent troops to the Southeast to remove them by force.[61] The Texas Senate, in making similar plans for the Texas tribes, merely followed the lead of the United States.

Despite the assurance in Article 5 of the treaty that the Texas government would protect the territory occupied by the Texas tribes from encroachment, in 1836 surveyors and settlers trespassed into their designated territory, destroyed crops, and stole horses and cattle. Texas officials left all of these crimes unpunished. Houston later remarked that the tribes' land was the "forbidden fruit in the midst of the garden; their blooming peach trees, their snug cabins, their well cultivated fields, and their lowing herds excite the speculators."[62] Some accused Texas senators of caving in to the special interests of the speculators and their own "personal aggrandizement." Houston warned the Texas Congress in December that if they failed to ratify the treaty, the tribes would declare war on the Republic with the backing of the Mexican army.[63]

The warning that only peace with the Texas tribes would stabilize the Republic and prevent a counterrevolution back-fired; critics later justified Indian removal when the tribes revolted against the Texans. When the Texas Senate refused to ratify the treaty, members of the Western Cherokee Union decided that they had no choice but to drive out the squatters by force. From the viewpoint of the Alabamas and Coushattas, they had trusted Houston in the belief that he had the authority to grant them titles to their lands. Had he not told the Alabamas and Coushattas and Cherokees in April 1836 that "all of my red brothers may rest satisfied that I will always hold you by the hand, and look at you as Brothers and treat you as such"? He added that he would "never lie to that treaty while I live, and it must stand as long as [a] good man lives and water runs."[64] After two years of fruitless waiting, however, the Alabamas and Coushattas and their allies grew impatient and wary of Houston's assurances. They no longer believed that his word bound the government of Texas.[65]

The Córdova Rebellion

Inspired by Vicente Córdova, a former judge and alcade who advocated a Mexican-controlled Texas, the Córdova Rebellion of 1838 gained the support of Mexicans, American Indians (including the Western Cherokee Union), African-Americans, and even alienated Anglo-Americans. The Mexican government supported the revolt in the hopes of weakening the new Republic enough to reclaim it. At a meeting with Córdova on July 9, 1838, Western Cherokee Union members agreed to "unite as soon as possible for action." Mexico had promised those who joined the rebellion "fee simple titles" to the land they occupied and claimed. Many pro-Mexican factions within the Union agreed to the bargain—they waged a "ceaseless and murderous war" upon Texans in return for legitimate title to their lands. The only drawbacks they likely foresaw were the casualties in raids, the possibility that Mexico, too, would break its agreement, and that if they lost to the Texans, they would face expulsion. Nevertheless, the choice seemed reasonable given their precarious situation after the Texas Senate's refusal to ratify the treaty.[66]

Chiefs Colita, Antone, and Duwali received several messages and visits from both Sam Houston and General Thomas Jefferson Rusk, then Texas Indian commissioner and commander of the Nacogdoches militia. They both tried to persuade the chiefs not to fight against the Texans. Colita expressed to the Texans that he and his people were "friendly," but both Rusk and Houston worried that the hostile actions of neighboring Anglo-Americans would provoke Alabama and Coushatta warriors to join Córdova. Agents therefore distributed gifts to various chiefs and hoped for the best.[67] Alabama and Coushatta leaders acted in unison and again successfully employed their diplomatic skills and brokered their relationship with the Western Cherokee Union. Yet despite talk of peace, war was inevitable. Most members of the Union participated in the Córdova Rebellion.

In an interesting turn of events, whereas their allies joined the Córdova Rebellion, the Alabamas and Coushattas, apart from a small number of Coushatta warriors, refused. Bound together through kinship and acting as a sovereign entity, the Alabamas and Coushattas reassessed their commitment to their Cherokee allies based on a calculation about their chances of maintaining their autonomy and of reaching their primary goal of remaining in East Texas. After the Texas Revolution, the Western Cherokee Union ceased to act as a powerful organization, so the Alabamas and Coushattas removed themselves from the alliance and pursued a separate policy, one that was contrary to the interests of the Union. It is not clear whether this was an official break, but chiefs Colita and Antone distanced their association with those involved in the Córdova Rebellion.

Those who joined the rebellion, notably the Cherokees, Delawares, Kickapoos, and a faction of Shawnees, instilled great fear among Anglo-Americans as warriors raided and destroyed settlements throughout Texas. Years of distrust, harsh treatment, and broken promises fueled the war. Those who avoided active participation in the war harbored Córdova's rebels in their villages, an act that Texans considered treasonous.[68] In a speech to Congress, Mirabeau Lamar, who succeeded Sam Houston as president of the Republic of Texas on December 10, 1838, imprudently responded to the revolt by calling for the extermination of the Texas tribes. Lamar urged Texans to end clemency toward all Indians, warning that "as long as we continue to exhibit our mercy without sh[o]wing our strength, so long will the Indian continue to bloody the edge of the tomahawk, and move onward in the work of rapacity and slaughter." He shouted that "it is time we should retaliate their warfare . . . in the persecution of an exterminating war upon their warriors."[69] The Texas tribes sealed their fate by associating themselves with the rebels, even if they had not committed warriors to the cause. The government commissioned General Rusk to extinguish the rebellion by force and to punish severely those involved.[70]

Despite many local successes, the Córdova Rebellion failed by March 1839, as did the Western Cherokee Union's fight to obtain title to their lands in East Texas. Mexico had given too little support, and the tribes lost their united front against the Texans. The Cherokees sued for peace, having experienced great suffering among their women and children for lack of food and supplies. Duwali wrote to Rusk expressing hope that it would "not be long before we shall se[e] our children grown up together in pea[c]e. . . . It is my wish for us all to do the best we can and liv[e] friendly together as brothers should."[71] Yet it was too late. Hatred and fear between the two cultures prevented such a union. After the tribes' participation in the Córdova Rebellion, whether direct or indirect, the Texas government had no incentive to ratify the treaty that recognized the Texas tribes' territorial claims. The failure left the Western Cherokee Union empty handed. President Mirabeau Lamar considered the revolt a direct challenge to the new Texas government and was determined to punish all Indian tribes, whether or not they had joined the insurrection.

Texans, having secured their independence, refused to recognize the rights of American Indians living within their borders. According to Lamar, they had "no legitimate rights of soil or sovereignty in this country."[72] In a letter to Duwali on May 26, 1839, he explained: "The Treaty alluded to, was a nullity when made [and] is inoperative now; [it] has never been sanctioned by this Government, and never will be." Lamar advised Duwali that it was useless to assume that the Texas tribes would ever receive the treaty lands: "Such hopes will only terminate in disappointment and despair."[73] Lamar added that even if the Texas Congress had ratified the treaty of 1836, the Texas tribes had "defiled it by robbery and murder and have forfeited all claims which might accrue under it, by leaguing with other Indians and Mexicans."[74] After he stigmatized the Texas tribes as traitors, the government not only denied them title to the lands they occupied, but also ordered their immediate expulsion from Texas. Speculators moved quickly; they marked and surveyed the lands that the Alabamas and Coushattas and others had fought so desperately to keep.[75]

Sam Houston rejected Lamar's course of action. In a speech to the Texas Senate in December 1840, he expressed sympathy with the Texas tribes for rising against their oppressors. He attributed the revolt to the unpunished encroachment by speculators and "land thieves" upon the tribes' lands. In his view, the bloodshed of the Córdova Rebellion "will rest upon our own shoulders," because the encroachment "was done in the face of a pledge made to the Indians by this government at the darkest hour ever known to the citizens of Texas." Had the tribes joined Santa Anna, they may have turned the tide of the Texas Revolution, but in return for neutrality, Houston declared: "They received a pledge from the provisional government of Texas that their rights should be guaranteed to them, and were dupes enough to believe it!"[76] Despite numerous speeches, Houston failed to persuade the government to side with the Alabamas and Coushattas and other Texas tribes.

After Texas secured its independence from Mexico, the Western Cherokee Union lost its status and influence. It was an all too familiar dilemma for the Alabamas and Coushattas: the French and Indian War and the peace that followed in 1763 also had left them empty handed. Their newly created center had been destroyed once again and would prove difficult to rebuild. Although principal chiefs Colita and Antone agreed to a treaty that guaranteed land in exchange for noninvolvement in the Revolution, Texas leaders denied their claim. The Western Cherokee Union had no recourse but to participate in a rebellion to reestablish their hegemony in East Texas. The confederation of Cherokees, Shawnees, Delawares, Kickapoos, and others who aided the Mexicans in the Córdova Rebellion had the strength of unity, but they ultimately failed to regain control of their territory. The Alabamas and the majority of Coushattas, however, removed themselves from the fight and opted for neutrality. It seems that chiefs Colita and Antone had reassessed their membership to the Union and, acting on the best interests of the collective whole, broke their partnership during the revolt. The Alabamas and Coushattas' alliance with the Texas tribes was ephemeral, like their unions with other tribes in the past. Outnumbered by Anglo-American settlers, the Alabamas and Coushattas had broken with the Western Cherokee Union because they understood that only an agreement with the Texas government would enable them to remain in their new homeland, and that they had no likelihood of obtaining it by force.

While diplomacy had worked in earlier decades, it was impossible to ignore American ideas of manifest destiny and their planned conquest of the western frontier. Anglo-Americans were too numerous, and, after the rebellion, settlement rapidly increased in East Texas. Even worse, the Alabamas and Coushattas realized that migration west was no longer an option. They had to end their diasporas in East Texas.

Colita, at this point over one hundred years old, gave the most dramatic and poignant account of Alabama and Coushatta relations with the white man in May 1839:

> I have given the White man my Lands—
> I have given them bread—
> and the former Big Captain [Sam Houston] told me that the
> White man should be my Friends.
> The white man lies; they are doing evil for good.
> I am for Peace and all my Indians are for peace, and if your Big
> Captain [Mirabeau Lamar] is determined to murder us and
> destroy our property we will be compelled to surrender and
> die like a Brave Nation should do.

Times was, when we could have driven the White man off—but
  we were their Friends and did not want to hurt the White man.
I will live here till I die which cannot be long and I want to
  know what is to become of my people—[77]

Colita's words echoed the Alabamas and Coushattas' century-long struggle to maintain their claim to land; they understood the value of their "property" in terms of survival. Colita had hoped for peace and cooperation with the white man, but he only saw deceit. He had provided protection for Americans needing aid in the Texas Revolution and had trusted Houston's word, but the outcome left him unsure how his people would endure the countless trials that awaited them. Yet the Alabamas and Coushattas continued to hold on to their goal of remaining in their homeland in East Texas.

It is here that the tale of Rabbit proves telling. When the contest with the two buffalo abruptly ended and they denied Rabbit access to water, Rabbit managed to return to the stream and gain access to the land in order to survive. Likewise, the Alabamas and Coushattas had no more power and Americans had control over their territory. Yet they too were clever. Although many perceived them as weak, the Alabamas and Coushattas would fight hard for their sovereignty and their rightful claim to land.

6

Journey's End

The ancestors of the Alabamas and Coushattas recalled the days long ago when they lived peacefully along a stream. Their lives changed when Big Man-Eaters lurked on the opposite side of the water and regularly invaded and killed many of them. The survivors organized town councils to figure out how to destroy their enemies but could never agree on a plan. One day, Rabbit decided to end the attacks. For three days, he wandered through the forest until he encountered Big Man-Eater. Rabbit told the Man-Eater about beautiful land that existed over the hills. Rabbit's vivid description intrigued the monster, so Rabbit agreed to take it there. They journeyed until sunset and camped at what Rabbit called "The Place of Hot Ashes." When Big Man-Eater fell asleep in front of the fire, Rabbit coated himself in cold ashes and then tossed hot ashes onto Big Man-Eater, severely burning him. Rabbit, pretending to be wounded, told Big Man-Eater that the land where they stayed had always been intolerable and therefore they must move on.[1]

The next night Rabbit convinced Big Man-Eater to make camp near a dead tree. As Big Man-Eater slept, Rabbit pushed over the tree, causing it to crush the monster. On the third day, Rabbit led the injured monster back home near the stream. Rabbit challenged Big Man-Eater to jump across the water to see who was better. As they both leapt to the other side, Rabbit quickly jumped back while singing a magical song. The stream then opened up and became an ocean, forever separating the Big Man-Eaters from the animals and the Alabamas and Coushattas.[2]

The story of Rabbit and Big Man-Eater echoes the early history of the Alabama and Coushatta people. The Big Man-Eater that resided on the opposite side of the water could be a metaphor for the white man, who repeatedly invaded their lands from initial contact to the nineteenth century. In the past, the Alabamas and Coushattas had been successful in coping with the western expansion by Anglo-Americans by re-creating new centers, where they benefited from neighboring Indian alliances and their position between contending nations. Yet the Alabamas and Coushattas knew that they could not simply continue to migrate west when their center collapsed. Instead, they searched for land within the southern woodlands that was similar to their ancient homeland and that they and outsiders would consider theirs to keep for future generations. They thought that they had finally found this refuge in East Texas. In the two decades following the Texas Revolution, however, the Alabamas and Coushattas struggled to survive while coping with a declining population and loss of status and influence among foreign emissaries. Their sovereignty and identity as a people were at stake, and they fought persistently against the designs of Texas and the United States to drive all American Indians beyond their borders. Alabama and Coushatta leaders such as Chief Colita learned through experience that they needed to speak the same language and negotiate with foreign powers in order to keep their territory. Like Rabbit in the folktale, the Alabamas and Coushattas would find a way out of their precarious situation.

Trapped

By 1840, the Alabamas and Coushattas discovered that Anglo-American settlers and government officials owned most of the territory they had previously occupied and claimed stretching from present-day Alabama to East Texas. Westward migration—a solution to the past problems of the Alabamas and Coushattas—seemed impossible. They hesitated to relocate farther west for fear of both losing their livelihood as cultivators and settling in the unfamiliar ecosystem of the western plains over which their enemies, the Comanches and Lipan Apaches, were dominant.

Despite past successes of averting Anglo-American encroachment, the Alabamas and Coushattas could no longer escape and re-create a new center without competing for land. They had struggled to maintain claims to their land before, but this time Texans boasted that they had subdued the American Indians and that the whole country of Texas was "open for the settlement of the white man."[3] Americans steadily immigrated into the Republic of Texas and quickly staked their claims as word spread about the availability of cheap, arable land. American settlement guaranteed the expansion of a growing nation and a booming southern economy. For southerners, the main appeal of Texas was the claim that it contained "more rich cotton and sugar land than all of the United States put together."[4] Moreover, land was cheap. Despite American Indian claims to these lands, in 1839 American settlers could purchase an acre for a minimum price of twenty-five cents to a maximum of five dollars; similar land in the United States ranged from five to fifty dollars.[5] With the exception of the Comanches who lived farther west, the only tribes that remained, according to Texans, were "too weak and too imbecile" to excite fear from potential settlers.[6]

The status of American Indian and Anglo-American relations by 1840 was consistent with this attitude. Given the rampant hostilities between the five "civilized" tribes and the Americans in the East, public administrators and government officials thought it impossible for American Indians and Anglo-Americans to coexist. Influential policy makers, such as T. Hartley Crawford, the commissioner of Indian affairs in Martin Van Buren's administration, argued in favor of Jackson's former policy of American Indian removal. Anglo-Americans generally believed that assimilating the Indians into white society and teaching them how to live as yeomen was impracticable—despite the southeastern peoples' long-standing traditions of land cultivation. Although Texas was not yet a part of the United States, American Indian removal of the southeastern tribes (Cherokees, Creeks, Choctaws, Seminoles, and Chickasaws) to Indian Territory in the 1830s influenced Texan politicians who had previously lived in the United States. It had convinced Mirabeau Lamar that the removal of Texas tribes was the best solution to the "Indian problem."[7]

These attitudes, combined with the increasing popularity of Texas, had a dramatic impact on the Republic's immigration. As the image of the Southwest improved, Anglo-Americans migrated west of the Mississippi in unprecedented numbers. Census reports from 1837 estimated the population of Texas at 40,000 inhabitants. Two years later, the population had climbed to over 250,000.[8] The new Republic beckoned to poor, landless white men and those who wished to start anew. Texas had become a land of opportunity for Anglo-Americans. The Alabamas and Coushattas, on the other hand, were only beginning a new struggle.

The Second American Indian Resistance in Texas

The wave of Anglo-American immigrants drove many American Indians to seek refuge farther west, into the hostile territory of their rivals. Southeastern tribes in Texas faced an uncertain future after the ill-fated Córdova Rebellion in 1839. Many Anglos boasted that Texas tribes had no legitimate rights to the soil, especially given the failed insurrection against the Republic. Lamar, who looked upon most American Indians with contempt, announced in May 1839 that anyone who had joined the revolt would "never be permitted to establish a permanent and independent jurisdiction within the inhabited limits of this [Texas] Government."[9] Lamar's harsh words stung; he added that their immigration to Texas was "unsolicited and unauthorized" and "has always been a source of regret to its more enlightened population."[10] The Cherokees, the revolt's primary instigators, were at the head of the list for immediate removal. Lamar allowed them to stay in Texas only until the government arranged to move them across the border into Indian Territory "without the necessity of shedding blood."[11] Their removal, like the removal of their brethren who walked the Trail of Tears years earlier, was certain.

In June, Lamar announced that other American Indians, such as the Alabamas, Coushattas, Delawares, and Shawnees, who mostly "have manifested a peaceful and friendly disposition," might stay in Texas temporarily. Yet he stressed that while they remained within the country, "any evidence of hostility on their part will cause their immediate punishment and expulsion." Moreover, he ordered the Indian agents assigned to the tribes not to give them any promises that they would be able "to identify themselves with the Country, or to claim any right in the Soil."[12] In sum, Texas would not acknowledge their title to their lands.

Continuing attacks by the Comanches and their allies, and by Mexican rebels who still refused to recognize Texas's independence, encouraged President Lamar to carry out his plan for Indian removal. On June 27, 1839, he set up a committee including the secretary of war, General A. Sidney Johnston, the vice president, David G. Burnet, and the chief justice, Thomas Rusk, to work out the details. Not surprisingly, the members of the weakened Western Cherokee Union refused to go peaceably. On July 15, Cherokee, Shawnee, Kickapoo, Delaware, and several Coushatta warriors, led by principal Cherokee chief Duwali, resisted the troops sent to escort them to Indian Territory. In response, Johnston ordered his troops to open fire. In the ensuing battle, the Texas troops killed at least fifty-five warriors and wounded eighty-eight.[13] Duwali, the Cherokees' beloved leader and fellow ally to the Alabamas and Coushattas, died in battle, and with his death came the end to the Western Cherokees' dominance among the Texas tribes. Troops pursued survivors for a week until they had driven them across the Texas border.[14] In their flight, the warriors left most of their belongings behind, including five kegs of powder, 250 pounds of lead, many horses, cattle, and corn. Their plan had failed, and they escaped in desperation.[15]

The staggering losses among the emigrant tribes ultimately destroyed the already failing Western Cherokee Union. Survivors dispersed in small parties and wandered in search of available land outside of Texas. Some bands sought refuge east near the Red River where remnants of the Chickasaws and Choctaws resided. Defeated Shawnees even volunteered to settle in Indian Territory in order to prevent further bloodshed. On August 7, 1839, Shawnee leaders met at Nacogdoches with Texas agents and signed a treaty for their removal beyond the Republic's territorial limits. The Texas government compensated the Shawnees for their improvements to the land, and allotted them 25,000 dollars to assist their permanent removal and to establish a reservation outside the Texas border.[16] They believed this was their last chance to survive.

A similar fate awaited the Cherokees, Delawares, and Kickapoos; their membership in the Western Cherokee Union ultimately failed to keep them in East Texas. Desperate, these remaining members of the defunct alliance and other remnant peoples made separate treaties with the Texas Republic. Many moved their families beyond the Texas border and attempted to create a new life. They found instead hardship and poverty and witnessed many deaths in their respective communities.

Colita's Resolution

The Alabamas and Coushattas, by contrast, fared better. Strong leadership was needed as their power weakened, and chiefs Colita and Antone became the voice for the Alabama and Coushatta people. Instead of making separate decisions based on town interests, as they had done in the eighteenth century, the Alabamas and Coushattas chose to work collectively. The Alabamas and Coushattas depended on each other more than before, especially as they realized that they had to stop moving and establish a permanent title to land. Chiefs Colita and Antone realized that peace with Anglo-Americans was the clear path to keeping their territory in East Texas, which explains their decision to break with the Western Cherokee Union during the Córdova Rebellion in 1838 and other skirmishes against the Texans. Even Duwali, however highly regarded, could not persuade Colita or Antone to join his cause. Thus, their survival as a sovereign entity was not attributable to military technology, skill in war, or economic might; it was skill in reading the political circumstances. They had joined the Western Cherokee Union at the right time, and had left it when, in their view, it tried to exceed its reach. Unlike their former allies, they pursued peace with their American neighbors and positioned themselves as allies to the Texans, not to other tribes.

Their decision to avoid participation in the revolts and to pursue peace with the Texans paid off. President Lamar allowed the Alabamas and Coushattas to stay in their villages near the Trinity and Neches rivers in Liberty County. He based this important decision on both the actions of and attitudes toward the Alabamas and Coushattas. First, Colita and his kinspeople had assisted Texan citizens in 1836 during the Texas Revolution and had frequently called for peace with the Texans. Colita skillfully made clear to Lamar that they were a small group with few allies. Second, Lamar, like other Texans, classified the various tribes based on the degree of white "civilization" that they had adopted. In Lamar's perspective, as well as that of many Anglo-Americans, American Indians were either "civilized" or "wild savages." Lamar called the latter "red barbarians."[17] The Alabamas and Coushattas were a settled people, focused on agricultural pursuits, and kept relatively peaceful relations with their Anglo-American neighbors. Their respective cultures had much in common, especially their dependence on land. Lamar and others therefore considered them as one of the more "civilized" Indian tribes: the presence of the Alabamas and Coushattas in East Texas, for the time being, was unobjectionable. Third, the Alabamas and Coushattas had witnessed a dramatic decline in their population during the previous two decades, owing to the stayers that remained behind in Louisiana (and those who remained there after the Texas Revolution), their struggles with enemy tribes, and their overall precarious situation. According to estimates in 1839, Alabama and Coushatta men numbered 107 and 46, respectively. Their total was approximately 280 persons.[18] Colita stressed that the Alabamas and Coushattas posed no threat to Texans.

If anything, Colita and Antone had convinced Lamar and other state representatives that if they forced the Alabamas and Coushattas to settle near the Texas borders like their former Cherokee allies, Indian-white relations would certainly deteriorate. Border raids by Texas tribes would not only continue, but also intensify. The Alabamas and Coushattas' temporary residence in Texas, on the other hand, might lessen the destructive raids on American settlements committed by former allies of the Western Cherokee Union.[19] Lamar made clear, however, that he still preferred Anglo-American to American Indian occupation of Texas. Yet his goal was to secure the borders and to protect settlers from the Mexicans and "hostile" tribes, both enemies of the Texas Republic. The Alabamas and Coushattas took advantage of the rumors that Mexican troops had allied with hostile tribes; these warnings circulated throughout the borders and instilled fear among Texans. Lamar's great concern for border security induced him to stress the importance of avoiding any confrontations with the peaceful or "civilized" tribes such as the Alabamas and Coushattas.[20] Yet maintaining peace between the two cultures was a difficult task.

Shortly after Lamar issued his approval for the Alabamas and Coushattas to remain in East Texas, news spread that a group of Texas citizens of Liberty County murdered five Coushattas accused of stealing horses. Chief Colita immediately visited agent Captain S. C. Hirams on May 24, 1839, and requested a meeting with President Lamar. According to Hirams, Colita advised him to "tell the Big Captain of your Nation I am a Friend to the White Man and have been so always, but the Indians are mad, five of the C[o]ushatta's are Killed." Colita stressed that the Anglos had falsely accused the Coushattas of stealing horses as "an excuse to murder & Rob the Indians." He thought that this wrongdoing was "not right and it will if persisted in cause a wound never to be heal'd[.] I'm now over one hundred years old. I am the White man's friend, but will not accuse my nation wrongfully."[21] Although Chief Colita pursued peace with the Anglos and their government, he would not ignore blatant attacks on his people, and he would assert their rights as a sovereign entity.

Despite the injustices committed by the Texans, Chief Colita and his kinspeople realized that it was in their best interests to remain at peace with Anglo-American settlers in order to stay in East Texas. War was not the solution to their problems. They had no allies, and white settlers outnumbered them. Colita therefore stressed his friendship with the Texans while maintaining the Coushattas' innocence in the dispute. Colita did not ask for the swift punishment of the Texans responsible for the murders; he had neither the leverage nor power to make such demands as he and his people once did. Yet Colita showed great diplomatic skill by acting swiftly and averted a Texan backlash against the Coushattas.

Regardless of the Alabamas and Coushattas' diminished power, President Lamar responded quickly to Colita's letter. On July 9, 1839, Lamar wrote that he regretted the dispute between the Coushattas and Anglo settlers, stating it was "bad—very bad." Each party was blaming the other for the crimes, and each felt maligned. Lamar seemed to sympathize with the Coushattas, acknowledging that both groups were to blame in the dispute: "Your people [are] running off the property of the whites; and the white men [are] resenting the injury with too much violence." To resolve the situation and prevent further occurrences, Lamar informed Colita that he had written to the Texans, advising them "to abstain for the future from interrupting the Indians in their neighborhood without first making known to me their cause of complaint." In return, Lamar expected that the Coushattas do the same and "conduct themselves with honesty and propriety and to refrain from all acts calculated to provoke the hostility of the whites."[22] Lamar informed Colita that he appointed Colonel Joseph Lindley as their Indian Agent to investigate the murders, to administer "impartial justice," to preserve peace, and to resolve the tensions between the Liberty County citizens and the Alabamas and Coushattas. Lamar ordered Lindley to extend the same protection to them as to the Texans to avoid another conflict. Colita, too, had to maintain order and peaceful relations among his people.[23]

When Lamar wrote to the citizens of Liberty County, he described the Alabamas and Coushattas as a small isolated group, and therefore asked them to refrain from hostilities. He claimed that it was unjust to pursue indiscriminate war upon such "vulnerable" people. He considered every "supposed" or "actual" violation made against the settlers by marginal elements of the group, but restrained settlers from committing wholesale atrocities in the name of white victims. Lamar made his point by asking the Texans, "Is it right, or in accordance with the liberal ideas of justice entertained by the white man, to punish indiscriminately the whole of a peaceful tribe for the misdeeds of a few bad men?"[24] Indeed, despite the actions of the few Coushatta warriors who had joined the Córdova Rebellion, neither the Alabamas nor Coushattas in aggregate were a threat to Texas settlers owing to their reduced population. Texans could safely live beside them. Lamar therefore ordered their Texan neighbors to act with respect and kindness toward the Alabamas and Coushattas.[25]

Thirty citizens of Liberty County responded quickly to Lamar's accusation that they had instigated hostilities against their Indian neighbors. They claimed that those who committed depredations against the Coushattas were angry white settlers from another county who sought to exterminate the tribes. Liberty citizens eventually convinced the men that the Coushattas "had done no harm" and were "friendly." The citizens further stressed to President Lamar that the Alabamas and Coushattas had lived, and would continue to live, in peace among the whites.[26] It was critical for Colita and others to maintain this new alliance with their host community and government in order to avoid removal to Indian Territory like the rest of the Texas tribes.

Liberty County citizens and the Alabamas and Coushattas cultivated a mutual friendship and experienced a relatively peaceful coexistence. Such a relationship was unusual considering the United States' and the Republic of Texas's Indian policies and general attitudes toward American Indians. The Alabamas and Coushattas disproved contemporary popular perceptions relating to their culture and defied public policy. They lived a similar lifestyle to that of their Anglo neighbors by spending their days cultivating the soil, as had their Mississippian ancestors. In their ethnocentric beliefs, Texas citizens probably considered the Alabamas and Coushattas as one of the few "civilized" tribes remaining in the Republic. They were a settled people who built log cabins and sold their crop surplus to the locals. The Alabamas and Coushattas had accomplished what politicians and public administrators had thought impossible. They had adapted to their surroundings by absorbing some aspects of Anglo culture (namely American trade goods) while keeping their sovereignty and identity intact.

The arrangement was reminiscent of the relationship the Alabamas and Coushattas had created with the French at Fort Toulouse in the eighteenth century; the two cultures not only lived together in relative peace, but also maintained a mutually beneficial relationship. In this case, Liberty citizens often employed skilled Alabamas and Coushattas to hunt, fish, and pick cotton in return for American trade goods. Although some disputes occurred occasionally, both cultures pursued amicable relations.[27]

Given rampant hostilities on the western borders at the time, this reciprocal relationship between these two cultures was rare. Remarkably, citizens of Liberty County lived in such close proximity to the villages that they at times defended the interests of the Alabamas and Coushattas. When Lamar appointed Joseph Lindley as their Indian agent, the citizens contested Lamar's decision, claiming that Lindley was incompetent, ignorant of the Alabama and Koasati languages, and a supporter of Indian removal. The citizens took the initiative when they nominated F. H. Rankin to act in his stead, believing that he was better qualified. Despite the citizens' protests, Lindley remained their agent.[28]

Despite Alabama and Coushatta hopes to remain in Texas, Lamar made no promises to them. He and fellow Texans encouraged Anglo-American settlement onto land formerly occupied by the emigrant tribes. Americans quickly claimed prime land near the Neches and Trinity rivers. Newly established towns surrounding both the Alabama and Coushatta villages flourished and, once again, created land disputes with the settlers.[29] The land grab in East Texas forced the Alabamas and Coushattas to take immediate action, only this time with limited bargaining power. Despite previous failed attempts, chiefs Colita and Antone petitioned the Fourth Texas Congress for official recognition to the lands they occupied.

The Committee on Indian Affairs read their case before the House on November 19, 1839. Congressman W. R. Moore of Polk County introduced a resolution authorizing the government to survey land to hold conditionally for the Alabamas and Coushattas. Upon investigating the claim, the committee concluded that they had only the right of occupancy. They deemed that the act passed in 1833 by the ayuntamiento of Liberty County (which had guaranteed the Alabamas and Coushattas land) was invalid. According to one congressman, I. W. Burton, they had no right to any land in Texas. He maintained that the county had no authority to grant them land and, at the same time, "preserve its good faith to legal land Claimants."[30] Burton loathed the idea of the Alabamas and Coushattas' occupation of quality land that in his opinion Anglo-Americans should settle.

Chiefs Colita and Antone continued to advance their cause despite these setbacks. Their skilled diplomacy ultimately paid off when they convinced the Fourth Congress that they had maintained peaceful relations with Texas citizens and had an "amicable disposition."[31] As a result, in 1840 the Texas Congress agreed after considerable debate that the Alabamas and Coushattas should reside in their long-occupied territory. Upon their resolution to pass an act that surveyed and granted lands to the Alabamas and Coushattas, they debated endlessly the location of the land grant. Some Congressmen considered a location near Texas's northern border. Advocates for the Alabamas and Coushattas, however, believed that if placed on the northern border (where they had no desire to relocate), they would be forced to raid border settlements in their weakened and impoverished state. They argued that it would force them to unite with their old allies, or worse, to join powerful tribes like the Comanches, who were enemies of the Republic.[32]

Although first considered unwarranted, reports confirmed these fears. Texas's secretary of war A. Sidney Johnston learned that Cherokee warriors on the northern border had courted with large presents their former rivals, the Comanches, "to enter with them in a war against the Republic."[33] Congressman

Burton was one of many who believed that if moved to the borders, the Alabamas and Coushattas would have increased opportunities to form an alliance with their former allies and Mexicans. If this occurred, Burton feared that these combined warriors had a potential of becoming "positive enemies of a formidable character."[34] The committee therefore took Lamar's earlier advice and noted that Anglo-American settlers located near Alabama and Coushatta villages must "in all good conscience" bear the inconvenience of having them as neighbors.[35] Liberty County did not protest the final decision.

Despite a few congressional representatives' attempts to nullify the bill entirely, it passed on January 14, 1840. On the same day, the Fourth Congress appropriated funds totaling $412.80 for Indian agent Thomas B. Stubblefield to survey the land grant. Stipulations included the Texas Republic's jurisdiction (including criminal) over the territory. Moreover, the act permitted the government to remove their community at any given time if deemed necessary: Texas congressional representatives had no intentions to give them a permanent title to the land. By November of 1840, the Alabamas and Coushattas claimed their designated land of merely two hundred acres, which included the long-standing Fenced-in Village on the Neches River and Battise and Colita villages on the Trinity River.[36] The amount allotted to them was diminutive compared to their previous claims to territory in East Texas, Louisiana, and Alabama.

To their disappointment, security eluded them once again. By 1841, the constant demand for land in East Texas led to Anglo encroachment onto their land reserve. The Alabamas and Coushattas were unable to keep squatters off their lands. Rumors circulated that a group of Texans had planned to exterminate them. Fearing for their lives, Alabama and Coushatta men and women abandoned their cabins, leaving behind valuable cattle and other domesticated animals. They felt they had no choice but to leave their villages for safer ground. Many, including Chief Colita, began a return movement; they found refuge with the stayers in Opelousas District, Louisiana, where a group of kinspeople continued to reside. Hoping to find a better situation in Opelousas, they were pleased to find refuge in Indian Village. Others decided to stay in Texas and fight for their land.[37]

This faction, mainly consisting of a small group of Coushatta warriors, made their presence known on the western Texas borders as they raided settlements and battled with Anglo settlers who, in the Coushattas' perspective, had stolen their lands and livelihood. In the summer of 1841, the Coushatta faction organized war parties with other disgruntled warriors from remnant American Indian communities on the Texas borders. According to some accounts, Mexican emissaries courted American Indian communities located near northern Texas and enlisted warriors in their ranks. Their sole purpose was to wage war against Texas, which had applied for annexation into the United States. Mexico had refused to recognize Texas independence, believing that Texas was still part of Mexican territory. Mexican agents obtained the support of the Kickapoos, Shawnees, Delawares, Coushattas, Cherokees, (all former Western Cherokee Union members), as well as factions of the Keechis, Chickasaws, and Choctaws.[38] The Texas government had taken their tribal lands, and participants in the rebellion desired to avenge the injustices committed against them.

The combined war party harassed and raided settlements on the Texas borders, many of the same lands that they had once occupied. The Coushattas and others were heavily armed with rifles and gunpowder provided by the Mexicans. According to witnesses, a party of Coushatta warriors had committed various depredations against the citizens of Fannin County. The warriors attacked settlements and stole property, including horses, cattle, and provisions. Reports also claimed that the warriors had murdered some Texans. A group of Texas citizens who hoped to end the raids offered to vacate the land given to the Alabamas and Coushattas, but the Coushatta warriors considered it an insincere gesture and refused to trust their word again. Encamped near the north bank of the Red River in Louisiana, they prepared for further engagements with the Anglos. Unbeknownst to a group of Coushattas, eight Texas citizens under the command of Captain Joseph Sowell pursued the war party. They encountered the allied warriors at their encampment and killed a number of them.[39] Those Coushattas who engaged in border raids poisoned Americans' perceptions of their commitment to peace. They had separated their cause from that of the collective whole and ultimately delayed the Alabamas and Coushattas' land claims in Texas.

The Petition to Sam Houston

While a faction of Coushattas continued to raid frontier settlements with their old allies, the Alabamas and the rest of the Coushattas remained in Opelousas, Louisiana. Yet their return movement was ill fated. Colita and his kinspeople trekked back to East Texas when sickness, disease, and unhealthy conditions plagued Peach Tree Village. Upon their arrival at the land appropriated for them by the Texas Congress, all remnants of their presence had disappeared. Anglo-American settlers occupied the territory and refused to leave. The precarious situation forced the Alabamas and Coushattas to settle other unoccupied lands near Cypress Bayou. Struggling to survive, they established a temporary village. Men built thirty houses and cleared one hundred acres of land for cultivation. They learned shortly after, however, that those lands already belonged to Anglo settlers. The Alabamas and Coushattas were once again in a "scattered and wandering condition from the Neches to [the] Trinity."[40] Their world was quickly falling apart, and finding a new solution to their dilemma was critical to their survival.

The itinerant existence of the Alabamas and Coushattas left them vulnerable. Their numbers steadily dwindled as they endlessly wandered the Louisiana-Texas border for available land; this instability exposed them to increased chances of sickness and disease. Their existence hung in an unsteady balance, so Chief Colita again employed diplomacy. Instead of choosing the warpath and fighting against the Texans, Colita focused on his alliance and friendship with influential Texas citizens to aid his kinspeople. His goal was clear: he planned to obtain the key to his people's survival—permanent title to land in East Texas. One of the first persons Colita approached by the close of 1841 was the Alabamas and Coushattas' long-standing ally and advocate, Sam Houston.

Houston, who had maintained a close relationship with the Alabamas and Coushattas since Texas's fight for independence, began his second term as president of the Republic of Texas in 1841. Immensely dissatisfied with Lamar's policy of Indian removal, Houston spent his second term cultivating better relations with the "hostile" tribes on the northern Texas border. He attempted to convince the Texas Congress that the best policy toward the tribes was peace, not war. The Mexican threat to reconquer Texas magnified as the Republic waited impatiently for the U.S. Congress to approve its annexation. Until Texas had the full support of the U.S. government, both Mexicans and their American Indian allies threatened the Republic. Houston therefore attempted to induce all tribes near the Texas borders, especially the numerous and powerful Comanches, to sign treaties of amity. Houston's efforts focused on the organization of a series of diplomatic meetings, including one at Tehuacana Creek, in order to establish peaceful relations with warring tribes.[41]

Though the Alabamas and Coushattas' situation was grave, Colita was chagrined when Houston paid them little attention. Houston made some effort to help his kinspeople when he ordered Indian agents to protect them, or at least to look out for their interests, but they received no immediate relief. Colita felt that Houston had failed to see the extreme gravity of their situation, so he visited Houston's wife, Margaret, and explained his people's worsened situation. Colita, who came from a matrilineal and somewhat matrilocal society, believed that Margaret would have the ability to influence Houston. As Colita expected, Margaret appealed to her husband on October 6, 1843, and informed him that the Alabamas and Coushattas had established camp near their home in Washington, Texas. According to Margaret, they had lived near Pine Island, but had abandoned the area when sickness decimated their population. They wanted to return to their homeland in East Texas. Margaret Houston lamented that they were "wretched looking objects[,] haggard from sickness and suffering. They [the Alabamas and Coushattas] are passing away, and soon the lone forests that they inhabit will know them no more!" She advised her husband to return home because she believed that Colita hoped to "have his wrongs redressed."[42] Chief Colita judiciously (albeit stubbornly) remained on their property until Sam Houston returned and listened to his grievances.

Owing to Houston's preoccupation with both tribal councils and the Texas Republic's annexation by the United States, the Alabamas and Coushattas waited almost a year before relief arrived. With only a few months remaining in his term as president of the Republic of Texas, Houston persuaded the superintendent of Indian affairs, Thomas G. Western, to appoint agent Joseph L. Ellis to investigate Colita's complaints. In October 1844, Ellis confirmed that Texans had occupied designated tribal lands in East Texas. Ellis ordered one claimant, Hamilton Washington, to leave immediately the land that had formerly been the Colita and Battise villages. Washington refused. To remedy the situation temporarily, Ellis persuaded Washington to allow Coushattas on his land to cultivate their fields and to build their houses on the east bank of the Trinity River. Ellis later presented them with hoes, axes, wedges, ploughs, and trace chains that helped the Coushattas double their crops of corn, peas, and potatoes compared to previous years. Upon further investigation, Ellis also found the former site of Fenced-in Village occupied by Anglo settlers. Like their Coushatta kinspeople, the Alabamas found a temporary settlement fifteen miles south of their old village on the Neches River in Liberty County. Here, ironically with the permission of the landowner, Doctor Wheat, the Alabamas constructed cabins, cleared fields, and planted corn.[43]

Both the Alabamas and Coushattas had reached an agreement, albeit temporary, with the Texans and ceased to roam the border between Texas and Louisiana. Their transience, however, had come at a great cost; their numbers had thinned beyond any recollection. By 1844, records reported that the Coushattas numbered only fifty warriors, around fifty women, and thirty to thirty-five children. The Alabamas in Texas had dwindled to twenty-eight warriors, twenty women, and around twenty children.[44]

Their decline in population may have resulted from disease, malnutrition, or starvation during their desperate search for available land. It is also likely that some of their families had traveled back to Louisiana to seek shelter once again among kinspeople. The Alabamas and Coushattas spent the next few years recuperating. They worked as independent farmers on their temporary lands and cultivated crops in order to feed their families. While they found some stability, they remained dissatisfied with the Texas government that had allowed others to take and occupy their lands. The Alabamas and Coushattas therefore continued their strategy of appealing to government agents and influential citizens in order to obtain an official endorsement of their claim to land in East Texas. They refused to surrender. However, Texas government officials, to whom chiefs Colita and Antone petitioned, were dealing with another crisis.

After the United States finally annexed Texas in December 1845, the government continued its aggressive policy of expansion under the presidency of James K. Polk. Popular sentiment advocated the U.S. domination over the Western Hemisphere and its destiny of becoming a continental power. The annexation of Texas, however, provoked Mexico into breaking diplomatic relations with the United States. Mexico viewed the annexation as a declaration of war. When both nations refused to resolve border disputes over Texas, the United States and Mexico engaged in a heated, bloody war that officially began on May 13, 1846.[45] Texans feared raids on their settlements by the western tribes; Mexican emissaries again courted various displaced tribes on the borders to aid their troops.[46] Yet many of the raiding groups had little power because of a lack of solidarity and decimated populations. Unlike past conflicts, the Mexicans and Texans yielded little, if anything, to American Indians in return for aid or neutrality. The Alabamas and Coushattas were too weak and therefore took no part in the Mexican War. The Treaty of Guadalupe Hidalgo, ratified March 10, 1848, ended the war; provisions stipulated that Mexico cede two-fifths of its territory (including California and New Mexico) to the United States. American Indians were absent in the negotiations, and the United States claimed their land by right of conquest.

The Alabamas and Coushattas were in no place to negotiate after the American victory. Another blow that challenged their optimism was the death of beloved Coushatta chief Colita on July 7, 1852, while on a hunting trip. Born in the town of Coosada in central Alabama around 1750, his esteemed leadership had brought the Alabamas and Coushattas closer together in desperate times, and was on the verge of achieving their goal of obtaining a permanent land grant. Chief Colita was from two worlds, one that he and his family had left behind in Alabama, and one that he helped create in Louisiana and Texas. Alabama and Coushatta men and women valued Chief Colita's efforts to maintain a peaceful existence with their American neighbors. In the *Texas Gazette* shortly after his death, the touching editorial on his life (namely his aid to Texas refugees during the Revolution) was evidence of his ability to persuade Texans that he and his people had made an effort to live peacefully among whites.[47]

There is little description relating to his burial, but true to their Mississippian origins, the Coushattas would have bestowed great honor because of his status as a principal chief. Based on traditional customs, Colita's kinsmen would have placed his knife, rifle, powder, bullets, a club or hatchet, a bow, a quiver of arrows, vermilion (to paint his body in the spirit world), a pipe, and tobacco in the grave. During the burial, they would lay out the body first (Coushattas used the expression *ballá:lin*), then bury him in a sitting position, turning his head toward the heavens.[48] Sadly, despite his efforts, Chief Colita never saw his people reach their goals.

Indian Removal

Former allies to the Alabamas and Coushattas, including remnants of the Delawares, Shawnees, Cherokees, and Kickapoos, also wandered the Texas borders during the 1840s. Many wished to settle in Indian Territory, but quickly discovered that other eastern tribes like the Chickasaws already had land claims issued by the U.S. government. The Chickasaws complained repeatedly to U.S. officials that these groups had no rights to settle on their lands and to raid their homesteads, so they asked for help in removing them.[49] Other small groups temporarily moved their families near Texas's borders. As they searched for available land, their precarious existence took heavy tolls on their populations. Neither Texas nor its citizens acknowledged a responsibility toward them; in their view, all the land belonged exclusively to Anglo-American settlers, and only by evicting American Indians could Texas fulfill the prophecy of manifest destiny.

When Texas joined the United States on December 29, 1845, the federal government assumed responsibility for Indian affairs with the aims of securing lands for settlers in Texas and removing the tribes who remained on its borders. By 1854, the Franklin Pierce administration proposed a solution to the "Indian problem" by which the federal department of Indian affairs (later known as the Bureau of Indian Affairs) designated available land on the Brazos River near the mouth of Clear Fork for two federally supervised reservations: the Brazos River Indian Reservation and the Clear Fork Reserves. The reservations allowed settlement for remnants of the southeastern and western tribes who had not yet moved to Indian Territory, including the Kickapoos, Shawnees, Cherokees, Delawares, Caddos, Wichita Wacos, Tawakonis, Tonkawas, and Comanches. A census in 1857 estimated that 982 members of different tribes lived on the Brazos Reservation. Most of them were destitute, and their population steadily declined as they experienced great hardship. Their Texan neighbors, who treated them with contempt, raided their homesteads and destroyed their crops.[50]

In May 1859, John Robert Baylor (who later commanded the Confederate forces in Texas) led 250 settlers in an attack on the Brazos Reservation in an attempt to exterminate all of the American Indians living there. Although the U.S. First Infantry prevented the massacre, many of the inhabitants who feared for their lives fled to Indian Territory or, like the Tonkawas, joined the Lipans in Mexico. In August, after only four years, the state government closed the reservation and forcibly removed the last tribes living in Texas into Indian Territory near present-day Anadarko, Oklahoma, where the tribes had to

adapt their culture and livelihood to the inhospitable and isolated terrain.[51] Their survival as a sovereign people was in jeopardy. Once Texas had secured its borders against Mexican
threats, the federal government concentrated on domestic affairs, including the final removal of all remnant tribes to Indian
Territory.

The Final Stand on the Big Sandy

The Alabamas and Coushattas were at journey's end, yet they
had not lost hope of remaining in their chosen homeland. In
1853, Chief Antone of the Alabamas, who helped fill the void of
Colita's leadership, and his subchiefs petitioned the Texas legislature to provide public land for a permanent, protective reserve in East Texas for his kinspeople. To achieve this end, Chief
Antone, like Colita, sought the help of Sam Houston. In his
desire to redress the wrongs committed by the Texas government against the Alabama and Coushatta people, Houston organized and conducted an interview between Chief Antone
and state representatives. The purpose of the meeting was to
record the injustices committed against his kinspeople and to
devise compensation for their losses. The council, held at Captain Samuel Power's home in Polk County, Texas, commenced
with Chief Antone describing how his people had suffered from
disease and exposure after the whites forced them from their
rightful land in Texas. He described the amount of territory they
had once claimed and now was gone since the founding of the
Texas Republic. When asked what they had recently lost, an
Alabama subchief responded that it amounted to a total of two
hundred acres of cleared and improved land, one hundred
head of cattle, and ten horses worth four hundred dollars; the
Alabamas understood the great value of their property. He further stated that they had never received any compensation
from the government or anyone else for these injustices.[52]

After agents recorded the information, Antone presented his
case to the Texas Legislature in the form of a memorial. The
memorial requested the donation of 1,280 acres of land for
their kinspeople to settle exclusively, a meager amount compared to their previous holdings. The issue of compensation

and resettlement was a difficult one. Texas agents had asked Chief Antone if they were willing to migrate to Indian Territory. Chief Antone's response was firm: "We are *not* willing to go there." They knew that leaving their homes in East Texas would drastically alter their customs and traditions as settled agriculturalists. They realized long ago that if their people migrated to Indian Territory—land that they considered nonarable—they would be forced to abandon their livelihoods as farmers or, worse, depend entirely on federal assistance. Such a drastic transition could be disastrous, so they refused to risk further endangering their traditions and, more importantly, their sovereignty. They preferred to live in a familiar environment that would allow them to continue their existence as they had for generations.[53]

Chief Antone instead requested that the Texas government establish a land reserve located on "Big Sandy" in Polk County, Texas, "on the eastern half, eighteen miles west of Moodville in what is known as the 'Big Thicket,' sixteen miles due north of Smithfield on the Trinity River."[54] To bolster their case, Antone petitioned the citizens of Polk County and adjoining counties; he tried to gain the support of the local community just as Chief Colita had done earlier. Antone and his subchiefs expressed a twin desire to establish permanent residence in the county and willingness to live in peace among the Texans, despite the numerous injustices committed against them by the Anglo-Americans. The citizens responded positively and signed the petition. They had no grievances against them settling near the Big Sandy. Like the Liberty County citizens before them, Polk County citizens considered the Alabamas and Coushattas as "friendly," "peaceful," and (reflecting their ethnocentric beliefs) "civilized."[55]

With support from Sam Houston and acquiescence from the local Anglo population, the Texas legislature granted the Alabamas 1,110 acres in Polk County, Texas, in 1854. As the first recipients of a state-regulated reservation in Texas, they had finally obtained an official title to land in East Texas that would remain, although in abridged form, to the present day. According to the state of Texas, "the Alabama Indians and their heirs forever in fee simple and in common with each other, and to use, occupy, enjoy[,] and cultivate as they may choose forever," these lands that the government would defend from any persons claiming the same land.[56]

One year later, in 1855, the Coushattas also secured a land grant from the State of Texas. The allotted 640 acres, however, had already been legally claimed by Texas settlers. Unable to find available land in East Texas, the majority of the Coushattas wandered across the state, homeless.[57] By 1861 approximately two hundred Coushattas occupied land near the Trinity River. Many had settled temporarily on the Alabama reservation; others found refuge at the Coushattas' village in western Louisiana. The Alabamas reported to Indian agent A. J. Harrison that they "are not only willing but extremely anxious for the Coshattie [*sic*] Indians to come and live with them."[58] By 1862, a significant portion of the Coushattas permanently settled with their Alabama kinspeople on the Big Sandy Reservation. The few remaining Coushattas chose to stay with the few families left in Louisiana who avoided detection by officials but continued to have contact (mostly through intermarriage) with their brethren in Texas. According to Harrison, the Alabamas and Coushattas had moved toward becoming "one nation or tribe," and were "all of the same kindred."[59] The Alabamas and Coushattas, a coalescent people, had finally merged into one entity on their lands in East Texas; it was a direct consequence of ending their diasporas.

The United States had removed most American Indians to Indian Territory before the close of the nineteenth century. Many of the southeastern peoples hoped to escape American expansion westward, but instead the U.S. government eventually forced them to remain on federal reservations. Anglo-Americans were rarely sympathetic to the plight of American Indians and most often were hostile and contemptuous. Although they inevitably encountered enemies in their path, the Alabamas and Coushattas created an anomalous, symbiotic relationship with many citizens of East Texas. Chiefs Colita and Antone committed to the path of peace and avoided later participation in alliances with the Mexicans or bellicose American Indian groups that attempted to reclaim their land in Texas. This alternative strategy provided the Alabamas and

Coushattas a meaningful connection with the Americans from whom they needed support.

Their relations with Anglo-American neighbors, their leaders' pursuit of peace between the two cultures, and their skillful diplomacy engendered support from influential Texas citizens and eventually won the Alabamas and Coushattas a permanent title to land. As many American Indians experienced subsequent diminution of their lands, so did the Alabamas and Coushattas. The amount of 1,100 acres was minuscule compared to the territory they had occupied and claimed for generations in Alabama, Louisiana, and Texas. That said, the Alabamas and Coushattas were the only successful American Indian community to remain in Texas on a reservation in the nineteenth century. This accomplishment, however, came at a great cost. Disease and starvation brought on by years of instability and periods of wandering in Texas significantly reduced their population. Many decades passed before they began to recover.

Conclusion

For generations, the Alabamas and Coushattas recounted the story of their ancestors' journey to the west. They remembered an earlier time when they ate acorns and cane sprouts, made fire with bass wood and a weed called *hassala'po*, and crafted bows and arrows. When they coalesced, the Alabamas and Coushattas constructed towns near the Alabama River and lived there for many years. Storytellers had a memory of one summer when an Alabama man wanted to go west; others wished to join him on his journey. A berdache (half-man, half-woman) asked him why he was leaving. The man replied, "I am going in order to kill turkey, deer, and other animals; after that I will return." The berdache tried to convince him to stay: "You are a man, but you want to run away. I will not run away. I will not run, although my grandfather used to say that the English are all hard fighters. When they come, I will take a knife, lie down under the bed, and keep striking at them until they kill me."[1] Although the berdache pressured his kinsmen to remain and fight against the English, the bulk of the Alabamas and Coushattas left their ancient homeland and traveled west to Louisiana.

The travelers started out in canoes on their long journey. They followed the river for a distance until they discovered a Choctaw village. To avoid conflict, they did not stay. Days later, they stopped at a white man's home and exchanged venison for corn. The white man told the travelers that he would show them a quicker route to their destination and then tied rope to their canoes and had his oxen pull them across to another river. Down the river, the group rested at a white blacksmith's trading post. They exchanged venison for knives, axes, and whiskey. A group of Choctaws told them, "There is no war here. There is peace. We are friends of the Alabamas." Happy to hear this, they drank whiskey with their new companions. As they got drunk, some of the men started to fight. Those who remained sober left for their canoes and continued to travel west. They eventually arrived in Louisiana at Bayou Boeuf, and then moved to Opelousas. They stayed for many years, but decided to settle farther west in Texas where they established Peach Tree Village, Cane Island, and Fenced-in Village. Despite the man's promise to the berdache, the Alabamas and Coushattas never returned to live in their shared sacred space along the Alabama River.[2]

The Alabamas and Coushattas' recollection of their journey to the west describes an exodus from their ancient homeland, adaptation to new spaces over many generations, and encounters with diverse peoples. The Alabamas and Coushattas created a coalescent community near the Alabama River, but they looked to the west when internal and external pressures took their toll. The berdache in the story refused to follow his kinspeople and remained in the homeland to fight the English, reminiscent of the stayers who faced forced removal to Indian Territory in the 1830s. As the travelers migrated west, they encountered both bellicose and amicable foreigners. Each culture had something to offer the other. The Alabamas and Coushattas' exchange of venison for corn reveals that they had increasing opportunities to hunt rather than farm. The white man's weapons, tools, and liquor altered their world, sometimes to the detriment of Alabama and Coushatta society. Despite the potential dangers ahead, they kept moving until they finally reached safer ground in East Texas. Only then did the

Alabamas and Coushattas create a permanent space so that future generations could survive and prosper.

The Alabamas and Cousahttas began their journey as two diasporic groups who shared a similar past. Both had origins in the same ancient southeastern community dating around 1050 C.E., and the Mississippian chiefdoms that followed it. They developed separately and distantly but still had common links. After the European encounter in the mid-sixteenth century, both suffered from disease, depopulation, and Indian slave raids. When these stresses crippled their respective communities, they began a diaspora in the late sixteenth and seventeenth centuries. The Coushattas migrated south from present-day Tennessee, and remnant groups that became the Alabamas moved east from present-day eastern Mississippi and western Alabama. It was a dangerous and unpredictable journey. They searched for a new space full of abundant game, clear running streams, and fertile soil—land that resembled the one they had left behind. These two diasporic groups—increasingly vulnerable in their newly found territory—established settlements near each other and quickly recognized the benefits of maintaining a lasting alliance. Although the Alabamas and Coushattas did not always make identical decisions, they generally worked together to benefit both of their interests. This plan was necessary as they confronted a new world.

From the sixteenth to the nineteenth centuries, Alabama and Coushatta migrations provided a unique mechanism to cope with European nations and later, the United States, as each fought to establish empires in North America. The Alabamas and Coushattas decided to migrate westward to construct a world in which they were at the center with competing forces on either side. They repeatedly developed diplomatic strategies as they traveled in and out of volatile, geopolitical zones from 1600 to 1840. As long as they could hunt game, gather similar foods, grow the same crops, and establish trade networks, the advantages of migration outweighed the costs. Juxtaposed between rival nations and empires, opportunities eventually faded and their sovereignty was in jeopardy. They resolved their dilemma by beginning their second migration as a diasporic group from Alabama to Louisiana, and their third from Louisiana to Texas. In each place, they remade their homeland and developed new centers. By adapting and changing with each movement, the Alabamas and Coushattas drew closer together and preserved their sovereignty, without outsiders' institutions or governments controlling them.

By the 1840s, however, Anglo-American settlement in the South expanded and enclosed most of the fertile land. The cost of learning how to live as free people in the more arid and vastly different ecosystems farther west proved too great; when they found new ground in East Texas, they planned to end their migrations. As had happened before, neighboring communities did not always welcome them. The Anglo-American community dominated state and local politics and many tried to remove all American Indians from their borders, despite the fact that many of the white settlers were also migrants from the East. Rather than moving on, however, the majority of the Alabamas and Coushattas chose the path of peace, even when many other American Indian tribes decided to fight. Long experience with European legal systems had taught Alabama and Coushatta leaders like chiefs Colita and Antone that they needed titles to the lands they claimed; traditional methods of marking territory with natural boundaries or barriers no longer prevented encroachment. Leaders instead needed to work with host communities and government authorities to ensure that others respected their territorial claims. Their last diplomatic maneuver, then, was to invoke an alliance with Anglo-Americans in order to obtain a permanent claim to land from the State of Texas, where they live today.

Migration and diaspora produced three specific patterns in Alabama and Coushatta history: it affected their culture, their political relationships, and their identity. The Alabamas and Coushattas experienced a new world after European contact. Over the centuries, the Alabamas and Coushattas altered their perspectives and transformed their worldviews in order to meet the demands of movement into new lands and the diverse peoples they encountered. They exchanged trade goods and ideas and forged new personal relationships with Europeans, Americans, and indigenous peoples. Social traditions are of course rarely static, and each major episode of Alabama and Coushatta relocation led to changes; they had to adjust to new environments in order to survive. Their experience in Texas, perhaps the most intrusive encounter with Anglo-Americans, in the end simply provided yet another example of cultural syncretism that characterized their existence since the eighteenth century. Yet despite the changes, elements of their culture endured. They kept intact many of the ancient Mississippian traditions that they both shared through common heritage, including matrilineal kinship systems, town organization, languages, ceramic technology, and settlement patterns. Even migration to new locations was a mechanism in ancient chiefdoms to cope with community stress or decline. The Alabama and Coushatta diaspora, then, was also part of the legacy of their Mississippian ancestors.

Migration and diaspora often left Alabama and Coushatta society in a precarious position, but also provided opportunities. Indeed, it led to a political watershed; the Alabamas and Coushattas skillfully used diplomacy in their contact with multiethnic peoples as their survival to the present indicates. Despite the attempts of European powers to turn American Indian communities against one another, the Alabama and Coushatta strategy throughout the early eighteenth to mid-nineteenth centuries was to create external alliances with neighboring groups. These unions were flexible and ephemeral and shared common goals: to learn and build trade networks and skills, to protect the people and their lands, and to provide political hegemony in the form of self-rule. Alabama and Coushatta membership in alliances with the Creek Confederacy, the Caddo Confederacy, and the Western Cherokee Union, lasted for years and even decades. When Alabama and Coushatta leaders judged that membership no longer benefited their interests, they disentangled themselves from their allies.

For smaller American Indian communities like those of the Alabamas and Coushattas, these alliances were critical to retain sovereignty. Their relationship with neighboring groups ultimately enhanced their status and power as British, French, Spanish, Mexican, and American emissaries vied for their allegiance throughout the eighteenth and nineteenth centuries in their newly created centers. Often, the Alabamas and Cou-shattas encouraged these rivalries and pursued neutrality during conflicts between foreign powers and consequently received gifts, trade, and protection. Ironically, exceptionally skillful Alabama and Coushatta leaders—Opoyheatly, Captain Pakana, The Mortar, The Wolf, Echean, Pia Mingo, Red Shoes, Antone, and Colita—anticipated wars, border disputes, or other conflicts among foreign nations and made the most of these opportunities.

In some situations, however, local self-government led to factionalism. From the mid-eighteenth to the early nineteenth centuries, each town's autonomy allowed its leaders to define communal interests, and some of these decisions led to short-term conflicts. Their bonds of kinship and their identity as a diasporic and coalescent people, however, proved stronger in the end than the temporary external divisions. Interestingly, as their various migrations led them farther into the west, town autonomy became secondary to the interests of the whole community. Strong and effective leadership by the principal chiefs Colita and Antone surpassed town leadership in the nineteenth century; it was in some ways a return to the centralized leadership under ancient chiefdoms. This Alabama and Coushatta unity was of prime importance as they confronted Anglo-Americans and enemy peoples that severely outnumbered them by the 1850s.

The most lasting effect of migration and diaspora was the creation of the Alabama and Coushatta identity. As they migrated farther away from their ancestral homeland, they created new sacred spaces. Yet based on their oral tradition recalled by Alabama and Coushatta storytellers, the memory of their homeland along the Alabama River retained importance and meaning. It was the sacred space where the Alabamas and Coushattas had coalesced and had created a lasting bond through their common ordeals. As they traveled to Louisiana, and later Texas, they established roots that became part of their shared experiences and history. They had united after their first migration and, over generations, incorporated each other's kinship systems and traditions. By the nineteenth century, their identity was distinguishable from other groups and reflected their commitment to migrate west. When their journey to the west ended, the Alabamas and Coushattas stayed connected by means of their shared ancestry, migrations, kinship ties, and claims to land.

Alabama and Coushatta identity, then, developed out of their shared migration and diaspora over a period of three hundred years. Movement and resettlement encouraged greater cohesiveness and support from within, and, if not for it, they may have never come together. Even the small population of Coushattas that stayed behind in Louisiana continued to make frequent contact with their sister villages in Texas. Intermarriage between the Alabamas and Coushattas perpetuated kinship ties that intertwined them, and this collective identity solidified as they shared experiences and kinship over generations, as they do today. Indeed, their journey to the west ultimately shaped their identity as a people. After their migrations ended, the Alabamas and Coushattas united permanently.

Since the sixteenth century, Alabama and Coushatta voices have echoed strength, strife, and survival. By tracing the history of the Alabamas and Coushattas and looking through different cultural, political, and social lenses, this study has unraveled how the Alabamas and Coushattas persistently sought to create a center that not only resembled their ancient homeland, but also one that they could keep on their own terms. The experiences of the Alabamas and Coushattas, from the days of their Mississippian chiefdoms to those of their nineteenth-century village settlements in Texas, are comparable to many indigenous peoples. They influenced and adapted to features of Euro-American culture while maintaining many traditional customs and practices, they utilized their influence to play foreign empires against each other, and they disputed European and, later, American claims to their land.

Yet the Alabamas and Coushattas accomplished what many American Indians could not in the face of great external pressures: they coalesced in their struggle to survive European encounters, journeyed west, claimed and received title to their lands in East Texas, maintained their sovereignty, and largely escaped forced removal to Indian Territory in Oklahoma. In this process, they continually avoided complete absorption into larger, more powerful entities despite their small population compared to other southeastern peoples, especially by the mid-nineteenth century. Their patterns of migration and diapora could have destroyed them, but they survived and remained together. Their union to each other was permanent, and the connection that developed out of their migrations is what makes them unique as a people. Indeed, we can learn much from the diasporic experiences of the Alabamas and Coushattas. Given the current frequency of dislocation and migration of many diverse peoples throughout the world, their story is especially compelling and enlightening.

Looking back at the Alabama and Coushatta creation story, only those who overcame the fear of hearing the hooting owls, echoing from all directions, emerged from their ancestral cave to begin a new life in a new world. These people became the Alabamas and Coushattas. Despite their repeated movement and the economic, social, and political hardships they encountered over five centuries, their connection to each other survived. The Alabamas and Coushattas demonstrated great resilience as they confronted many challenges. Today they hold a deep connection to the lands they had and now occupy, and they continue to endure and thrive as a sovereign people.

Epilogue

In the years following the American Civil War, the Alabamas and Coushattas continued to occupy their land in East Texas and western Louisiana. They cultivated small plots of arable land, raised cattle, horses, and other domesticated animals, and maintained good relations by providing labor to the neighboring Anglo-American communities.[1] Their lives, however, began to change dramatically as non-Indians surrounded them and completely permeated their world. In the past, they could have escaped and re-created their world on their own terms by migrating farther west, but this was no longer possible. Their journey had ended. By the turn of the twentieth century, the pernicious effects of the state and federal governments' solution to the "Indian problem" began to seep into the culture that Alabama and Coushatta ancestors had created so long ago.

Transition

For three centuries, the Alabamas and Coushattas had remained relatively isolated from the influence of government agencies and formal foreign institutions largely because of their migrations. When the Alabamas and Coushattas could no longer escape westward, they faced many challenges to their ancient beliefs. Beginning in the 1880s, Christian missionaries settled in both Alabama and Coushatta communities and dramatically altered their lives. Within thirty years, Christianity replaced most Native religious beliefs. Presbyterian missionary C. W. Chambers and his family arrived at the Texas village of the Alabamas and Coushattas in 1899, built a mission chapel and day school, and stayed until 1937. In addition to his proselytizing, Chambers promoted health care and established formal, Western-based education. The Louisiana Coushattas had a similar experience when Christian missionary Lyda Averill Taylor lived among them in the 1930s.[2]

Over the decades, continual exposure to missionaries and Anglo-American culture crowded out the oral tradition of the Alabamas and Coushattas. Their ancient practices of passing down myths and folktales, legends, worldviews, and beliefs to younger generations were diminishing. Moreover, Christian teachings slowly began to alter Alabama and Coushatta perspectives and beliefs, transforming many of their stories. Religious syncretism appeared in their creation myths, including an account of how their forbears and animals escaped to a raft when the floods came—a story very much reminiscent of Noah's ark.[3] By the late 1800s, the Alabamas and Coushattas had experienced the full impact of cultural suppression by whites. According to Howard Martin, "the missionaries had come with new myths and new tales, and museum collectors came and hauled off their past and their artifacts by the wagonload." He lamented that "many of these stories belong to a period which is long past and cannot be repeated in our world."[4]

Rapid Alabama and Coushatta social changes caught the attention of whites from Texas and throughout the United States, who viewed these changes as a positive transformation. James McLaughlin, an inspector from the U.S. Department of the Interior, arrived at the Alabama and Coushatta Texas reservation in September 1918. He reported that 132 Alabama and Coushatta men and women met him at the chapel, "all neatly dressed as white persons." The men wore their hair short and women had theirs coifed just as their white counterparts in neighboring settlements.[5]

One of the most striking transformations was language. Many Alabamas and Coushattas spoke English well, and the rest could understand enough to allow them to interact with their neighbors. This was a departure from the past. Very few Alabamas and Coushattas, outside of chiefs or village representatives, had understood the English language when they first moved onto their reservation in Texas in the mid-1800s. Before their final settlement, they had incorporated aspects of French, Spanish, and English vocabulary and concepts into their own Native languages. Institutional agencies and government officials, however, discouraged the use of traditional languages, restrictions that their counterparts in Oklahoma also experienced. Interaction in church, school, and work was in English. Over time, it became their main form of communication with outsiders, and eventually each other—especially among the younger generations.[6]

Incorporating English into their lexicon promoted meaningful and more frequent interaction with their white neighbors. According to McLaughlin, the Alabamas and Coushattas were "well spoken of by whites of the surrounding country, for whom many of them work in the woods and on farms." The white neighbors' description of "their Indians" was "chaste, virtuous, docile, law abiding and easily controlled, but very backward in an agricultural way, due to lack of knowledge of practical farming and conservation of the soil."[7] This attitude was in typical ethnocentric terms, but considering the ubiquitous racism of the early twentieth century toward American Indians, could be viewed as favorable for the time.

The Alabamas and Coushattas had experienced a staggering transformation. McLaughlin reported his observations to the U.S. Secretary of the Interior and recommended federal funding for the Alabama-Coushatta Tribe of Texas; they had met the U.S. government's qualifications for assistance. If we take McLaughlin's report at face value, all Native traditions were lost; in fact, Alabama and Coushatta culture remained intact, albeit in a mixed form. Early missionaries built a church on the site of the old dancing grounds, but they practiced many of their ancient dances discretely in the woods.[8] Changes to their culture certainly occurred, yet just as in the past, both the Alabamas and Coushattas combined new values with their traditional practices and beliefs.

Awakening

From the 1930s to the 1950s, paternalistic federal and state legislation replaced missionary activity as the salient external influence on Alabama and Coushatta culture. The most noted change took place in 1934 after the passage of the Indian Reorganization Act, also known as the Indian New Deal. By 1938, the Alabama-Coushattas of Texas incorporated and elected a tribal council and drafted a constitution preserving tribal sovereignty. Federal termination of responsibilities toward American Indians soon followed, and from 1955 to 1987, the Alabama-Coushattas of Texas were under state jurisdiction.

Historian Jonathan Hook has argued that following the era of self-determination in the late 1960s and 1970s, the Alabamas and Coushattas experienced an ethnogenesis, a "formulation of a new ethnic identity," as well as an ethnic regenesis—a reemergence of their cultural past.[9] Tribal members focused on reclaiming lost traditions, beliefs, and practices, and firmly established their right to home rule as a sovereign entity.

One of the concerns resulting from this awakening was the diminishing use of ancestral languages and oral traditions. In the past, outsiders often aided the preservation of Alabama and Coushatta traditions by compiling folktales and stories. For example, John Swanton, an ethnologist from the Bureau of American Ethnology, visited the tribe in 1911, 1912, and 1932. He met with community members interested in preserving their past. Throughout his visit, Chief Charles Martin Thompson (Sun-Ke) introduced Swanton to Alabama and Coushatta elders; Swanton later recorded some of their oral traditions, including stories, songs, and dances.[10] In the 1930s, Howard Martin followed Swanton and interviewed and recorded more extensively nineteen Alabama and Coushatta elders. This older generation remembered traditions that predated missionaries who arrived in the 1880s; they related original, authentic versions of oral traditions and linguistic details.[11]

In the 1990s, tribal members took control over efforts to revive their Native languages. Although the Alabama and Koasati languages are different—they are pairs of dialects—constant exposure to each other's language over three centuries led Alabama speakers to freely borrow words and grammar from Koasati, and vice versa. Alabama and Coushatta men and women intermarried in their gradual journey west, so many today speak both Alabama and Koasati.[12] Recent publications of the Alabama and Koasati dictionaries have aided the teaching of both languages to younger generations. Cora Sylestine—who spent fifty years compiling the information with countless Alabama and Coushatta contributors—completed, with Heather K. Hardy and Timothy Montler, the first Alabama-English dictionary in 1993 (it is now available on the World Wide Web). She began the project when "the language of her people might be lost over the generations."[13] Although she died before its release, her contributions to the preservation of the Alabama language are endless. Soon after, with the assistance of Bel Abbey, Martha John, and Ruth Poncho, and other Native speakers, Geoffrey Kimball completed a Koasati-English dictionary in 1994. Like the Alabama dictionary, it contains current as well as defunct words and phrases, pronunciation, and grammar. Both dictionaries include references to traditional narratives, ancient customs and concepts, and medicinal uses and practices. These sources will no doubt help ensure that the Alabama and Koasati languages are not lost forever. Alabama and Coushatta members, however, have stressed that the elders must teach their languages to the younger generations; they should not learn it simply from a book.[14]

Despite these efforts, many challenges still exist. Tribal members no longer teach the Alabama and Koasati languages as first languages, albeit for practical reasons. Their Native languages subsequently have been lost in many families, especially to those under the age of forty-five. In 2000, Chief Clayton Sylestine of the Alabama-Coushattas of Texas reminisced that when he was a boy in the 1940s, he learned the "Indian names of nature," but that now "I'm not sure I could tell you in English."[15] Yolanda Poncho, the curator of the Alabama-Coushatta museum in Texas, remembered her grandmother telling her stories in Koasati: "None of this has been written down. If we want to remember it, we have to pass it down."[16] Many of the young know very little of the ancient languages of Alabama or Koasati, but the reservation's cultural committee now offers Alabama and Koasati language classes for children and adults. Today, roughly one-third of those who live on the reservation can speak Alabama or Koasati.

Just as the community has struggled with preserving its language and culture, the Alabamas and Coushattas' claim to their homelands has been beleaguered by decades-long problems and controversies. Local, state, and national headlines continue to document the ongoing issues. Reports about them began as early as 1854 when they received 1,110 acres of land in East Texas. After many decades, on December 7, 1918, Franklin K. Lane, secretary of the U.S. Department of the Interior, recommended a purchase of additional land for the Alabamas and Coushattas of Texas in order to improve their economic conditions. By 1928, tribal leaders helped organize a delegation to receive federal funds to purchase additional lands and to provide for its infrastructure. Federal involvement with tribal lands ended in 1954 when the Alabama-Coushattas of Texas terminated their relationship with the U.S. government. Their reservation now includes 4,600 acres.[17]

Over the last decade, the Alabama-Coushattas of Texas have been negotiating with government officials regarding use of their reservation; the limits of tribal sovereignty are at issue. In 1999, they organized local and state support in their conflict with John Cornyn, then attorney general of Texas, now a Republican U.S. senator. Dubbed "The Last of the Indian Fighters" by the tribe, Cornyn questioned the Alabama-Coushattas' right to have a casino on their reservation. The building in question, known as the Alabama-Coushatta Entertainment Center, was a small casino compared to most. Despite their efforts, Texas officials closed the casino in 2002 after only nine months of operation. Tribal revenues were significantly curtailed by this action, but the Texas government provided no compensation for the tribe's loss.[18]

Indeed, the casino had provided a potential solution to economic hardship that plagued the Alabama-Coushattas of Texas. Seventy tribal members formed the majority of the casino staff; after the opening of the casino, the unemployment rate dropped from 47 percent to 18 percent. According to tribal member Kevin Battise, profits from the casino's eight-month run were earmarked for housing and education. Battise stated in July 2002: "Education is a big need on our reservation. Only 1 percent [of the 998 members] has a four-year degree." Poverty continues to confront tribal members and their families. The Alabama-Coushatta per capita income in 2003 was $10,465 versus a $15,834 average in the United States, and a $19,617 average in Texas.[19]

Following the loss of their casino, in October 2002 the Alabama-Coushattas of Texas finally learned the outcome of their 1983 lawsuit against the U.S. government. The U.S. Court of Federal Claims, after nearly twenty years of review, ruled that the U.S. Congress should award them over $270 million in the wake of past federal infringements including the unlawful extraction of oil, gas, and timber, and non-Indian seizure of Alabama-Coushatta lands without compensation. According to the ruling, the U.S. government failed to secure the tribe's land from 1845 to 1954 when they were under federal jurisdiction and care. The Alabama-Coushattas therefore still hold aboriginal title to possess and occupy 5.5 million acres in East Texas.[20]

The Court's ruling is nonbinding, and it is unknown if Congress will provide compensation. The only positive indicator is that Congress rarely ignores Court recommendations. In the event that Congress does not act, the Alabama-Coushattas only recourse is filing another lawsuit claiming ownership to ancestral homelands in Louisiana and Texas. Ronnie Thomas, chairman of the Alabama-Coushatta Tribal Council, summarized his people's stance in the *Austin American-Statesman*: "All we know is, it's 5 million acres, and that's worth a lot. We're not willing to give that up for nothing."[21] If the Alabama-Coushattas bring this lawsuit to court, over 500,000 individuals living on their ancestral tribal lands could be affected. In true irony, these Texans may be denied titles to land that they now occupy, which would spell disaster for real estate values in affluent developments such as The Woodlands (north of Houston). Open land in and around Huntsville State Park also could be affected. In the end, Congress has "power of the purse," and the settlement is still pending.[22]

Likewise, the Coushattas of Louisiana, who hold 3,000 acres in Allen Parish, have experienced great strain in their community in the past few years. Although they have enjoyed great success and wealth with their modern casino in Kinder, Louisiana (bringing in approximately $300 million per year), reports of corruption have plagued them. The struggle over the casino has divided the Coushatta community, and many tribal members are calling for reform. The Coushattas are currently involved in a $32 million lawsuit with two Washington lobbyists including Jack Abramoff, a top aid to the indicted former Republican majority leader, Tom Delay, who secured a private meeting for them with President George W. Bush to discuss antitax legislation. The Coushattas' lawsuit charges that the defendants conducted fraud and money laundering. In 2006, Abramoff pleaded guilty to unrelated federal charges of fraud and corruption and was sentenced in March of that year to over five years in prison. Interestingly, in July 2006, the Alabama-Coushattas of Texas filed a separate lawsuit against Abramoff, former Christian Coalition leader Ralph Reed, and his associates. The Alabama-Coushattas accused them of fraud and racketeering in a conspiracy to shut down their casino, which happened to benefit Abramoff's other tribal clients (including the Coushattas of Louisiana). They are seeking restitution for the millions of dollars lost since the casino closed in 2002.[23]

Steadfast Bonds of Kinship

Despite repeated attacks on Alabama and Coushatta culture, language, and claim to land in the late nineteenth and twentieth centuries, close ties kept their identity intact and strengthened their resolve toward revitalization. The Alabamas and Coushattas had maintained kinship connections since the 1700s, if not earlier. Matrilineal clans helped define personal identity and linked families to their ancestors. By the twentieth century, the Alabama and Coushatta kinship bonds remained strong, but long-established ideas had undergone some significant transformations. The traditional determinant of membership into the Alabama and Coushatta community for centuries had been the matrilineal kinship system; individuals traced their ancestry through the mother's clan. Although Alabama and Coushatta clans still exist and continue to hold meaning to tribal members, non-Indian influences have encouraged Western patrilineal systems. For example, in the 1990s, the Alabama-Coushattas of Texas introduced the "No Clan" that includes those who have a genetic connection to tribal relatives through their father, not their mother. Moreover, in response to John Collier's Indian New Deal of the 1930s and its provisions to preserve Indian ancestry, the Alabama-Coushattas passed a requirement of 100 percent blood quantum for tribal membership. This meant that both parents of applicants to the tribe had to be full-blooded American Indians, with at least one Alabama or Coushatta parent. If a tribal member marries a non-Indian, the couple cannot live on the reservation. Today over half of its members live on the Alabama-Coushatta Reservation in Texas; the rest are scattered around the country.[24] Clan ties still extend to the Coushattas in Louisiana. Both groups also continue to intermarry as they did after their seventeenth-century diaspora.

The Alabamas and Coushattas today continue to support a thriving community. There are currently 1,000 enrolled members of the Alabama-Coushatta Tribe of Texas, and around 1,000 registered members of the Coushattas of Louisiana. Just as they had over four centuries ago, they remain connected to each other. Looking ahead toward the challenges in the twenty-first century, the Alabamas and Coushattas' commitment to their identity and sovereignty will in all likelihood ensure that they will endure and create a better world for future generations. If this book helps outsiders to appreciate the rich cultural traditions that have survived despite centuries of migration and diaspora, or, better still, serves in some way to reinforce the remarkable longevity of that culture—then its purpose will have been fulfilled.

Notes

Introduction

1. Howard N. Martin, "A Journey to the Sky," in *Myths and Folktales of the Alabama-Coushatta Indians* (Austin, Tex.: Encino Press, 1977), 24–27.

2. Ibid.

3. Ibid.

4. Ibid.

5. Studies on the Alabamas and Coushattas have focused on the twentieth century, including, most recently, Jonathan Hook's *The Alabama-Coushatta Indians* (College Station: Texas A&M University Press, 1998). While Hook offers thoughtful analysis, the brevity of his study leaves many unanswered questions. For a more in-depth critique of Hook's work, see my review of the book in the *Alabama Review* (February 1999). Other studies that briefly discuss the Alabamas and Coushattas include Harriet Smither's "The Alabama Indians of Texas," *Southwestern Historical Quarterly* (October 1932): 83–108. It is one of the few scholarly works that summarizes the history of the Alabamas to 1931. Other brief histories include Dorman H. Winfrey's article, "The Alabama-Coushattas," in *Indian Tribes of Texas* (Waco, Tex.: Texian Press, 1971), 5–14; and David Agee Horr, ed., *Alabama-Coushatta (Creek) Indians* (New York: Garland, 1974).

6. For a detailed discussion of Alexander McGillivray and his claim to

the Creek Nation, see Michael D. Green, *The Politics of Indian Removal: Creek Government and Society in Crisis* (Lincoln: University of Nebraska Press, 1982), 33–43.

7. Joshua Piker, *Okfuskee: A Creek Indian Town in Colonial America* (Cambridge, Mass.: Harvard University Press, 2004); Jason Baird Jackson, *Yuchi Ceremonial Life: Performance, Meaning, and Tradition in a Contemporary American Indian* (Lincoln: University of Nebraska Press, 2005); and Steven C. Hahn, *The Invention of the Creek Nation, 1670–1763* (Lincoln: University of Nebraska Press, 2004). Another study that looks inside the Creeks by focusing on the Yamacraws is Julie Anne Sweet's *Negotiating for Georgia: British-Creek Relations in the Trustee Era, 1733–1752* (Athens: University of Georgia Press, 2005).

8. Recent literature on the Texas tribes includes David La Vere's *Contrary Neighbors: Southern Plains and Removed Indians in Indian Territory* (Norman: University of Oklahoma Press, 2000), *The Texas Indians* (College Station: Texas A&M University Press, 2004), and *Life among the Texas Indians: The WPA Narratives* (College Station: Texas A&M University Press, 1998); Gary Clayton Anderson's *The Conquest of Texas: Ethnic Cleansing in the Promised Land, 1820–1875* (Norman: University of Oklahoma Press, 2005); F. Todd Smith's *From Dominance to Disappearance: The Indians of Texas and the Near Southwest, 1786–1859* (Lincoln: University of Nebraska Press, 2005), and *The Wichita Indians: Traders of Texas and the Southern Plains, 1540–1845* (College Station: Texas A&M University Press, 2000); Dianna Everett's *The Texas Cherokees: A People Between Two Fires, 1819–1840* (Norman: University of Oklahoma Press, 1995); and Mary Whatley Clarke's *Chief Bowles and Texas Cherokees* (Norman: University of Oklahoma Press, 2001).

9. Robin Cohen identifies these characteristics as the "fibers" that intertwine to make and strengthen a "diasporic rope." Cohen, *Global Diasporas: An Introduction* (Seattle: University of Washington Press, 1997), 180–87; Nicholas Van Hear, *New Diasporas: The Mass Exodus, Dispersal and Regrouping of Migrant Communities* (Seattle: University of Washington Press, 1998), 5.

10. The most recent studies include Marc S. Rodriguez, ed., *Repositioning North American Migration History: New Directions in Modern Continental Migration, Citizenship and Community* (Rochester, N.Y.: University of Rochester Press, 2004); James N. Gregory, *The Southern Diaspora: How Great Migrations of Black and White Southerners Transformed America* (Chapel Hill: University of North Carolina Press, 2006); Isidore Okpewho, Carole Boyce Davies, and Ali Alamin Mazrui, eds., *The African Diaspora: African Origins and New World Identities* (Bloomington: Indiana University Press, 2001); Bertrand Van Ruymbeke and Randy J. Sparks, eds., *Memory and Identity: The Huguenots in France and the Atlantic Diaspora* (Columbia: University of South Carolina Press, 2003); Samdar Lavie and Ted Swedenburg, eds., *Displacement, Diaspora, and Geographies of Identity* (Durham, N.C.: Duke University Press, 1996).

11. Van Hear, *New Diasporas*, 62.

12. The historical sources include the Archives des Colonies C13 Series; the British Public Records, Colonial Office Series; the Bexar Archives; the *American State Papers*; the Archivo General de Mexico, Fomento y Colonization; the Nacogdoches Archives; and various papers from Indian agents, military officers, and politicians, found at the following repositories: Center for Louisiana Studies in Lafayette, La.; Historic New Orleans Collection; British Public Records Office, London; Library of Congress, Washington, D.C.; Center for American History, Austin, Tex.; and the Clements Center for Southwest Studies, Dallas, Tex.

13. Although some scholars believe that the use of oral tradition is not in keeping with an accurate portrayal of history and therefore should not be used, I believe we must incorporate these stories to preserve American Indian voices and perspectives. One must always keep in mind, however, that these traditions may have been altered as a result of European contact and pressures to assimilate.

Chapter 1

1. "Origin of the Alabama and Coushatta Tribes," in Howard N. Martin, *Myths and Folktales of the Alabama-Coushatta Indians of Texas* (Austin, Tex.: Encino Press, 1977), 3.

2. Adam King, *Etowah: The Political History of a Chiefdom Capital* (Tuscaloosa: University of Alabama Press, 2003), 4–7, 15; David Anderson, *Savannah River Chiefdoms: Political Changes in the Late Prehistoric Southeast* (Tuscaloosa: University of Alabama Press, 1994), 7–9.

3. King, *Etowah*, 4–7; Charles Hudson, *The Southeastern Indians* (Knoxville: University of Tennessee Press, 1976), 77; Charles Hudson, *Knights of Spain, Warriors of the Sun: Hernando De Soto and the South's Ancient Chiefdoms* (Athens: University of Georgia Press, 1997), 23; Paul D. Welch, *Moundville's Economy* (Tuscaloosa: University of Alabama Press, 1991), 2, 7, 9; David G. Anderson, "Fluctuations between Simple and Complex Chiefdoms: Cycling in the Late Prehistoric Southeast," in *Political Structure and Change in the Prehistoric Southeastern United States*, ed. John F. Scarry (Gainesville: University Press of Florida, 1996), 232, 237.

4. Patricia Galloway, *Choctaw Genesis, 1500–1700* (Lincoln: University of Nebraska Press, 1995), 336; David J. Hally, "Platform-Mound Construction and the Instability of Mississippian Chiefdoms," in Scarry, *Political Structure and Change*, 93–94, 97; Susan C. Power, *Early Art of the Southeastern Indians: Feathered Serpents and Winged Beings* (Athens: University of Georgia Press, 2004), 63; Hudson, *Southeastern Indians*, 78; Elman R. Service, *Primitive Social Organization* (New York: Random House, 1962), 144.

5. Vernon James Knight Jr. and Patricia Galloway have both suggested that origin myths of southeastern peoples may shed light on their historical past as Mississippian mound builders. Vernon James Knight Jr., "Symbolism of Mississippian Mounds," in *Powhatan's Mantle: Indians in the Colonial Southeast*, ed. Peter H. Wood, Gregory A. Waselkov, and M. Thomas Hatley (Lincoln: University of Nebraska Press, 1989), 279–91.

6. Craig T. Sheldon, "The Mississippian-Historic Transition in Central Alabama" (Ph.D. diss., University of Oregon, 1974), 9.

7. Ned J. Jenkins, "Early Creek Origins: The Moundville Connection," Alabama Museum of Natural History Bulletin (in press).

8. Sheldon, "The Mississippian-Historic Transition," 9; Welch, *Moundville's Economy*, 23–26; Hudson, *Knights of Spain*, 252.

9. Vernon James Knight Jr. and Vincas P. Steponaitis, "A New History of Moundville," in *Archaeology of the Moundville Chiefdom*, ed. Vernon James Knight Jr. and Vincas P. Steponaitis (Washington, D.C.: Smithsonian Institution Press, 1998), 1–25.

10. Vincas P. Steponaitis, *Ceramics, Chronology, and Community Patterns: An Archaeological Study at Moundville* (New York: Academic Press, 1983), 168; Anderson, *Savannah River Chiefdoms*, 147; Welch, *Moundville's Economy*, 23, 183–90; Hudson, *Southeastern Indians*, 85–86.

11. Knight and Steponaitis, "A New History of Moundville," 1–25; Anderson, *Savannah River Chiefdoms*, 148–50; Christopher S. Peebles, "The Rise and Fall of the Mississippian in Western Alabama: The Moundville and Summerville Phases, A.D. 1000 to 1600," *Mississippi Archaeology* 22 (1987): 1–31; Christopher S. Peebles, "Moundville from 1000 to 1500 A.D. as Seen from 1840 to 1985 A.D.," in *Chiefdoms in the Americas*, ed. Robert D. Drennen and Carlos A. Uribe (Lanham, Md.: University Press of America, 1987), 21–41.

12. The Alibamu and Miculasa simple chiefdoms on the Tombigbee River acted independently of the Moundville chiefdom during its paramountcy and likely were unaffected by Moundville's collapse. See Jenkins, "Early Creek Origins"; Sheldon, "The Mississippian-Historic Tradition," 120; Galloway, *Choctaw Genesis*, 63–64; John Cottier, "The Alabama River Phase: A Brief Description of a Late Phase in the Prehistory of South Central Alabama," appendix to *Archaeological Salvage Investigations in the Miller's Ferry Lock and Dam Reservoir, 1968* (Moundville: University of Alabama, 1970), 120; Steponaitis, *Ceramics, Chronology, and Community Patterns*, 169; Anderson, "Fluctuations between Simple and Complex Chiefdoms," 250; Anderson, *Savannah River Chiefdoms*, 7, 13, 149.

13. The variant spellings of Coushattas are "Coste" or "Acoste" by the Spanish; "Conchatys" by the English, and sometimes "Conchaques" by the French. Swanton first identified Coste as "Koasati" (Coushatta). See John R. Swanton, *Early History of the Creek Indians and Their Neighbors*, Bureau of American

Ethnology Bulletin 73 (Washington, D.C.: U.S. Government Printing Office, 1922), 201. Chester B. DePratter, Charles M. Hudson, and Marvin Smith identified the site on Bussell Island as Coste. See their chapter, "The Hernando de Soto Expedition: From Chiaha to Mabila," in *Alabama and the Borderlands*, ed. R. Reid Badger and Lawerence A. Clayton (Tuscaloosa: University of Alabama Press, 1985), 114; Lawrence A. Clayton, Vernon James Knight Jr., and Edward C. Moore, eds., *The De Soto Chronicles: The Expedition of Hernando De Soto to North America in 1539–1543*, 2 vols.(Tuscaloosa: University of Alabama Press, 1993), 1:232.

14. Not much is known about the industry or production of the Coste chiefdom, outside of pottery. Unlike the abundant burials found at Moundville, there are no graves in these communities; they had a burial custom of defleshing the body and encapsulating the bones in ossuaries. Thomas M. N. Lewis, *The Prehistory of the Chickamauga Basin in Tennessee*, 2 vols. (Knoxville: University of Tennessee Press, 1995), 1:6–7, 13, 245; Clayton, Knight, and Moore, *De Soto Chronicles*, 1:232; Marvin T. Smith, *Aboriginal Culture Change in the Interior Southeast* (Athens: University of Georgia Press, 1988), 139.

15. Ned Jenkins argues that the Coste origins can be found in the Moundville variant, which helps explain Alabama and Coushatta similarities in their ceramics and languages prior to their coalescence. See Jenkins, "Early Creek Origins"; Smith, *Aboriginal Culture Change*, 139; Lewis, *Prehistory of the Chickamauga Basin*, 1:6–7, 13, 245; Marvin T. Smith, *Coosa: The Rise and Fall of a Southeastern Mississippian Chiefdom* (Gainesville: University Press of Florida, 2000), 80.

16. Hudson, *Knights of Spain*, 50; David Ewing Duncan, *Hernando de Soto: A Savage Quest in the Americas* (New York: Crown, 1995), 242–43.

17. Soto had previously visited neighboring Chiaha. Many peoples that Soto encountered accepted his demands for slaves and supplies out of fear, but the people of Chiaha resisted. They had refused to give Soto thirty women as slaves and abandoned their village to avoid conflict. Soto searched the neighboring villages and destroyed large maize fields along the way to Coste. Clayton, Knight, and Moore, *De Soto Chronicles*, 1:88–91, 282–83.

18. Ibid., 1:282.

19. Ibid., 1:88–91, 282–83. *Barbacoa* is an Arawak word describing a "weight-bearing framework raised up on posts." Many southeastern groups grilled their food on such structures, which could be large or small. It is from "barbacoa" that we get the name "barbecue" and the technique. Hudson, *Knights of Spain*, 156, 158.

20. Clayton, Knight, and Moore, *De Soto Chronicles*, 2:321 (quote); 1:90–91, 282–83.

21. Ibid., 1:283 (quote), 90–91; Hudson, *Knights of Spain*, 205–7.

22. Clayton, Knight, and Moore, *De Soto Chronicles*, 1:284.

23. Ibid., 1:88–91, 2:282–83; Hudson, *Knights of Spain*, 205–7.

24. Hudson, *Knights of Spain*, 256–59.

25. There is still much speculation on the ancient Tombigbee chiefdoms. See John Blitz, *Ancient Chiefdoms of the Tombigbee* (Tuscaloosa: University of Alabama Press, 1993); Hudson, *Knights of Spain*, 262–65, 271–74. For a discussion of the Chicaza paramount chiefdom, see Robbie F. Ethridge, *From Chicaza to Chickasaw*, (Chapel Hill: University of North Carolina Press, forthcoming).

26. The territory that Soto had traversed was probably only a part of the Alibamu domain; the location of the palisade may indicate that they stayed there as a refuge during hunting trips. Word probably spread that foreign intruders were in their midst, and consequently, the chief of the Alibamus sent warriors to ambush the Spaniards at the empty fort. Clayton, Knight, and Moore, *De Soto Chronicles*, 1:109, 110; Hudson, *Knights of Spain*, 271.

27. Clayton, Knight, and Moore, *De Soto Chronicles*, 1:109, 110, 237, 2:379–80; Hudson, *Knights of Spain*, 271.

28. Clayton, Knight, and Moore, *De Soto Chronicles*, 2:381.

29. Ibid., 1:110, 237–38, 2:380–81.

30. For a detailed account of Soto's expedition, see ibid. and Hudson, *Knights of Spain*.

31. Yet another loss was the disappearance of some cultural practices, including facets of art, religion, philosophy, and knowledge. Smith, *Aboriginal Culture Change*, 55; Alfred W. Crosby Jr., *The Columbian Exchange* (Westport, Conn.: Greenwood Press, 1972), 40, 44, 51. For a detailed study of American Indian depopulation from Old World diseases, see Henry F. Dobyns, "Estimating Aboriginal American Population: An Appraisal of Techniques with a New Hemispheric Estimate," *Current Anthropology* 7 (1966): 395–416; and Dobyns, *Their Number Become Thinned* (Knoxville: University of Tennessee Press, 1983).

32. Paul Kelton has suggested that European epidemic diseases made no significant impact on American Indian communities until after 1696. See Paul Kelton, "The Great Southeastern Smallpox Epidemic," in *Transformation of the Southeastern Indians, 1540–1760*, ed. Robbie Ethridge and Charles Hudson (Jackson: University Press of Mississippi, 2002), 21–38.

33. "Why Sickness Still Exists on the Earth," in Martin, *Myths and Folktales*, 8.

34. Ibid., 8–9.

35. Charles Hudson, *The Juan Pardo Expeditions: Exploration of the Carolinas and Tennessee, 1566–1568* (Washington, D.C.: Smithsonian Institution Press, 1990), 3–18; Dennis Reinhartz and Gerald D. Saxon, eds., *The Mapping of the Entradas into the Greater Southwest* (Norman: University of Oklahoma Press, 1998), 75.

36. Eric Hinderaker and Peter C. Mancall, *At the Edge of Empire: The Backcountry in British North America* (Baltimore: Johns Hopkins University Press,

2003), 73–75; Alan Gallay, *The Indian Slave Trade: The Rise of the English Empire in the American South, 1670–1717* (New Haven, Conn.: Yale University Press, 2002), 46.

37. For a discussion on the shift of the Native mind-set regarding capital, see Christina Snyder, "Captives of the Dark and Bloody Ground: Identity, Race, and Power in the Contested American South" (Ph.D. diss., University of North Carolina, Chapel Hill, 2007); Gallay, *Indian Slave Trade*, 29, 46.

38. Hinderaker and Mancall, *At the Edge of Empire*, 73–75; Gallay, *Indian Slave Trade*, 46.

39. Historians have pointed out that, contrary to popular belief, seventeenth-century European weapons were no match for the more accurate bows and arrows; European firearms were loud and novel but not very effective in battle. Gallay, *Indian Slave Trade*, 15, 41, 129.

40. Robbie Ethridge, "The Making of a Militaristic Slaving Society: The Chickasaws and the Colonial Indian Slave Trade," in *The Indian Slave Trade in Colonial America*, ed. Alan Gallay (Lincoln: University of Nebraska Press, forthcoming); Gallay, *Indian Slave Trade*, 15, 41, 129.

41. Pierre Le Moyne d'Iberville, *Iberville's Gulf Journals*, trans. and ed. Richebourg Gaillard McWilliams (Tuscaloosa: University of Alabama Press, 1981), 119.

42. Lewis, *Prehistory of the Chickamauga Basin*, 6–13, 245.

43. British Public Records Office, South Carolina Colonial Entry, September 30, 1683, Book 1: 257–58, South Carolina Department of Archives and History, Columbia, South Carolina; Hinderaker, *At the Edge of Empire*, 73–75; Gallay, *Indian Slave Trade*, 55–57; Eric E. Bowne, *The Westo Indians: Slave Traders of the Early Colonial South* (Tuscaloosa: University of Alabama Press, 2005), 1–10.

44. Entries for June 1 and 4, 1680, *Journal of the Grand Council of South Carolina, August 25, 1671–June 24, 1680*, ed. Alexander S. Salley Jr. (Columbia: Historical Commission of South Carolina, 1907), 84, 85.

45. British Public Records Office, South Carolina Colonial Entry, June 3, 1684, Book 1: 289–90; Alexander S. Salley Jr., *Journal of the Commons House of Assembly of South Carolina for 1703* (Columbia: Historical Commission of South Carolina, 1934), 75–76.

46. For details on these factors seen in a shatter zone, see Sheri M. Shuck-Hall, "Diaspora and Coalescence of the Alabamas and Coushattas in the Southeastern Shatter Zone," in *Mapping the Mississippian Shatter Zone: The European Invasion and Regional Instability in the American South*, ed. Robbie Ethridge and Sheri M. Shuck-Hall (Lincoln: University of Nebraska Press, forthcoming).

47. Scholars do not yet have an exact date as to when the peoples from the Tombigbee and Black Warrior rivers moved near the Alabama River, except

that it took place between Soto's entrada and 1700. Jenkins, "Early Creek Origins"; Mark F. Boyd, ed. and trans., "Expedition of Marcos Delgado from Apalache to the Upper Creek Country in 1686," *Florida Historical Quarterly* 16 (1937): 2–32.

48. In 1686 Delgado listed Alabama villages on the upper Alabama River; he also noted that the Coushattas had united with and established villages among the Alabamas by this time as well. Boyd, "Expedition of Marcos Delgado," 19; Guillaume Delisle, "Carte de la Louisiane et du cours du Mississippi," Texas State Historical Association, Center for American History, University of Texas at Austin, 1981; entry for January 13, 1693, in Alexander S. Salley Jr., *Journals of the Commons House of Assembly of South Carolina for the Four Sessions of 1693* (Columbia: Historical Commission of South Carolina, 1907), 11–13; Vernon J. Knight Jr. and Sherée L. Adams, "A Voyage to the Mobile and Tomeh in 1700, with Notes on the Interior of Alabama," *Ethnohistory* 28 (1981): 179–94.

49. Oral tradition was critical to the survival of American Indian societies. Both the Alabamas and Coushattas had storytellers who portrayed values, history, and traditions; the Coushattas called them *a:łí:kan*, and the Alabamas, *náasifatli*. Martin, *Myths and Folktales*, 3; Geoffrey D. Kimball, *Koasati Dictionary* (Lincoln: University of Nebraska Press, 1994), 14; Bill Grantham, *Creation Myths and Legends of the Creek Indians* (Gainesville: University Press of Florida, 2002), 8, 30.

50. Swanton, *Early History of Creek Indians*, 192.

51. Ned Jenkins has argued that the Alabama language is most closely associated with that spoken in the ancient Moundville culture. He also suggests that the Alabamas had lived near the Creeks for two hundred years when their language was first recorded and classified as part of the eastern branch but was likely a western Muskogean language prior to their diaspora. See Jenkins, "Early Creek Origins."

52. Karen Jacque Lupardus, "The Language of the Alabama Indians" (Ph.D. diss., University of Kansas, 1982), 1, 4; Cora Sylestine, Heather K. Hardy, and Timothy Montler, *Dictionary of the Alabama Language* (Austin: University of Texas Press, 1993), xi–xii.

53. Caleb Swan, "Position and State of Manners in and Arts in the Creek, or Muscogee Nation in 1791," in *Historical and Statistical Information Respecting the History, Condition, and Prospects of the Indian Tribes of the United States*, ed. Henry Rowe Schoolcraft (Philadelphia: J. B. Lippincott, 1855), 5:257.

54. Ibid.; entries for February 29 and March 1, 1702, in *Iberville's Gulf Journals*, ed. Richebourg Gaillard McWilliams (Tuscaloosa: University of Alabama Press, 1981), 167–8.

55. Kimball, *Koasati Dictionary*, 187.

56. Sylestine, Hardy, and Montler, *Dictionary of the Alabama Language*, 140–41; Grantham, *Creation Myths*, 8.

57. Kimball, *Koasati Dictionary*, 323–24; Sylestine, Hardy, and Montler, *Dictionary of the Alabama Language*, 552; Lupardus, "The Language of the Alabama Indians," 1, 4; Howard N. Martin, "Ethnohistorical Analysis of Documents Relating to the Alabama and Coushatta Tribes of the State of Texas," in *Alabama-Coushatta (Creek) Indians*, ed. David Agee Horr (New York: Garland, 1974), 192.

58. Kimball, *Koasati Dictionary*, 323–24; Sylestine, Hardy, and Montler, *Dictionary of the Alabama Language*, 552.

59. Kimball, *Koasati Dictionary*, 54; Nancy Shoemaker, *A Strange Likeness: Becoming Red and White in Eighteenth-Century North America* (New York: Oxford University Press, 2004), 16–17.

60. Hernando de Soto saw the town of "Tasqui" near the Hiwassee River in Tennessee during his entrada, and Charles Hudson believes that there is no doubt that this town is the same as Taskigi, where the Koasati language was spoken. Hudson, *Juan Pardo Expeditions*, 109; Galloway, *Choctaw Genesis*, 177–79; Smith, *Coosa*, 80; Treaty of Friendship and Commerce with the Alabama Indians, March 27, 1760, British Public Records Office, Colonial Office, Class 5 (PRO, CO5), 221–27; Boyd, "Expedition of Marcos Delgado," 2–32; Guillaume Delisle, "Carte du Mexique et de la Floride," (1703) and Nicholas de Fer, "Le Cours de Missisipi ou de St. Louis," (1718), The Historic New Orleans Collection, Williams Research Center; Pedro Oliver to Baron de Carondelet, December 1, 1793, *Spain in the Mississippi Valley, 1765–1794*, Annual Report of the American Historical Association for the Year 1945, ed. Lawrence Kinnaird (Washington, D.C.: U.S. Government Printing Office, 1946), 231; Knight and Adams, "A Voyage to the Mobile and Tomeh," 179–94; Bernard Romans, *A Concise Natural History of East and West Florida*, (Gainesville: University of Florida Press, 1962), 332; Amos J. Wright Jr., *Historic Indian Towns in Alabama, 1540–1838* (Tuscaloosa: University of Alabama Press, 2003), 17, 50–52, 60, 150–51, 162, 186.

61. The map of the Alabama Nation in 1717 included in this book indicates only approximate locations based on the available evidence. There is much speculation and thus, some disagreement, among scholars on the names, identities, and locations of Alabama towns. For example, according to Amos Wright Jr., Alabama villages may have included Pawokti, located on the east bank of the Alabama River near present-day Montgomery, and Nitahauritz, or Bear Fort, which was the southernmost Alabama village downriver on the west bank of the Alabama and below the Cahaba River. Wright also believes that another group established Tamahita (near the town of Coosada) by 1761, and had 18 warriors according to that year's census report. Also connected to this

village was Woksoyudshi (Okchauitci), which was situated on the Coosa River about two miles south of Wetumpka. Archaeologists, however, have not discovered these village sites. See Wright, *Historic Indian Towns in Alabama*, 17, 50–52, 60, 150–51, 162, 186.

62. Wetumpka (Wetumpkee) may have also been an Alabama town, considering its close proximity to Pakana. Over time the Alabamas and Coushattas occupied two distinct locations, one along east-southeast of the Tallapoosa River and another along the Coosa River. Delgado, "Expedition of Marcos Delgado," 2–32; Treaty of Friendship and Commerce with the Alabama Indians, March 27, 1760, PRO CO5; Knight and Adams, "A Voyage to the Mobile and Tomeh," 179–94; Galloway, *Choctaw Genesis*, 177–79; Wright, *Historic Indian Towns in Alabama*, 17, 50–52, 60, 114, 150–51, 162.

63. Wright, *Historic Indian Towns in Alabama*, 17, 50–52, 60, 114, 150–51, 162.

64. Ibid.

65. Ibid.; Vaudreuil to Maurepas, June 15, 1748, Archives des Colonies, Manuscript Series C13A (AC-C13A), 32:102–4; Beauchamp's Journal, 1746, in *Mississippi Provincial Archives: French Dominion (MPAFD)*, ed. and trans. Dunbar Rowland, A. G. Sanders, and Patricia Galloway, vols. 4–5 (Baton Rouge: Louisiana State University Press, 1984), 4:276; Diron d'Artaguette to Maurepas, October 17, 1729, AC-C13A, 12:148–59.

66. John Stuart, journal entry for March 7, 1772, in *Documents of the American Revolution 1770–1783*, ed. Kenneth G. Davies, 20 vols. (Dublin: Irish University Press, 1972–79), 5:261; Kimball, *Koasati Dictionary*, 274; Power, *Early Art of the Southeastern Indians*, 163–69; Charles M. Hudson, *Conversations with the High Priest of Coosa* (Chapel Hill: University of North Carolina Press, 2003), 153–75; Swan, "Position and State of Manners," 5:264; Romans, *Concise Natural History*, 144–45; Hudson, *Southeastern Indians*, 213, 218, 221; John Reed Swanton, *The Indians of the Southeastern United States*, Bureau of American Ethnology Bulletin 137 (Washington, D.C.: Smithsonian Institution Press, 1979), 276.

67. James Adair, *The History of the American Indians*, ed. Samuel Cole Williams (1775; repr., New York: Argonaut Press, 1966), 6; Jean Chaudhuri and Joyotpaul Chaudhuri, *A Sacred Path: The Way of the Muscogee Creeks* (Los Angeles: University of California, Los Angeles, American Indian Studies Center, 2001), 75–77; Marvin T. Smith, *Archaeology of Aboriginal Culture Change in the Southeast* (Athens: University of Georgia Press, 1987), 89, 93–98; Gregory A. Waselkov, Brian M. Wood, and Joseph M. Herbert, *Colonization and Conquest: The 1980 Archaeological Excavations at Fort Toulouse and Fort Jackson, Alabama* (Montgomery, Ala.: Auburn University), 5, 8, 9; King, *Etowah*, 137.

68. André Pénicaut, *Fleur de Lys and Calumet: Being the Pénicaut Narrative of*

French Adventure in Louisiana, trans. and ed. Richebourg Gaillard McWilliams (Tuscaloosa: University of Alabama Press, 1988), 63–64, 164–165; Lamothe Cadillac to Pontchartrain, Fort Louis, October 26, 1713, in *MPAFD*, trans. and ed. Dunbar Rowland and A. G. Sanders, vols. 1–3 (Jackson: Mississippi Department of Archives and History, 1927–32), 2:162–65.

69. John H. Blitz and Karl G. Lorenz, *The Chattahoochee Chiefdoms* (Tuscaloosa: University of Alabama Press, 2006), 12–22; King, *Etowah*, 4–10; Anderson, *Savannah River Chiefdoms*, 1–10.

70. The Alabama term *imafaakachi* means to be a clan member. Children often asked their parents of which clan they were members: "Nàasok chali amayiksamo?" or "What is my clan?" Sylestine, Hardy, and Montler, *Dictionary of the Alabama Language*, 75, 472; Kimball, *Koasati Dictionary*, 27.

71. Kimball, *Koasati Dictionary*, 10, 50, 274, 275; Martin, *Myths and Folktales*, 3; Hudson, *Southeastern Indians*, 193–94.

72. Kimball, *Koasati Dictionary*, 10, 50, 274, 275; Martin, *Myths and Folktales*, 3; Hudson, *Southeastern Indians*, 193–94.

73. Ernest Sickey's Testimony to the U.S. Claims Court, November 29, 1983, no. 123: 50, Richard Yarborough Collection, Center for American History, University of Texas at Austin; George Peter Murdock, *Social Structures*, (New York: Free Press, 1965), 70, 76; Fred B. Kniffen, Hiram R. Gregory, and George A. Stokes, *The Historic Indian Tribes of Louisiana: From 1542 to the Present* (Baton Rouge: Louisiana State University Press, 1987), 223–26.

74. Waselkov, Wood, and Herbert, *Colonization and Conquest*, 9; Kniffen, Gregory, and Stokes, *Historic Indian Tribes of Louisiana*, 223–26; Hudson, *Southeastern Indians*, 194–98, 236.

75. John Phillip Reid, *A Law of Blood: The Primitive Law of the Cherokee Nation* (New York: New York University Press, 1970), 37.

76. Ibid.; Hudson, *Southeastern Indians*, 193.

Chapter 2

1. John Reed Swanton, *Early History of the Creek Indians and Their Neighbors*, Bureau of American Ethnology Bulletin 73 (Washington, D.C.: U.S. Government Printing Office, 1922), 192.

2. Paul Kelton, "The Great Southeastern Smallpox Epidemic, 1696–1700: The Region's First Major Epidemic?" in *The Transformation of the Southeastern Indians, 1540–1760*, ed. Robbie Ethridge and Charles Hudson (Jackson: University of Mississippi Press, 2002), 21–37. For the mourning wars, see Daniel Richter, *Ordeal of the Longhouse: The Peoples of the Iroquois League in the Era of European Colonization* (Chapel Hill: University of North Carolina Press, 1992).

3. Jean-Batiste Bénard de La Harpe, *Historical Journal of the Settlement of the*

French in Louisiana, ed. Glenn R. Conrad (Lafayette: University of Southwestern Louisiana, 1971), 62–63. For a brief but detailed study on the Apalachee chiefdom, see John F. Scarry, "The Apalachee Chiefdom: A Mississippian Society on the Fringe of the Mississippian World," in *The Forgotten Centuries: Indians and Europeans in the American South, 1521–1704*, ed. Charles Hudson and Carmen Chaves Tesser (Athens: University of Georgia Press, 1994), 327–56.

4. Steven Hahn has argued that these alliances (except the Cherokees) created a unified front in the viewpoint of the English, hence coining these peoples part of the "Creek Nation." For a detailed study of the development of the Creek Nation, see Steven Hahn, *Invention of the Creek Nation, 1670–1763* (Lincoln: University of Nebraska Press, 2004).

5. Alexander S. Salley Jr., *Journal of the Commons House of Assembly of South Carolina for 1703* (Columbia: Historical Commission of South Carolina, 1934), 121 (quote); La Harpe, *Historical Journal*, 62–63, 66–67, 76, 79.

6. La Harpe, *Historical Journal*, 62–63, 66–67, 76, 79; Salley, *Journal of the Commons House of Assembly of South Carolina for 1703*, 79; General Assembly Commons House Journals, September 2, 1703, Green Copy no. 2, 293, 295, Manuscript Collection, South Carolina Department of Archives and History, Columbia.

7. La Harpe, *Historical Journal*, 62–63 (quote), 66–67, 76, 79.

8. Alexander S. Salley Jr., *Journal of the Commons House of Assembly of South Carolina for 1701* (Columbia: Historical Commission of South Carolina, 1925), 4–5.

9. William L. McDowell Jr., ed., *The Colonial Records of South Carolina: Journals of the Commissioners of the Indian Trade, September 20, 1710–August 29, 1718* (Columbia: South Carolina Department of Archives and History, 1955), 72; Kathryn E. Holland Braund, *Deerskins and Duffels: The Creek Indian Trade with Anglo-America, 1685–1815* (Lincoln: University of Nebraska Press, 1993), 29.

10. Richebourg Gaillard McWilliams, ed., *Iberville's Gulf Journals* (Tuscaloosa: University of Alabama Press, 1981), 3–4. For a guide to Iberville's early years, see Nellis M. Crouse, *Le Moyne d'Iberville: Soldier of New France* (Ithaca, N.Y.: Cornell University Press, 1954); and Guy Frégault, *Pierre Le Moyne d'Iberville* (Montreal: Fides, 1968).

11. Patricia Dillon Woods, *French-Indian Relations on the Southern Frontier, 1699–1762* (Ann Arbor, Mich.: University Microfilms International Research Press, 1980), 20–21; Mathé Allain, *"Not Worth a Straw": French Colonial Policy and the Early Years of Louisiana* (Lafayette: Center for Louisiana Studies, University of Southwestern Louisiana, 1988), 52; Jay Higginbotham, *Old Mobile: Fort Louis de la Louisiane, 1702–1711* (Tuscaloosa: University of Alabama Press), 23, 24.

12. La Harpe, *Historical Journal*, 62–66; Swanton, *Early History of the Creek Indians*, 194; Higginbotham, *Old Mobile*, 24, 25, 31–32, 53.

13. Entry, March 14, 1699, in McWilliams, *Iberville's Gulf Journals*, 59.

14. André Pénicaut, *Fleur de Lys and Calumet: Being the Pénicaut Narrative of French Adventure in Louisiana*, trans. and ed. Richebourg Gaillard McWilliams (Tuscaloosa: University of Alabama Press, 1988), 63–64; entry, March 26, 1702, in McWilliams, *Iberville's Gulf Journals*, 173; La Harpe, *Historical Journal*, 59–60.

15. Iberville had smoked peace calumets with many southeastern peoples, and he always believed that it was an agreement of friendship and alliance. Entry, February 17, 1699, in McWilliams, *Iberville's Gulf Journals*, 46.

16. Alan Gallay, *Indian Slave Trade: The Rise of the English Empire in the American South, 1670–1717* (New Haven, Conn.: Yale University Press, 2002), 109–11.

17. Entry, March 26, 1702, in McWilliams, *Iberville's Gulf Journals*, 173; La Harpe, *Historical Journal*, 62–66; Pénicaut, *Fleur de Lys and Calumet*, 63–64.

18. Pénicaut, *Fleur de Lys and Calumet*, 65; Bienville to Pontchartrain, September 6, 1704, in *Mississippi Provincial Archives: French Dominion, 1701–1729 (MPAFD)*, ed. Dunbar Rowland and Albert G. Sanders, vols. 1–3 (Jackson: Mississippi Department of Archives and History, 1929), 3:19–23; Bienville to Pontchartrain, August 20, 1709, in Rowland and Sanders, *MPAFD*, 3:136–37; *Thomas Nairne's Muskhogean Journals: The 1708 Expedition to the Mississippi River*, ed. Alexander Moore (Jackson: University Press of Mississippi, 1988), 76; Bienville to Minister, September 6, 1704, Archives des Colonies, Manuscript Series C13A (AC-C13A), 1:449.

19. Moore, *Thomas Nairne's Muskhogean Journals*, 76; Higginbotham, *Old Mobile*, 87, 123–125.

20. Pénicaut, *Fleur de Lys and Calumet*, 65–66, 124; Bienville to Minister, September 6, 1704, AC-C13A, 1:449.

21. Pénicaut, *Fleur de Lys and Calumet*, 65, 66 (quote), 124; Bienville to Minister, September 6, 1704, AC-C13A, 1:449.

22. Pénicaut, *Fleur de Lys and Calumet*, 68–69 (quote), 123.

23. Ibid.

24. Ibid.; John Phillip Reid, *A Law of Blood: The Primitive Law of the Cherokee Nation* (New York: New York University Press, 1970), 37.

25. Pénicaut, *Fleur de Lys and Calumet*, 65–67; La Harpe, *Historical Journal*, 62–66; interviews of Sissy Abbey, July 14, 1938, and Jeff Abbey, July 8, 1938, in Lyda Averill Taylor Papers (Taylor Papers), Center for American History, University of Texas at Austin; Geoffrey D. Kimball, *Koasati Dictionary* (Lincoln: University of Nebraska Press, 1994), 27, 48, 130; David Lewis Jr. and Ann Jordon, *Creek Indian Medicine Ways: The Enduring Power of Muskoke Religion* (Albuquerque: University of New Mexico Press, 2002), 80.

26. Pénicaut, *Fleur de Lys and Calumet*, 68–69, 123.

27. La Harpe, *Historical Journal*, 66, 68, 73; Pénicaut, *Fleur de Lys and Calumet*, 72–73, 123–25; La Salle to Minister, Fort Louis, May 12, 1709, in *General Correspondence of Louisiana: 1678–1763*, ed. Dunbar Rowland (New Orleans: Polyanthos, 1976), 66; d'Artaguette to Minister, August 6, 1709, AC-C13A, 2:53; La Salle to Minister, May 12, 1709, AC-C13A, 2:395.

28. Pénicaut, *Fleur de Lys and Calumet*, 72–73, 123–125; La Salle to Minister, Fort Louis, May 12, 1709, Rowland, *General Correspondence of Louisiana*, 66; d'Artaguette to Minister, August 6, 1709, AC-C13A, 2:53; La Salle to Minister, May 12, 1709, AC-C13A, 2:395.

29. Robin F. A. Fabel and Robert Rea, "Lieutenant Thomas Campbell's Sojourn among the Creeks, November 1764–May 1765," *Alabama Historical Quarterly* 36, no. 2 (Summer 1974): 97–111; 109 (quote); interviews of Sissy Abbey, July 14, 1938, and Jeff Abbey, July 8, 1938, in Taylor Papers.

30. Bernard Romans, *A Concise Natural History of East and West Florida* (Gainesville: University of Florida Press, 1962), 134, 144, 146, 147, 240, 325; interviews of Sissy Abbey, July 14, 1938, and Jeff Abbey, July 8, 1938, in Taylor Papers; Kimball, *Koasati Dictionary*, 27, 48, 130; Lewis and Jordon, *Creek Indian Medicine Ways*, 80.

31. Pénicaut, *Fleur de Lys and Calumet*, 72–73, 123–25; La Salle to Minister, Fort Louis, May 12, 1709, in Rowland, *General Correspondence of Louisiana*, 66; d'Artaguette to Minister, August 6, 1709, AC-C13A, 2:53; La Salle to Minister, May 12, 1709, AC-C13A, 2:395.

32. Pénicaut, *Fleur de Lys and Calumet*, 126–30; Higginbotham, *Old Mobile*, 383–85.

33. Pénicaut, *Fleur de Lys and Calumet*, 164.

34. McDowell, *Journals of the Commissioners of the Indian Trade*, 4, 10, 11.

35. Ibid., 31.

36. Ibid.

37. Ibid.

38. Ibid., 32.

39. Ibid., 31.

40. For further information on John Wright and the commissioners' struggle to pass another Indian trade act, see Gallay, *Indian Slave Trade: The Rise of the English Empire in the American South*, 245–49; McDowell, *Journals of the Commissioners of the Indian Trade*, 30–32.

41. McDowell, *Journals of the Commissioners of the Indian Trade*, 43, 48, 49 (quote).

42. La Harpe, *Historical Journal*, 91; Pénicaut, *Fleur de Lys and Calumet*, 164; Hahn, *Invention of the Creek Nation*, 82–83; Daniel H. Usner Jr., *Indians, Settlers, and Slaves in a Frontier Exchange Economy: The Lower Mississippi*

Valley before 1783 (Chapel Hill: University of North Carolina Press, 1992), 28; Braund, *Deerskins and Duffels*, 34.

43. La Harpe, *Historical Journal*, 84.

44. Ibid.

45. Pénicaut, *Fleur de Lys and Calumet*, 165.

46. Lamothe Cadillac to Pontchartrain, Fort Louis, October 26, 1713, in Rowland and Sanders, *MPAFD* 2:162–65; Bienville to Pontchartrain, September 1, 1715,in Rowland and Sanders, *MPAFD* 3:188; Pénicaut, *Fleur de Lys and Calumet*, 164–65.

47. Pénicaut, *Fleur de Lys and Calumet*, 165.

48. Thomas J. Pluckhahn, *Kolomoki: Settlement, Ceremony, and Status in the Deep South, 350–750* (Tuscaloosa: University of Alabama Press, 2003), 8–9, 86.

49. La Harpe, *Historical Journal*, 175.

50. Howard N. Martin, *Myths and Folktales of the Alabama-Coushatta Indians of Texas* (Austin, Tex.: Encino Press, 1977), xxvii–xxviii, 2–3; Gregory A. Waselkov, Brian M. Wood, and Joseph M. Herbert, *Colonization and Conquest: The 1980 Archaeological Excavations at Fort Toulouse and Fort Jackson, Alabama* (Montgomery, Ala.: Auburn University), 71–73.

51. Martin, *Myths and Folktales*, xxvii–xxviii, 2–3.

52. Cora Sylestine, Heather Hardy, and Timothy Montler, *Dictionary of the Alabama Language* (Austin: University of Texas Press, 1993), 484; John Reed Swanton, *Myths and Tales of the Southeastern Indians*, Bureau of American Ethnology Bulletin 88 (Washington, D.C.: U.S. Government Printing Office, 1929), 153; Bill Grantham, *Creation Myths and Legends of the Creek Indians* (Gainesville: University Press of Florida, 2002), 21–25.

53. Martin, *Myths and Folktales*, 24–27.

54. Jean-Bernard Bossu, *Jean-Bernard Bossu's Travels in the Interior of North America, 1751–1762*, trans. and ed. Seymour Feiler (Norman: University of Oklahoma Press, 1962), 145.

55. La Harpe, *Historical Journal*, 194 (quote); Waselkov, Wood, and Herbert, *Colonization and Conquest*, 71–73.

56. La Harpe, *Historical Journal*, 194; Waselkov, Wood, and Herbert, *Colonization and Conquest*, 71–73.

57. Beauchamp to Maurepas, January 25, 1741, in *MPAFD*, ed. and trans. Dunbar Rowland, A. G. Sanders, and Patricia Galloway, vols. 4–5 (Baton Rouge: Louisiana State University Press, 1984), 4:172–174; Daniel H. Thomas, *Fort Toulouse: The French Outpost at the Alabamas on the Coosa* (Tuscaloosa: University of Alabama Press, 1989), 30–31. Waselkov, Wood, and Herbert, *Colonization and Conquest*, 93.

58. Deliberations of the Navy Council, Paris, September 1, 1716, in Rowland,

General Correspondence of Louisiana, 72. More studies on the French population at Fort Toulouse are needed, especially in looking at marriages, births, and deaths recorded in parish registers in Mobile. These records are now located in the archives of the Diocese of Mobile.

59. Caleb Swan, "Position and State of Manners in and Arts in the Creek, or Muscogee Nation in 1791," in *Historical and Statistical Information Respected the History, Condition, and Prospects of the Indian Tribes of the United States*, ed. Henry Rowe Schoolcraft (Philadelphia: J. B. Lippincott, 1855), 5:272.

60. Interview of Jeff Abbey, July 25, 1938, in Taylor Papers.

61. La Vente to Pontchartrain, March 2, 1708, in Rowland and Sanders, *MPAFD*, 2:31 (quote); Thomas, *Fort Toulouse*, 40–41. Charles O'Neill, *Church and State in French Colonial Louisiana* (New Haven, Conn.: Yale University Press, 1966), 250.

62. La Vente to Pontchartrain, March 2, 1708, in Rowland and Sanders, *MPAFD*, 2:31; Memorandum of B. Tartarin, Jesuit, 1738[?], in Rowland, *General Correspondence of Louisiana*, 124; Waselkov, Wood, and Herbert, *Colonization and Conquest*, 93; O'Neill, *Church and State*, 74, 87, 107; Guillaume Aubert, "'The Blood of France'": Race and Purity of Blood in the French Atlantic World," *William and Mary Quarterly* 61, no. 3 (2004): 439–78.

63. Benjamin Hawkins, *A Sketch of The Creek Country, in the Years 1798 and 1799* (1848; repr., Savannah: Georgia Historical Society, 1916), 73; James Adair, *The History of the American Indians*, ed. Samuel Cole Williams (1775; repr., New York: Argonaut Press, 1966), 147; interview of Jeff Abbey, July 25, 1938, in Taylor Papers.

64. Sylestine, Hardy, and Montler, *Dictionary of the Alabama Language*, 45; Hawkins, *Sketch of The Creek Country*, 73; Adair, *History of the American Indians*, 147.

65. Records that recognized intermarriage with the French are too vague or incomplete to determine their tribal affiliation. Quite often, Native women were listed as "slave" or "Indienne." For further details of possible intermarriages, see the following records: Etienne Teysseir to Magdelaine René de Mandevillle, September 18, 1725; Pierre Paquet to Magdelaine Baudrau, August 26, 1726; Philippe Fonteneau dit St. Philippe to Marie Brignac, May 24, 1747; and baptism of Charles Aigron, December 3, 1736, all in Jacqueline Olivier Vidrine, ed., *Love's Legacy: The Mobile Marriages Recorded in French, Transcribed with Annotated Abstracts in English, 1724–1786* (Lafayette: University of Southwestern Louisiana, 1985), 20, 21, 52, 53, 126, 127, 264, 265.

66. Marriage announcement of Mathias Berthelot to Margueritte Panyoüäsas, June 16, 1738, in Vidrine, *Love's Legacy*, 164–65; Perier and De La Chaise to the Directors of the Company of the Indies, New Orleans, March 25, 1729, in Rowland and Sanders, *MPAFD*, 2:636–37.

67. Adair, *History of the American Indians*, 6; Jean Chaudhuri and Joyotpaul

Chaudhuri, *A Sacred Path: The Way of the Muscogee Creeks* (Los Angeles: University of California, Los Angeles, American Indian Studies Center, 2001), 75–77; Marvin T. Smith, *Archaeology of Aboriginal Culture Change in the Southeast* (Athens: University of Georgia Press, 1987), 89, 93–98; Waselkov, Wood, and Herbert, *Colonization and Conquest*, 5, 8, 9.

68. Mr. Thomas Jones to Harman Verelest, February 23, 1738, in Allen D. Candler, Kenneth Coleman, and Milton Ready, eds. *The Colonial Records of the State of Georgia* (*CRGA*), 28 vols. (Atlanta: C. P. Byrd, 1904–16; repr., Athens: University of Georgia Press, 1974–76), 22:88; Jones to Verelest, October 6, 1740, in ibid., 22:428.

69. Large households often included orphans or former prisoners of war, mainly women, who had been adopted into the matrilineage. Women's separation from men even applied during menstruation; they retreated to the woods and stayed in a menstruation hut, similar to those of the Mississippian culture. During the menstruation period they built a fire, cooked meals (making sure to avoid eating salt), and remained isolated until their cycle finished. Ernest Sickey's Testimony to the U.S. Claims Court, November 29, 1983, no. 123: 50, Richard Yarborough Collection, Center for American History, University of Texas at Austin; interview of Sissy Abbey, July 9, 1938, in Taylor Papers; Patricia Galloway, "Where Have All the Menstrual Huts Gone? The Invisibility of Menstrual Seclusion in the Late Prehistoric Southeast," in *Women In Prehistory: North America and Mesoamerica*, ed. Cheryl Claassen and Rosemary A. Joyce (Philadelphia: University of Pennsylvania Press, 1997): 47–62; George Peter Murdock, *Social Structures* (New York: Free Press, 1965), 70, 76; Swan, "Position and State of Manners," 262, 272; Charles Hudson, *The Southeastern Indians* (Knoxville: University of Tennessee Press, 1976), 260; Fred B. Kniffen, Hiram R. Gregory, and George A. Stokes, *The Historic Indian Tribes of Louisiana: From 1542 to the Present* (Baton Rouge: Louisiana State University Press, 1987), 223–26; Robbie Ethridge, *Creek Country: The Creek Indians and Their World* (Chapel Hill: University of North Carolina Press, 2003), 74.

70. She also had complete control over her reproductive rights, and, though rare, could abort or kill her newborn; Caleb Swan recorded that a discontented woman practiced infanticide as an act of revenge against her husband. Unhappy marriages at times led to adultery, however, and many southeastern communities punished adulteresses by cropping their hair or allowing the husband to beat his wife and cut off her ears. Alabama and Coushatta oral tradition supports this practice, but Benjamin Hawkins, who lived among the Alabamas and their neighbors in the late eighteenth century, reported that the Alabama towns did not abide by this law. Interview with Sissy Abbey, July 9, 1938, in Taylor Papers; Benjamin Hawkins, *The Letters, Journals, and Writings of Benjamin Hawkins*, ed. C. L. Grant, 2 vols. (Savannah, Ga.: Beehive Press, 1980), 1:296, 321; Hawkins, *Sketch of The Creek Country*, 73–74; Swan, "Posi-

tion and State of Manners," 272, 278; Gregory Waselkov and Kathryn E. Holland Braund, eds., *William Bartram on the Southeastern Indians* (Lincoln: University of Nebraska Press, 1995), 58.

71. According to Alabama and Coushatta oral tradition, when ready to have a child, a woman escaped to the woods alone. Using little medicine, she squatted to her heels and delivered the child. She bit or cut the umbilical cord, then wrapped her child and went home. A Coushatta remedy to ease childbirth was a medicinal concoction made by boiling basswood bark (*batahkô*) in water; women drank it until the child was born. Another medicine used to remove the afterbirth was made from boiling four roots of cocklebur. Alabama and Coushatta women buried the umbilical cord after waiting four days, which they believed protected the newborn from sickness and fear. Newborns were considered the reincarnation of their mothers' ancestors, so they needed no other charms or amulets for protection. Kimball, *Koasati Dictionary*, 43, 78; interview of Sissy Abbey, July 9, 1938, in Taylor Papers; Kniffen, Gregory, and Stokes, *Historic Indian Tribes of Louisiana*, 224, 225.

72. Children were given a name once they reached four years of age (symbolic of the four cardinal directions). Interview of Sissy Abbey, July 9, 1938, in Taylor Papers; Sylestine, Hardy, and Montler, *Dictionary of the Alabama Language*, 53.

73. Kimball, *Koasati Dictionary*, 43, 78; interview of Sissy Abbey, July 9, 1938, in Taylor Papers; Kniffen, Gregory, and Stokes, *Historic Indian Tribes of Louisiana*, 224, 225; John Reed Swanton, *Social Organization and Social Usages of the Indians of the Creek Confederacy*, Bureau of American Ethnology Bulletin 42 (1928; repr., New York: Johnson Reprint Co., 1970), 79, 80, 337, 377; Hudson, *Southeastern Indians*, 186; Elman R. Service, *Primitive Social Organization* (New York: Random House, 1962), 106.

74. Edward J. Cashin, *Lachlan McGillivray, Indian Trader: The Shaping of the Southern Colonial Frontier* (Athens: University of Georgia Press, 1992), 71–72; Mary Ann Oglesby Neely, "Lachlan McGillivray: A Scot on the Alabama Frontier," *Alabama Historical Quarterly* 36, no. 1 (Spring 1974): 5–14.

75. "Archaeological Excavation of Alabama Burial Mound, East Texas" (1983), Richard Yarborough Collection, Center for American History, University of Texas at Austin; Bienville and Salmon to Minister, New Orleans, April 12, 1735, and September 4, 1735, in Rowland, *General Correspondence of Louisiana*, 120; interviews of Jeff Abbey, July 15, 1938, and Sissy Abbey, July 9, 1938, in Taylor Papers.

76. William L. McDowell Jr., ed., *The Colonial Records of South Carolina: Documents Relating to Indian Affairs, 1750–1765*, 2 vols. (Columbia: South Carolina Department of Archives and History, 1958, 1970), 1:312, 2:104; Joshua Piker, *Okfuskee: A Creek Indian Town in Colonial America* (Cambridge, Mass.: Harvard University Press, 2004), 124.

77. Journal of John Stuart, February 24, 1772, in *Documents of the American Revolution 1770–1783*, ed. Kenneth G. Davies, 20 vols. (Dublin: Irish University Press, 1972–79), 5:256–58.

78. Savannah Council, July 14, 1763, in Candler, Coleman, and Ready, *CRGA*, 9:70–71.

79. Ibid.

80. Diron d'Artaguette to Maurepas, October 24, 1737, in Rowland, Sanders, and Galloway, *MPAFD*, 4:146.

81. Ibid.

82. Vaudreuil to Rouillé, June 24, 1750, in Rowland, Sanders, and Galloway, *MPAFD*, 5:45.

83. Kimball, *Koasati Dictionary*, 31, 107, 264; Sylestine, Hardy, and Montler, *Dictionary of the Alabama Language*, 66, 528.

84. Kimball, *Koasati Dictionary*, 60, 122, 231–32; Sylestine, Hardy, and Montler, *Dictionary of the Alabama Language*, 523, 626.

85. Kimball, *Koasati Dictionary*, 41, 44, 235; Sylestine, Hardy, and Montler, *Dictionary of the Alabama Language*, 79, 88, 89, 408, 411.

86. Col. William Stephens's Journal, September 28, 1741, in Candler, Coleman, and Ready, *CRGA*, 5:511; Mr. Jno. Dobell to the Trustees, October 29, 1745, in ibid., 24:433.

87. Gallay, *Indian Slave Trade*, 341.

88. Mr. Jno. Dobell to the Trustees, October 29, 1745, in Candler, Coleman, and Ready, *CRGA*, 24:432–33.

89. Meeting of the Common Council of the Trustees of Georgia, May 23, 1745, in ibid., 2:457; Perrier to the Minister, January 19, 1732, AC-C13A, 14:43; Perrier to the Minister, May 14, 1732, AC-C13A, 14:64; Crémont to the Minister, May 15, 1732, AC-13A, 14:112; Beauchamp to Maurepas, November 5, 1731, AC, C13-A, 13:199; Waselkov, Wood, and Herbert, *Colonization and Conquest*, 41–50.

90. Bienville to the Minister, April 14, 1735, AC-C13A, 20:33; Bienville to Maurepas, February 10, 1736, in Rowland and Sanders, *MPAFD*, 1:290.

91. According to Vaudreuil, the Tallapoosas had allowed the British to build the fort only because they feared a war with the Choctaws, the French, and the Spanish. Vaudreuil to Maurepas, February 12, 1744, in Rowland, Sanders, and Galloway, *MPAFD*, 4:214–24. Waselkov, Wood, and Herbert, *Colonization and Conquest*, 45–46.

92. Col. William Stephens's Journal, July 11, 1739, in Candler, Coleman, and Ready, *CRGA*, 4:421.

93. Col. William Stephens's Journal, September 28, 1741, in ibid., 5:511; Mr. Jno. Dobell to the Trustees, October 29, 1745, in ibid., 24:433.

94. Mr. Jno. Dobell to the Trustees, October 29, 1745, in ibid., 24:433.

95. Gov. James Glen to President and Assistants of Georgia, October 1750, in ibid., 26:64.

96. Mr. Jno. Dobell to the Trustees, October 29, 1745, in ibid., 24:432–33.

97. Gov. James Glen to President and Assistants of Georgia, October 1750, in ibid., 26:64–65.

98. Pénicaut, *Fleur de Lys and Calumet*, 209.

99. Bienville on the Indians, May 15, 1733, in Rowland and Sanders, *MPAFD*, 1:193.

100. Pénicaut, *Fleur de Lys and Calumet*, 246.

101. Vaudreuil to Rouillé, June 24, 1750, in Rowland, Sanders, and Galloway, *MPAFD*, 5:47.

102. Diron d'Artaguette to Maurepas, September 1, 1734, in Rowland and Sanders, *MPAFD* 1:253; La Harpe, *Historical Journal*, 194. For more details regarding the French plans at Fort Toulouse, see the following: Duclos to Pontchartrain, Dauphine Island, June 7, 1716, in Rowland and Sanders, *MPAFD*, 3:203–5; Hubert to the Council, October 26, 1717, in Rowland and Sanders, *MPAFD* 2:250; De l'Epinay and Hubert to Minister, May 30, 1717, in Rowland, *General Correspondence of Louisiana*, 76; Guénot and Massi to Lépinay, October 8, 1717, AC-C13A, 5:119; Pénicaut, *Fleur de Lys and Calumet*, 165; De Lamothe to Cadillac, Fort Louis, September 21, 1714, in Rowland, *General Correspondence of Louisiana*, 70; Thomas, *Fort Toulouse*, 11; Waselkov, Wood, and Herbert, *Colonization and Conquest*, 47.

103. La Harpe, *Historical Journal*, 193.

104. Ibid., 156.

105. Vaudreuil and Salmon to Maurepas, July 21, 1743, in Rowland, Sanders, and Galloway, *MPAFD*, 4:207–10; 208–9 (quote).

106. La Harpe, *Historical Journal*, 216.

107. Babe Descloseaux to the Minister, October 25, 1748, AC-C13A, 32:222.

108. Ibid.

109. Château Memoirs, January 13, 1723, AC-C13A, 6:402; Le Conceal, February 4, 1723, AC-C13A, 6:404; Perrier and Salmon to the Minister, November 25 and December 5, 1731, AC-C13A, 14:172; Bienville and Salmon to the Minister, April 5, 1734, AC-C13A, 18:62–68; Vaudreuil to Maurepas, February 12, 1744, in Rowland, Sanders, and Galloway, *MPAFD*, 4:222–23; Vaudreuil to Roiled, September 22, 1749, in Rowland, Sanders, and Galloway, *MPAFD*, 5:36.

110. Vaudreuil and Salmon to Maurepas, July 21, 1743, in Rowland, Sanders, and Galloway, *MPAFD*, 4:207–10; 209 (quote); Bienville to Maurepas, 14 April 1735, in Rowland and Sanders, *MPAFD*, 1:258.

111. Edmund Atkin to William Pitt, March 27, 1760, British Public Record Office, Colonial Office, Class 5 Files: the French and Indian War, 64:222.

112. Bienville to Maurepas, April 23, 1735, in Rowland and Sanders, *MPAFD*, 1:260–62; 261 (quote).

113. Bienville to Maurepas, April 30, 1735, in Rowland and Sanders, *MPAFD*, 1:263–64; 263 (quote).

114. Vaudreuil and Salmon to Maurepas, July 21, 1743, in Rowland and Sanders, *MPAFD*, 4:208–9.

Chapter 3

1. Howard N. Martin, *Myths and Folktales of the Alabama-Coushatta Indians of Texas* (Austin, Tex.: Encino Press, 1977), 8.

2. Diron d'Artaguette to Maurepas, October 24, 1737, in *Mississippi Provincial Archives: French Dominion (MPAFD)*, trans. and ed. Dunbar Rowland, A. G. Sanders, and Patricia Galloway, vols. 4–5 (Baton Rouge: Louisiana State University Press, 1984), 4:149.

3. Diron d'Artaguette to Maurepas, October 24, 1737, in Rowland, Sanders, and Galloway, *MPAFD*, 4:142–54; Gregory Waselkov, "Indian Maps of the Colonial Southeast," in *Powhatan's Mantle: Indians in the Colonial Southeast*, ed. Peter H. Wood, Gregory Waselkov, and M. Thomas Hatley (Lincoln: University of Nebraska Press, 1989), 292–343.

4. Diron d'Artaguette to Maurepas, October 24, 1737, in Rowland, Sanders, and Galloway, *MPAFD*, 4:142–44 (quote); Allan Gallay, *Indian Slave Trade: The Rise of the English Empire in the American South, 1670–1717* (New Haven, Conn.: Yale University Press, 2002), 142–43.

5. King's Paper, May 29, 1738, in *MPAFD*, trans. and ed. Dunbar Rowland and A. G. Sanders, vols. 1–3 (Jackson: Mississippi Department of Archives and History, 1927–32), 1:369.

6. Bienville to Maurepas, April 14, 1735, in Rowland and Sanders, *MPAFD*, 1:256; Noyan to Maurepas, November 8, 1734, in Rowland, Sanders, and Galloway, *MPAFD*, 4:139.

7. Louboey to Maurepas, October 12, 1739, in Rowland and Sanders, *MPAFD*, 1:405; Bienville to Maurepas, April 14, 1735, in Rowland and Sanders, *MPAFD*, 1:254–60; Bienville to Maurepas, April 23, 1735, in Rowland and Sanders, *MPAFD*, 1:260–61.

8. Diron d'Artaguette to Maurepas, October 24, 1737, in Rowland, Sanders, and Galloway, *MPAFD*, 4:142–52; Crémont to Maurepas, February 21, 1737, in Rowland, Sanders, and Galloway, *MPAFD*, 4:140–42; Diron d'Artaguette to Maurepas, May 8, 1737, in Rowland and Sanders, *MPAFD*, 1:340–41; Bienville to Minister, New Orleans, August 25, 1735, in *General Correspondence of Louisiana: 1678–1763*, ed. Dunbar Rowland (New Orleans: Polyanthos, 1976), 120.

9. Diron d'Artaguette to Maurepas, October 24, 1737, in Rowland, Sanders, and Galloway, *MPAFD*, 4:142–52, 147 (quote); Crémont to Maurepas, February 21, 1737, in Rowland, Sanders, and Galloway, *MPAFD*, 4:140–42; Diron d'Artaguette to Maurepas, May 8, 1737, in Rowland and Sanders, *MPAFD*, 1:340–41; Bienville to Minister, New Orleans, August 25, 1735, in Rowland, *General Correspondence of Louisiana*, 120.

10. Diron d'Artaguette to Maurepas, October 24, 1737, in Rowland, Sanders, and Galloway, *MPAFD*, 4:147 ("What" quote) and 149 ("Would hope" quote).

11. Ibid., 4:151.

12. Ibid., 4:148–49.

13. Ibid., 4:151.

14. Ibid., 4:147.

15. Ibid.

16. Crémont to Maurepas, February 21, 1737, *MPAFD*, in Rowland, Sanders, and Galloway, 4:140–42; Diron d'Artaguette to Maurepas, May 8, 1737, *MPAFD*, in Rowland and Sanders, 1:340–41; Bienville to Minister, New Orleans, August 25, 1735, in Rowland, *General Correspondence of Louisiana*, 120.

17. Kathryn E. Holland Braund, *Deerskins and Duffels: The Creek Indian Trade with Anglo-America, 1685–1815* (Lincoln: University of Nebraska Press, 1993), 4–5; Vernon James Knight Jr., "The Formation of the Creeks," in *The Forgotten Centuries: Indians and Europeans in the American South, 1521–1704*, ed. Charles Hudson and Carmen Chavez Teaser (Athens: University of Georgia Press, 1994), 373–91; Gallay, *Indian Slave Trade: The Rise of the English Empire in the American South, 1670–1717*, 133–34.

18. Gregory Waselkov and Kathryn E. Holland Braund, eds., *William Bartram on the Southeastern Indians* (Lincoln: University of Nebraska Press, 1995), 108, 146, 155, 156; Braund, *Deerskins and Duffels*, 6–7, 139–41; Jean Chaudhuri and Joyotpaul Chaudhuri, *A Sacred Path: The Way of the Muscogee Creeks* (Los Angeles: University of California, Los Angeles, American Indian Studies Center, 2001), 70–73.

19. Southeastern peoples including the Creeks, Cherokees, Choctaws, Chickasaws, and Seminoles also practiced the Green Corn Ceremony. Chaudhuri and Chaudhuri, *Sacred Path*, 52–53; Marvin T. Smith, *Coosa: The Rise and Fall of a Southeastern Mississippian Chiefdom* (Gainesville: University Press of Florida, 2000), 64–66; Marvin T. Smith, *Archaeology of Aboriginal Culture Change in the Southeast* (Athens: University of Georgia Press, 1988), 59, 89, 93–98; Michael D. Green, *The Politics of Indian Removal: Creek Government and Society in Crisis* (Lincoln: University of Nebraska Press, 1982), 13–16; Braund, *Deerskins and Duffels*, 140–41.

20. James Crawford, *The Mobilian Trade Language* (Knoxville: University of Tennessee Press, 1978), 34, 54, 100.

21. Vaudreuil and Salmon to Maurepas, July 21, 1743, in Rowland, Sanders, and Galloway, *MPAFD*, 4:210.

22. Jean-Bernard Bossu, *Jean-Bernard Bossu's Travels in the Interior of North America, 1751–1762*, trans. and ed. Seymour Feiler (Norman: University of Oklahoma Press, 1962), 154.

23. Steven Hahn, *Invention of the Creek Nation, 1670–1763* (Lincoln: University of Nebraska Press, 2004), 67.

24. Bienville to Maurepas, April 30, 1735, in Rowland and Sanders, *MPAFD*, 1:263–64.

25. Vaudreuil to Maurepas, March 15, 1747, in Rowland, Sanders, and Galloway, *MPAFD*, 4:306.

26. Mr. Jno. Dobell to the Trustees, October 29, 1745, in Allen D. Candler, Kenneth Coleman, and Milton Ready, eds. *The Colonial Records of the State of Georgia (CRGA)*, 28 vols. (Atlanta: C. P. Byrd, 1904–16; repr., Athens: University of Georgia Press, 1974–76), 24:432.

27. Ibid., 24:433.

28. Gregory A. Waselkov, Brian M. Wood, and Joseph M. Herbert, *Colonization and Conquest: The 1980 Archaeological Excavations at Fort Toulouse and Fort Jackson, Alabama* (Montgomery, Ala.: Auburn University), 56.

29. A British source from 1761 credits 320 hunters to the six villages: 35 in Okchai, 20 in Little Okchai, 70 in Wetumpka (or Tompowa), 30 in Pakana, 40 in Taskigi, and 125 in Soosawtee (in all probability the village of Coosada, which was at times also listed as Coushettee). In 1764, the British listed a total of 440 Alabama and Coushatta warriors. Creek Villages and their Population, January 24, 1764, in *Mississippi Provincial Archives: English Dominion, 1763–1766 (MPAED)*, ed. Dunbar Rowland (Nashville, Tenn.: Brandon Printing Company, 1911), 94; Edmond Atkin, *The Edmond Atkin Report and Plan of 1755*, ed. Wilbur Jacobs (Lincoln: University of Nebraska Press, 1967), 62; Daniel H. Thomas, *Fort Toulouse: The French Outpost at the Alabamas on the Coosa* (Tuscaloosa: University of Alabama Press, 1989), 12, 13, 51.

30. Edmond Atkin, *Edmond Atkin Report*, 62.

31. Treaty of Friendship and Commerce with the Alabama Indians, March 27, 1760, British Public Records, Colonial Office, Class 5 (PRO, CO5), fols. 221–22.

32. Edmund Atkin to British Licensed Traders, September 7, 1759, PRO, CO5, vol. 64, fols. 216–18.

33. Edmund Atkin to British Licensed Traders, September 7, 1759, PRO, CO5, vol. 64, fol. 216.

34. Edmond Atkin to British Licensed Traders (or their substitutes at their stores) in the Upper Creek Country, September 7, 1759, PRO, CO5, 64:216–18; Edmund Atkin to William Pitt, March 27, 1760, PRO, CO5, 64:245–54; James Adair, *The History of the American Indians*, ed. Samuel Cole Williams (1775; repr., New York: Argonaut Press, 1966), 270.

35. Treaty of Friendship and Commerce with the Alabama Indians, March 27, 1760, PRO, CO5, vol. 64, fols. 221–23 (quotes).

36. Ibid., 64:225.

37. It is presumed that Opoyheatly, at this point an elderly man, died shortly after he signed the treaty. Ibid., 64:223–25, 227.

38. Edmond Atkin to British Licensed Traders (or their substitutes at their stores) in the Upper Creek Country, September 7, 1759, PRO, CO5, vol. 64, fols.

216–18; Edmund Atkin to William Pitt, March 27, 1760, PRO, CO5, vol. 64, fols. 245–54; Adair, *History of the American Indians*, 268–72.

39. Louboey to Maurepas, January 4, 1740, in Rowland and Sanders, *MPAFD*, 1:415.

40. Vaudreuil and Salmon to Maurepas, July 21, 1743, in Rowland, Sanders, and Galloway, *MPAFD*, 4:209.

41. Kerlérec to Berryer, August 4, 1760, in Rowland, Sanders, and Galloway, *MPAFD*, 5:258–61; Kerlérec to Berryer, June 12, 1760, in Rowland, Sanders, and Galloway, *MPAFD*, 5:251–53; Adair, *History of the American Indians*, 201–3; Tom Hatley, *The Dividing Paths: Cherokees and South Carolinians Through the Era of the Revolution* (New York: Oxford University Press, 1992), 156–61.

42. Kerlérec to Berryer, June 12, 1760, in Rowland, Sanders, and Galloway, *MPAFD*, 5:252.

43. Kerlérec to Berryer, July 12, 1761, in Rowland, Sanders, and Galloway, *MPAFD*, 5:273–74.

44. Governor's Council at Savannah, July 3, 1761, in Candler, Coleman, and Ready, *CRGA*, 8:524.

45. Governor's Council at Savannah, January 4, 1763, in ibid., 9:16–17.

46. Lawrence Kinnaird, ed., "Spain in the Mississippi Valley, 1765–1794," in *Annual Report of the American Historical Association* (Washington, D.C.: U.S. Government Printing Office, 1946–49), 1:xv; Daniel Usner, *Indians, Settlers, and Slaves in a Frontier Exchange Economy: The Lower Mississippi Valley before 1783* (Chapel Hill: University of North Carolina Press, 1992), 105.

47. Governor's Council at Savannah, January 4, 1763, in Candler, Coleman, and Ready, *CRGA*, 9:12–14.

48. Minutes of Council with Choctaws, November 14, 1763, in Rowland, Sanders, and Galloway, *MPAFD*, 5:294–301, 296–97 (quote).

49. Ibid.

50. Minutes of the Congress at Pensacola, May 26, 1765, in Rowland, *MPAED*, 194–95.

51. Entry, July 14, 1764, in Carl Brasseaux, trans. and ed., *A Comparative View of French Louisiana, 1699 and 1762: The Journals of Pierre Le Moyne d'Iberville and Jean-Jaques-Blaise d'Abbadie (D'Abbadie's Journal)* (Lafayette: Center for Louisiana Studies, 1979), 123 (quotes); Minutes of the Congress at Pensacola, May 26, 1765, in Rowland, *MPAED*, 1:194–95.

52. Governor's Council at Savannah, July 14, 1763, in Candler, Coleman, and Ready, *CRGA*, 9:72–73.

53. Ibid., 9:73.

54. Ibid., 9:72–73.

55. Governor's Council at Savannah, October 10, 1759, in ibid., 8:167.

56. Entry, March 14, 1764, in Brasseaux, *D'Abbadie's Journal*, 111–12; Major Farmar to James Germany, January 10, 1764, in Rowland, *MPAED*, 18.

57. Robin F. A. Fabel and Robert Rea, "Lieutenant Thomas Campbell's Sojourn among the Creeks, November 1764–May 1765," *Alabama Historical Quarterly* 36, no. 2 (Summer 1974): 97–111.

58. Speeches at the Congress of Pensacola, May 28, 1765, in Rowland, *MPAED*, 199.

59. Ibid. (quote); Speeches at the Congress of Pensacola, May 27, 1765, in Rowland, *MPAED*, 190–93.

60. Speeches at the Congress of Pensacola, May 29, 1765, in Rowland, *MPAED*, 204.

61. Sometime in late 1773, after a congress held in Augusta in June that year, The Mortar died. Ibid.

62. Topoye to John Stuart, June 23, 1766, PRO, CO5, vol. 64, fols. 475–77.

63. Alabama and Coushatta society, like most in the Southeast, equated the father's role as one who delivers kindness and generosity without any obligations to reciprocate. Stuart, however, misread the gesture, assuming that they would behave like good "red children" and obey the British. John Stuart to Topoye, June 23, 1766, PRO, CO5, vol. 64, fols. 479–82, 477 (quote); Patricia Galloway, "'The Chief Who is Your Father': Choctaw and French Views of the Diplomatic Relation," in Wood, Waselkov, and Hatley, *Powhatan's Mantle*, 264–65.

64. Topoye to John Stuart, June 23, 1766, PRO, CO5, vol. 64, fols. 475–77, 477 (quote).

65. John Fitzpatrick, *The Merchant of Manchac: The Letterbooks of John Fitzpatrick, 1768–1790*, ed. Margaret Fisher Dalrymple (Baton Rouge: Louisiana State University Press, 1978), 198; Entry, April 6, 1784, in Brasseaux, *D'Abbadie's Journal*, 114.

66. Archibald Robertson, *Archibald Robertson: His Diaries and Sketches in America, 1762–1780*, ed. Harry M. Lydenberg (New York: New York Public Library, 1971), 12–15; Robin F. A. Fabel, *Colonial Challenges: Britons, Native Americans, and Caribs, 1759–1775* (Gainesville: University Press of Florida, 2000), 18–20, 39, 43.

67. George Gauld, "A Survey of the Coast of West Florida from Pensacola to Cape Blaise," Special Collections, University of West Florida, Pensacola; John D. Ware, *George Gauld: Surveyor and Cartographer of the Gulf Coast* (Gainesville: University Press of Florida, 1982), 62 (quote).

68. John Thomas to John Stuart, December 1771, in *Documents of the American Revolution, 1770–1783*, ed. Kenneth G. Davies, 20 vols. (Dublin: Irish University Press, 1972–79), 3:267; Fitzpatrick, *Merchant of Manchac*, 198; John Sibley, "Historical Sketches of Several Indian Tribes in Louisiana South of the Arkansas River, and Between the Mississippi and the River Grand, 5 April 1805," *American State Papers: Indian Affairs, Class II, 1789–1814* (Washington, D.C.: Gales and Seaten, 1832), 1:724.

69. Oliver to Carondelet, June 11, 1793, in Kinnaird, "Spain in the Mississippi Valley," 3:168; Villebeuvre to Gayoso, August 30, 1793, in "Papers from the Spanish Archives Relating to Tennessee and the Old Southwest, 1783–1800," ed. D. C. Corbitt, *East Tennessee Historical Society Publications* 35 (1963): 85–86.

70. Benjamin Hawkins, *A Sketch of The Creek Country, in the Years 1798 and 1799* (1848; repr., Savannah: Georgia Historical Society, 1916), 35; Sibley, "Historical Sketches," 1:724; Dan Flores, "The Red River Branch of the Alabama-Coushatta Indians: An Ethnohistory," *Southern Studies* 16 (Spring 1977): 58.

71. Reginald Horsman, "The Indian Policy of an 'Empire of Liberty,'" in *Native Americans and the Early Republic*, ed. Frederick Hoxie, Ronald Hoffman, and Peter Albert (Charlottesville: University Press of Virginia, 1999), 37; Reginald Horsman, *Expansion and American Indian Policy, 1783–1812* (East Lansing: Michigan State University Press, 1967).

72. Merritt B. Pound, *Benjamin Hawkins, Indian Agent* (Athens: University of Georgia Press, 1951), 224–25.

73. Treaty with the Creeks: Articles of Agreement and Capitulation, August 9, 1814, Richard Yarborough Collection, Center for American History, University of Texas at Austin. For further details, see Calvin Martin, *Sacred Revolt: The Muskogees' Struggle for a New World* (Boston: Beacon Press, 1991); Frank L. Owsley Jr., *Struggle for the Gulf Borderlands: The Creek War and the Battle of New Orleans, 1812–1815* (Gainesville: University Press of Florida, 1981); and Gregory Dowd, *A Spirited Resistance: The Native American Struggle for Unity, 1745–1815* (Baltimore: Johns Hopkins University, 1992).

74. Sibley, "Historical Sketches," 1:724.

Chapter 4

1. Howard N. Martin, "The Origin of Corn and Tobacco," in *Myths and Folktales of the Alabama-Coushatta Indians of Texas* (Austin, Tex.: Encino Press, 1977), 5–6.

2. John Sibley, "Historical Sketches of Several Indian Tribes in Louisiana South of the Arkansas River, and Between the Mississippi and the River Grande, 5 April 1805," in *American State Papers: Indian Affairs, Class II, 1789–1814* (Washington, D.C.: Gales and Seton, 1832), 1:724.

3. Bernard Romans, *A Concise Natural History of East and West Florida* (1775; repr., Gainesville: University of Florida Press, 1962), 145; Benjamin Hawkins, *A Sketch of The Creek Country, in the Years 1798–1799* (1848; repr., Spartanburg, S.C.: The Reprint Company, 1982), 35–36.

4. Such year-round primary responsibilities required women to learn to cooperate with each other. Women passed down to their daughters and female kin craft skills such as basket weaving. Women drew strength and sup-

port from one another; younger women looked to their elder clanswomen for both instruction and praise. Bonds between Alabama and Coushatta women in this matrilocal society gave them autonomy and a knowledge of their own abilities without needing the approval of men.

5. Interview of Sissy Abbey, July 7–9, 1938, in Lyda Averill Taylor Papers (Taylor Papers), Center for American History, University of Texas at Austin; Geoffrey D. Kimball, *Koasati Dictionary* (Lincoln: University of Nebraska Press, 1994), 4, 5.

6. David H. Jurney and Timothy K Pertula, "Nineteenth Century Alibamu-Koasati Pottery Assemblages and Culinary Traditions" (paper presented at the 1995 Meeting of the Louisiana Archaeological Society, Natchitoches, Louisiana). For further details, see David H. Jurney and Timothy K. Perttula, "Nineteenth-Century Alibamu-Koasati Pottery Assemblages and Culinary Traditions," *Southeastern Archaeology* 14 (Summer 1995): 17–30; and Timothy Perttula, "Material Culture of the Koasati Indians of Texas," *Historical Archaeology* 28 (1994): 65–77.

7. Annie Heloise Abel, ed., *A Report From Natchitoches in 1807 by Dr. John Sibley* (New York: New York Museum of the American Indian, Heye Foundation, 1922), 25, 97n18.

8. Sibley, "Historical Sketches," 1:730.

9. Women cut the meat into thin slabs and pounded it flat and added vegetable salt made out of moss found at the bottom of riverbeds. To make their task easier, they used what the Coushattas called a meat drying tool, *a:nipü stittaksolühka* (sometimes made from bear grass leaves), to thread the meat and hang it from the rack. The women then dried it over a fire, making jerky that stayed fresh for four to six months. Kimball, *Koasati Dictionary*, 16; Romans, *Concise Natural History*, 93–94; Charles Hudson, *The Southeastern Indians* (Knoxville: University of Tennessee Press, 1976), 257, 300.

10. Women first soaked the hides in water for many hours, often overnight. After the skins were completely saturated, they placed a large, thick log (approximately two and a half feet in diameter) into the ground at an angle. Women then placed a wet skin over the log and began scraping it with a knife to remove the hair. The smooth skins were soaked in water containing deer brains, then removed and stretched. They repeated this process until the skins were pliable. Women made holes and threaded the sides of the skins and tied the two ends to two sticks placed into the ground. As the skins stretched, women rubbed each side with a stick. To make clothing, Alabama and Coushatta women used a sharp stick as an awl and thread made of twisted weeds to sew the skins. Romans, *Concise Natural History*, 146; interview of Sissy Abbey, July 7–9, 1938, in Taylor Papers; Cora Sylestine, Heather Hardy, and Timothy Montler, *Dictionary of the Alabama Language* (Austin: University of Texas Press, 1993), 535.

11. Sibley, "Historical Sketches," 1:724.

12. David La Vere, *The Caddo Chiefdoms: Caddo Economies and Politics, 700–1835* (Lincoln: University of Nebraska Press, 1998), 109, 139.

13. Robin Cohen, *Global Diasporas: An Introduction* (Seattle: University of Washington Press, 1997), ix.

14. Thomas Jefferson to Congress Recommending A Western Exploring Expedition, January 18, 1803, in *The Essential Thomas Jefferson*, ed. John Gabriel Hunt (New York: Gramercy Books, 1994), 207–8; Thomas Jefferson to Congress: Third Annual Message, October 17, 1803, in Hunt, *The Essential Thomas Jefferson*, 215; Joyce Purser, "The Administration of Indian Affairs in Louisiana, 1803–1820," *Louisiana History* 5 (Fall 1964): 401–19.

15. James Madison to William C. C. Claiborne, July 10, 1801, and Claiborne to Madison, November 18, 1803, in *Official Letter Books of W. C. C. Claiborne, 1801–1806*, ed. Dunbar Rowland, 6 vols. (Jackson: Mississippi Department of Archives and History, 1917), 1:1, 284–85; War Department to John Sibley, October 17, 1805, in Abel, *Report from Natchitoches*, 90n13. Purser, "Administration of Indian Affairs in Louisiana," 401–2.

16. Dan Flores, ed., *Jefferson and Southwestern Exploration: The Freeman and Custis Accounts of the Red River Expedition of 1806* (*Freeman and Curtis Accounts*) (Norman: University of Oklahoma Press, 1984), 24–29; John Francis Bannon, ed., *Bolton and the Spanish Borderlands* (Norman: University of Oklahoma Press, 1964), 53.

17. Manuel Salcedo to Pedro Cevallos, New Orleans, August 20, 1804, in *Before Lewis and Clark: Documents Illustrating the History of the Missouri, 1785–1804*, ed. Abraham P. Nasatir, 2 vols. (St. Louis: St. Louis Historical Documents Foundation, 1952), 2:745–50, 750 (quote).

18. Nemesio Salcedo to the Governor of Texas, July 15, 1805, Bexar Archives Translations, Center for American History, University of Texas, Austin, series II, 8:146.

19. Flores, *Freeman and Custis Accounts*, 38.

20. Ibid., 88, 132n16.

21. Ibid., 145–48, 146 (quote), 160n3.

22. According to Dan Flores, the settlement was on Cedar Bluffs, directly across the river from present-day Gilliam, Louisiana. Flores, *Freeman and Custis Accounts*, 148–49, 149n39.

23. Ibid., 157.

24. Ibid., 161–64.

25. Ibid.

26. Nemesio Salcedo to William Claiborne, September 18, 1806, Nacogdoches Archives Calendar, Center for American History, University of Texas at Austin, 256:117. For further details relating to the Red River expedition and the

Spanish confrontation with Freeman's exploration party, see Carl Newton Tyson, *The Red River in Southwestern History* (Norman: University of Oklahoma Press, 1981), 73–77.

27. Flores, *Freeman and Custis Accounts*, 286.

28. Journal entry, February 13, 1807, in Abel, *Report From Natchitoches*, 12–13.

29. Interview of Jeff Abbey, July 8, 1938, in Taylor Papers; James Adair, *The History of the American Indians*, ed. Samuel Cole Williams (1775; repr., New York: Argonaut Press, 1966), 417; Hudson, *Southeastern Indians*, 254–57.

30. Journal entries, February 13, 1807, and April 7, 1807, in Abel, *Report From Natchitoches*, 12–13, 19–20.

31. Journal entry, April 7, 1807, in Abel, *Report from Natchitoches*, 19–20, 20 (quote).

32. The complexities of Alabama and Coushatta blood law has not been studied. John Phillip Reid gives an excellent analysis on Cherokee blood law and posits that the Creek Nation had similar practices and laws. It is assumed here that Alabama and Coushatta law is comparable to that of the Cherokees. John Phillip Reid, "The Cherokee Thought: An Apparatus of Primitive Law," in *Ethnology of the Southeastern Indians: A Source Book*, ed. Charles M. Hudson (New York: Garland, 1985): 281–302; Hudson, *Southeastern Indians*, 229–30.

33. Journal entry, May 15, 1807, in Abel, *Report from Natchitoches*, 23–24.

34. Journal entries, June 8, 1807, and June 14, 1807, in Abel, *Report From Natchitoches*, 30–37.

35. Journal entries, June 8, 1807, August 18, 1807, and November 10, 1807, in Abel, *Report From Natchitoches*, 30–31, 56–59, 82–83.

36. Antonio Cordero to Nemesio Salcedo, October 30, 1807, Bexar Archives (BX), Center for American History, University of Texas at Austin,8:139–40.

37. Ibid.

38. Ibid.

39. Miguel Díaz de Luna's Memorandum, May 15, 1810, BX, 45:231; Nemesio Salcedo to Royal Tribunal of Consulate of Veracruz, December 25, 1808, Consulado de Veracruz to Salcedo, January 11, 1809, and Nemesio Salcedo to Royal Tribunal, February 28, 1809, all in Panton and Leslie Papers, Auburn University, vol. 193; Nemesio Salcedo to Cordero, August 7, 1807, Nacogdoches Archives Calendar, 256:397; Abraham P. Nasatir, *Borderland in Retreat: From Spanish Louisiana to the Far Southwest* (Albuquerque: University of New Mexico Press, 1976), 132–33.

40. Journal entries, June 8, 1807, August 18, 1807, and November 10, 1807, in Abel, *Report from Natchitoches*, 30–31, 56–59, 82–83.

41. Journal entry, May 20, 1807, in Abel, *Report from Natchitoches*, 25, 95, 97n18.

42. Ibid.

43. Journal entries, June 14, 1807, July 21, 1807, and September 1 1807, in Abel, *Report from Natchitoches*, 38–39, 46–47, 67.

44. William Claiborne to James Madison, New Orleans, July 11, 1808, in Rowland, *Official Letter Books*, 183–84; Thomas Jefferson to U.S. Congress, November 8, 1808, in Panton and Leslie Papers, 1:438–45.

45. William Claiborne to Henry Dearborn, Opelousas, August 8, 1808, in Rowland, *Official Letter Books*, 4:186.

46. Ibid., 4:185.

47. William Claiborne to Henry Dearborn, Secretary at War, New Orleans, November 5, 1808, in Rowland, *Official Letter Books*, 4:237–39.

48. Ibid., 4:238.

49. Nancy Shoemaker, *A Strange Likeness: Becoming Red and White in Eighteenth-Century North America* (New York: Oxford University Press, 2004), 23.

50. Thomas Jefferson, "Message from the President of the U.S. Transmitting a Letter from Gov. Claiborne on the Small Tribe of Alibama Indians on the Western Side of the Mississippi," December 30, 1808, *Pamphlets in American History* (Washington, D.C.: A.& G. Wat Printers, 1809), Group I: 962; Dan Flores, "The Red River Branch of the Alabama-Coushatta Indians: An Ethnohistory," *Southern Studies* 16 (Spring 1977): 66.

51. Salcedo to Bonaviá, April 24, 1809, Nacogdoches Archives (NA), Center for American History, University of Texas at Austin, 11:254.

52. Pedro Lopea Prieto to Manuel de Salcedo, July 3, 1809, BX, 42:20–21; Mariano Varela to Bernardo Bonaviá, July 13, 1809, BX, 42:127–36; Manuel do Salcedo to Bernardo Bonavía, July 15, 1809, BX, 42:165–68.

53. Journal Entry, November 10, 1807, in Abel, *Report From Natchitoches*, 82–83.

54. A small group of forty Choctaws also migrated west and established a village on the Neches, twelve miles below an Alabama village. Salcedo to Bonaviá, April 24, 1809, NA, 11:254; Dianna Everett, *The Texas Cherokees: A People Between Two Fires, 1819–1840* (Norman: University of Oklahoma Press, 1990), 21.

55. Salcedo to Bonaviá, April 24, 1809, NA, 11:254; Everett, *Texas Cherokees*, 21.

56. Jedediah Morse, "A Report to the Secretary of War of the United States on Indian Affairs, 1822," Richard Yarborough Collection, Center for American History, University of Texas at Austin, 373; George Gray to the Secretary of War, December 30, 1824, in *The Territorial Papers of the United States: The Territory of Arkansas, 1819–1825*, ed. Clarence Edwin Carter (Washington, D.C.: U.S. Government Printing Office, 1953), 19:739–40.

Chapter 5

1. "The Buffalo Tug-of-War," in Howard N. Martin, *Myths and Folktales of the Alabama-Coushatta Indians of Texas* (Austin, Tex.: Encino Press, 1977), 30–31.

2. Ibid.

3. F. Todd Smith, *The Wichita Indians: Traders of Texas and the Southern Plains* (College Station: Texas A&M University Press, 2000), 116–17; Dianna Everett, *The Texas Cherokees: A People Between Two Fires, 1819–1840* (Norman: University of Oklahoma Press, 1990), 9–11; Mary Whatley Clarke, *Chief Bowles and the Texas Cherokees* (Norman: University of Oklahoma Press, 1971), 11–15.

4. Everett, *Texas Cherokees*, 9–11; Clarke, *Chief Bowles*, 11–15.

5. Jedediah Morse, "A Report to the Secretary of War of the United States on Indian Affairs, 1822," Richard Yarborough Collection, Center for American History, University of Texas at Austin, 258–59, 373. For more details about the Comanche-related tribes, see Thomas W. Kavanaugh, *Comanche Political History: An Ethnohistorical Perspective, 1707–1875* (Lincoln: University of Nebraska Press, 1996).

6. Everett, *Texas Cherokees*, 29–30.

7. Juan Antonio Padilla, "Texas in 1820," trans. M. A. Hatcher, *Southwestern Historical Quarterly* 23 (1919): 47–68.

8. Manuel de Mier y Teran to Commandant General Inspector de los Estados Internos de Oriente, July 31, 1830, leg. 5, exp. 34, in Archivo General de Mexico (AGM), Fomento y Colonization, Center for American History, University of Texas at Austin; Juan Nepomuceno Almonte to M. Stokes and J.F. Schermerhorn, June 18, 1834, AGM, leg. 8, exp. 65; Sam Houston to Lewis Cass, July 30, 1833, in *The Writings of Sam Houston, 1821–1847*, ed. Amelia W. Williams and Eugene C. Barker, 8 vols. (Austin: University of Texas Press, 1938–41), 2:15–16; Stephen Austin to Jared E. Groce, October 18, 1823, *The Austin Papers: Annual Report of the American Historical Association for the Year 1922*, ed. Eugene Barker, 2 vols. (Washington D.C.: U.S. Government Printing Office, 1928), 2:701–2; Governor Miller to the Secretary of War, June 20, 1820, in Carter, *Territorial Papers of the United States*, 19:191–92; Morse, "Report on Indian Affairs," 258–59, 373; Report of Standing Committee on Indian Affairs, October 12, 1837, in *The Indian Papers of Texas and the Southwest, 1825–1916*, ed. Dorman H. Winfrey and James M. Day, 5 vols. (Austin: Texas State Historical Commission, 1995), 1:22–26.

9. David La Vere, *Contrary Neighbors: Southern Plains and Removed Indians in Indian Territory* (Norman: University of Oklahoma Press, 2000), 24–26.

10. Herman R. Friis, "The Image of the American West at Mid-Century (1840–1860)," in *The Frontier Re-Examined*, ed. John Francis McDermott (Chi-

cago: University of Illinois Press, 1967), 49–53; George William Bonnell, *To-pographical Description of Texas* (1840; repr., Waco, Tex.: Texian Press, 1961), 10–11; William Kennedy, *Texas: The Rise, Progress, and Prospects of the Republic of Texas*, 2 vols. (London: R. Hastings, 1841), 1:14–15, 122; Francis Moore Jr., *Map and Description of Texas* (1840; repr., Waco, Tex.: Texian Press, 1965), 8, 23; Frederic Gaillardet, *Sketches of Early Texas and Louisiana*, ed. and trans. James L. Shepherd III (Austin: University of Texas Press, 1966), 68–69. Chester Newell, *History of the Revolution in Texas* (1838; New York: Arno Press, 1973), 13, 130–31, 137.

11. Bernard Romans, *A Concise Natural History of East and West Florida* (1775; repr., Gainesville: University Press of Florida, 1962), 134, 146, 147.

12. Ibid.; Geoffrey D. Kimball, *Koasati Dictionary* (Lincoln: University of Nebraska Press, 1994), 274; Interviews of Jeff Abbey, July 15, 1938, and Sissy Abbey, July 7, 1938, in Lyda Averill Taylor Papers (Taylor Papers), Center for American History, University of Texas at Austin.

13. Interview of Jeff Abbey, July 8, 1938, in Taylor Papers; Benjamin Hawkins, *The Letters, Journals, and Writings of Benjamin Hawkins*, ed., C. L. Grant, 2 vols. (Savannah, Ga.: Beehive Press, 1980), 1:295–96; Robbie Ethridge, *Creek Country: The Creek Indians and Their World* (Chapel Hill: University of North Carolina Press, 2003), 95.

14. The Alabama and Coushatta oral tradition of "Corn Woman" symbolized the importance placed on the woman providing food for her family. In this story, an old woman takes care of some orphans and feeds them by rubbing herself "as one rubs roasting ears"; she was corn. She declares that she is their mother and makes corn bread for them. Afterward, she tells the children to gather the hard corn kernels and sweep them into a corncrib outside. The next morning, the children returned to the corncrib to find it full of corn. Corn Woman represented the Earth Mother who provided food to the Alabamas and Coushattas. The emphasis placed on women within the structure of Alabama and Coushatta society signified their importance within the community. "Corn Woman," in John Reed Swanton, *Myths and Tales of the Southeastern Indians*, Bureau of American Ethnology Bulletin 88 (Washington, D.C.: U.S. Government Printing Office, 1929), 168; Amelia Rector Bell, "Separate People: Speaking of Creek Men and Women," *American Anthropologist* 92 (1990): 332–45; Kimball, *Koasati Dictionary*, 38; Cora Sylestine, Heather Hardy, and Timothy Montler, *Dictionary of the Alabama Language* (Austin: University of Texas Press, 1993), 632.

15. The Alabamas called it *hoɫka*, while the Coushattas knew it as *cawáhka*. They ate it hot or cold to accompany their meals, and often let it sour for up to three days; at this stage, it had a bitter taste and beerlike odor. Young women began to make their own sofkey when they reached the age of courtship; if a

young woman decided to prepare the dish for a young man, it would begin a relationship that possibly led to marriage. Preparing meals was a key responsibility for a woman, so if she was a poor cook, she had to go to a medicine maker to take out the bad medicine from within her. Romans, *Concise Natural History*, 144–46; Caleb Swan, "Position and State of Manners in and Arts in the Creek, or Muscogee Nation in 1791," in *Historical and Statistical Information Respecting the History, Condition, and Prospects of the Indian Tribes of the United States*, ed. Henry Rowe Schoolcraft (Philadelphia: J. B. Lippincott, 1855), 5:274; Kimball, *Koasati Dictionary*, 38; Sylestine, Hardy, and Montler, *Dictionary of the Alabama Language*, 78, 632; Charles Hudson, *The Southeastern Indians* (Knoxville: University of Tennessee Press, 1976), 285, 304–5; Gregory Waselkov and Kathryn E. Holland Braund, eds., *William Bartram on the Southeastern Indians* (Lincoln: University of Nebraska Press, 1995), 165; Kathryn Holland Braund, "Guardians of Tradition and Handmaidens to Change: Women's Roles in Creek Economic and Social Life during the Eighteenth Century," *American Indian Quarterly* 14 (Summer 1990): 242–43; Bell, "Separate People," 332–45.

16. According to reports, the Coushattas had acquired a taste for alcohol more than the Alabamas, but the evidence does not indicate how much. Morse, "A Report on Indian Affairs," 258.

17. Morse, "A Report on Indian Affairs," 258; Sylestine, Hardy, and Montler, *Dictionary of the Alabama Language*, 592; Cheryl Claassen, "Women's Lives in Prehistoric North America," in *Women in Prehistory*, ed. Cheryl Claassen and Rosemary A. Joyce (Philadelphia: University of Pennsylvania Press, 1997), 70; Hudson, *Southeastern Indians*, 295, 297.

18. J. Francisco Madero's Report (Madero's Report), Manuel de Mier y Teran to Ecsmo. Sr. Srio. de Relaciones Ints. y Esteriores, July 4, 1831, AGM, leg. 4, exp. 10; Gustav Dresel, *Houston Journal: Adventures in North America and Texas, 1837–1841*, ed. and trans. Max Freund (Austin: University of Texas Press, 1954), 65–66.

19. Dresel, *Houston Journal*, 65.

20. Madero's Report, AGM, leg. 4, exp. 10; Dresel, *Houston Journal*, 33, 65–66.

21. Madero's Report, AGM, leg. 4, exp. 10.

22. One of the first important colonizers, Austin's estate (mostly land) was appraised at $527,485 in 1837. Gregg Cantrell, *Stephen F. Austin: Empresario of Texas* (New Haven, Conn.: Yale University Press, 1999), 379; Newell, *History of the Revolution in Texas*, 16–17; Mattie Austin Hatcher, *The Opening of Texas to Foreign Settlement, 1801–1821* (1927; repr., Philadelphia: Porcupine Press, 1976), 284–86.

23. Hatcher, *The Opening of Texas*, 284–86.

24. Ibid.

25. Austin to Alcalde, May 24, 1824, in Barker, *Austin Papers*, 2:800; Smith, *Wichita Indians*, 114–15.

26. Austin to Mateo Ahumada, April 30, 1826, in Barker, *Austin Papers*, 2:1315–16.

27. Ibid; Smith, *Wichita Indians*, 119; J. Child to Austin, February 1, 1824, in Barker, *Austin Papers*, 2:735; Austin to Saucedo, September 8, 1825, in Barker, *Austin Papers*, 2:1194–95; Austin to Saucedo, May 19, 1826, in Barker, *Austin Papers*, 2:1341–44.

28. A. Houren, "The Causes and Origin of the Decree of April 6, 1830," *Southwestern Historical Quarterly* 16 (1913): 378–442; Everett, *Texas Cherokees*, 61–62.

29. Don Ramon Musquiz to Jose Maria Letona, September 25, 1831, in Winfrey and Day, *Indian Papers of Texas*, 1:2–3.

30. Notice of Appointment from José Maria Letona to Don Ramon Musquiz, March 22, 1832, in Winfrey and Day, *Indian Papers of Texas*, 1:4; José de Las Piedras to Don Ramon Musquiz, May 7, 1832, in Winfrey and Day, *Indian Papers of Texas*, 1:5.

31. Letters to the Alcalde of Nacogdoches from Ruiz, February 20, 1835, in Winfrey and Day, *Indian Papers of Texas*, 6–7.

32. Concession of Land to the Peaceful Coushatta and Alabama tribes, July 4, 1831, AGM, leg. 4, exp. 10; José Maria Letona to Commandant General, September 1, 1831, in Winfrey and Day, *Indian Papers of Texas*, 1:1–2. Sam Houston on Behalf of the Cherokee Land Bill, said before the Fourth Congress of the Republic of Texas, 22 December 1839, in Williams and Barker, *Writings of Sam Houston*, 2:328–29, 342–43; Sam Houston's Speech Concerning the Cherokee Bill, House of Representatives, December 4, 1840, in Williams and Barker, *Writings of Sam Houston*, 2:355–56; Sam Houston to the Texas Senate, May 21, 1838, in Williams and Barker, *Writings of Sam Houston*, 4:55–56; Tadeo Ortiz to President of Mexico, February 2, 1833, AGM, leg. 7, exp. 57; José Maria Diaz Noriega to the Supreme Governor General, AGM, leg. 9, exp. 68.

33. Sam Houston to the Texas Senate, May 21, 1838, in Williams and Barker, *Writings of Sam Houston*, 4:55.

34. Sylestine, Hardy, and Montler, *Dictionary of the Alabama Language*, 395.

35. Antonio Tenorio to the Military Commander of Coahuila and Texas, April 9, 1835, in Jenkins, *Military Papers of the Texas Revolution*, 1:61–62, 62 (quote); Sam Houston to the Texas Senate, May 21, 1838, in Williams and Barker, *Writings of Sam Houston*, 4:55; Ruiz to Alcalde, February 20, 1835, in John H. Jenkins, ed., *Military Papers of the Texas Revolution, 1835–1836*, 10 vols. (Austin, Tex.: Presidial Press, 1973), 1:22.

36. Tenorio to the Military Commander of Coahuila and Texas, April 9, 1835, in Jenkins, *Military Papers of the Texas Revolution*, 1:62 (quote).In 1834, the

commissioner of colonization, Juan Almonte, estimated the Indian population (Cherokees and associate bands) at approximately 4,500. This included five hundred Cherokees, five hundred Choctaws, six hundred Creeks, four hundred Shawnees, eight hundred Kickapoos, one hundred Tejas, three hundred Nacogdoches, five hundred Coushattas and Alabamas, and five hundred Caddos. Almonte, "Statistical Report on Texas," ed. Carlos Casteneda, *Southwestern Historical Quarterly* 28 (1924): 222; Tenorio to the Military Commander of Coahuila and Texas, April 9, 1835, in Jenkins, *Military Papers of the Texas Revolution*, 1:61–62; Report of the Secretary of War, June 16, 1835, AGM, leg. 9, exp. 70; Governor of the State of Coahuila and Texas to the Secretary of War, July 15, 1835, AGM, leg. 9, exp. 57; Antonio Tenorio to the Secretary of War, April 9, 1835, AGM, leg. 9, exp. 57.

37. T. R. Fehrenbach, *Lone Star: A History of Texas and the Texans* (New York: Macmillan, 1968), 185–89; Everett, *Texas Cherokees*, 1990), 67–68.

38. Domingo de Ugartechea to Ellis Peter Bean, March 26, 1835, in Jenkins, *Military Papers of the Texas Revolution*, 1:44.

39. Pedro Ellis Bean to Ugartechea, August 18, 1835, Nacogdoches Archives, Center for American History, University of Texas at Austin, 82:249.

40. Domingo de Ugartechea to Martin Perfecto de Cos, May 15, 1835, Bexar Archives (BX), Center for American History, University of Texas at Austin, 165:146–48; Martin Perfecto de Cos to Domingo de Ugartechea, May 23, 1835, BX, 165:271; Domingo de Ugartechea to Peter Ellis Bean, June 4, 1835, BX, 165:481–82; Ruiz to the Alcalde of Nacogdoches, February 20–July 29, 1835, MS. Indian Papers, Texas State Archives. Austin, Texas.

41. Sublet et al. to Committee of Public Safety, September 22, 1835, in Jenkins, *Military Papers of the Texas Revolution*, 1:480–81 (quote); Appointment of Sam Houston, John Forbes, and John Cameron as Indian Commissioners, December 22, 1835, in Winfrey and Day, *Indian Papers of Texas*, 1:10; Appointment of Sam Houston, John Forbes, and John Cameron as Indian Commissioners by Henry Smith, December 28, 1835, in Winfrey and Day, *Indian Papers of Texas*, 1:11.

42. H. P. N. Gammel, *The Laws of Texas, 1822–1897*, 10 vols. (Austin, Tex.: Gammel Book Company, 1898), 1:546–47.

43. James Reily to General Rusk, April 22, 1838, Rusk Papers, Center for American History, University of Texas at Austin; Sam Houston to Andrew Jackson, May 11, 1829, in Williams and Barker, *Writings of Sam Houston*, 1:132–33; Sam Houston's Certificate of Citizenship in the Cherokee Nation, October 21, 1829, in Williams and Barker, *Writings of Sam Houston*, 1:143; Tah-Lohn-Tus-Ky [Sam Houston] on the Indians, for the *Arkansas Gazette*, June 22, 1830, in Williams and Barker, *Writings of Sam Houston*, 1:155–87; John Hoyt Williams, *Sam Houston: A Biography of the Father of Texas* (New York: Simon and Schuster, 1993), 21–27.

44. Treaty with Cherokees and Their Associate Bands Residing in Texas, February 23, 1836, Manuscript Collection, Texas State Archives; Sam Houston to Henry Smith, February 29, 1836, in Williams and Barker, *Writings of Sam Houston*, 1:356–60.

45. Treaty with Cherokees and Their Associate Bands Residing in Texas, February 23, 1836; Sam Houston to Henry Smith, February 29, 1836, in Williams and Barker, *Writings of Sam Houston*, 1:356–60.

46. Treaty with Cherokees and Their Associate Bands Residing in Texas, February 23, 1836.

47. Ibid.; Sam Houston to Henry Smith, February 29, 1836, in Williams and Barker, *Writings of Sam Houston*, 1:356–60.

48. Prairie View Malone, *Sam Houston's Indians: The Alabama-Coushatti* (San Antonio, Tex.: Naylor Company, 1960), 21–22.

49. Antonio López de Santa Anna to Ministry of War and Marine, February 16, 1836, in *The Mexican Side of the Texas Revolution (1836), By the Chief Mexican Participants*, comp. and trans. Carlos E. Castaneda (Washington, D.C.: Documentary Publications, 1971), 66; Thomas Toby and Brother to D.G. Burnet, July 23, 1836, enclosure: to Mr. P.P. Rea, July 1, 1836, in *Official Correspondence of the Texan Revolution*, vol. 2, ed. William C. Binkley (New York: D. Appleton-Century Company, 1936), 888.

50. Entry for April 18 and 22, 1836, in José Enrique de la Pena, *With Santa Anna in Texas: A Personal Narrative of the Revolution*, ed. and trans. Carmen Perry (College Station: Texas A&M University Press, 1975), 113, 116.

51. Martin, *Folktales of the Alabama-Coushatta Indians*, 61–63.

52. Ibid., 79–81.

53. Ibid.

54. Ibid.

55. Almonte, "Statistical Report on Texas," 222.

56. Inaugural address of Sam Houston, President of the Republic of Texas, October 22, 1836, in Williams and Barker, *Writings of Sam Houston*, 1:448.

57. Ibid.; Sam Houston to the Texas Senate, May 21, 1838, in Williams and Barker, *Writings of Sam Houston*, 4:55–60.

58. Report of Standing Committee on Indian Affairs, October 12, 1837, in Winfrey and Day, *Indian Papers of Texas*, 1:26–27.

59. Ibid.

60. Scholarship has focused on the question of why the federal government forcefully removed Native Americans to Indian Territory and their motivation for doing so. Scholars have also debated the issue of President Andrew Jackson's concern for the welfare of Native Americans and whether it was true sincerity or mere rhetoric. A group of historians have argued that the key motivation for Indian removal was ruthless aggression and limitless greed for Indian lands. Among these are Mary E. Young, *Redskins, Ruffleshirts, and*

Rednecks (Norman: University of Oklahoma Press, 1961); Reginald Horsman, *Race and Manifest Destiny: The Origin of American Racial Anglo-Saxonism* (Cambridge, Mass.: Harvard University Press, 1981); Francis Jennings, *The Founding of America* (New York: W. W. Norton, 1993). Revisionist historians, on the other hand, argue that Jackson's primary goal of Indian removal was to preserve the security of the United States and its American Indian inhabitants. See Robert Remini, *The Legacy of Andrew Jackson: Essays on Democracy, Indian Removal, and Slavery* (Lincoln: University of Nebraska Press, 1988); Francis Paul Prucha, *Indian Policy in the United States: Historical Essays* (Lincoln: University of Nebraska Press, 1981); Prucha, *The Great Father* (Lincoln: University of Nebraska Press, 1984).

61. Favorable terms promised to many of the tribes in the treaties were broken. American Indian emigrants to Indian territory faced unnecessary hardship and death. The most infamous was the thousand-mile "Trail of Tears" westward, in which only 8,000 out of 12,000 Cherokees survived. Robert Leitch Wright, *The Only Land They Knew: The Tragic Story of the American Indians in the Old South* (New York: Free Press, 1980), 283–84.

62. Ibid., 4:60.

63. Ibid.; Sam Houston to the Texas Senate, December 20, 1836, in Williams and Barker, *Writings of Sam Houston*, 1:518–19; James Reily to General Rusk, April 22, 1838, in Rusk Papers.

64. Sam Houston to Colonel Bowl, Great Chief of the Cherokees, April 13, 1836, in Williams and Barker, *Writings of Sam Houston*, 1:409.

65. Sam Houston to the Alabama and Coushatta Indians, November 12, 1838, in Williams and Barker, *Writings of Sam Houston*, 2:293–94; Sam Houston to Colonel Bowl (Cherokee), August 14, 1838, in Rusk Papers; Sam Houston to Big Mush, Chief of the Cherokees, August 10, 1838, Williams and Barker, *Writings of Sam Houston*, 2:269–70; General Rusk to Sam Houston, August 16, 1838, in Rusk Papers; General Rusk to Colonel Bowles (Cherokee), August 13, 1838, in Rusk Papers.

66. No known sources suggest that the Alabamas joined the Córdova Rebellion. Sources only note a few Coushatta warriors taking part in the raids. Sources also fail to mention how many Coushatta warriors engaged in the revolt. Vincente Córdova to Manuel Flores, July 19, 1838, in Winfrey and Day, *Indian Papers of Texas*, 1:8 (quotes); James T. De Shields, *Border Wars of Texas*, ed. Matt Bradley (1912; repr., Austin, Tex.: State House Press, 1993), 245–47; Paul D. Lack, "The Córdova Revolt," in *Tejano Journey, 1770–1850*, ed. Gerald E. Poyo (Austin: University of Texas Press, 1996), 89; Elisha Clapp to General Rusk, October 3, 1838, in Rusk Papers.

67. S. Hiram to Sam Houston, August 17, 1838, in Rusk Papers; General Rusk to Colonel Bowles, October 9, 1838, in Rusk Papers. Sam Houston to General Rusk, August 26, 1838, in Rusk Papers.

68. Citizens of the Town of Houston to Sam Houston, August 25, 1838, in Rusk Papers; Minutes of the Council Creek, July 11, 1839, in Rusk Papers.

69. Mirabeau Lamar to Both Houses of Congress, December 21, 1838, in *The Papers of Mirabeau Buonaparte Lamar* (*Lamar Papers*), ed. Charles Adams Gulick Jr. and Katherine Elliot, 6 vols. (Austin, Tex.: A. C. Baldwin and Sons, 1921–28), 2:352–53.

70. Texas House of Representatives Resolution, November 10, 1838, in Rusk Papers.

71. Colonel Bowles to General Rusk, May 26, 1839, in Rusk Papers.

72. Mirabeau Lamar to Chief Bowles, May 26, 1839, in Winfrey and Day, *Indian Papers of Texas*, 1:61–66, 62 (quote).

73. Ibid., 62.

74. Ibid. (quote); Mirabeau Lamar to Colonel Bowles and Other Head Men, May 26, 1839, in *Lamar Papers*, 2:590–94.

75. Minutes of the Council Creek, July 11, 1839, in Rusk Papers; Treaty with the Cherokees and their Associate Bands, Camp Johnston, July 14, 1839, in Rusk Papers.

76. Sam Houston's Speech Concerning the Cherokee Land Bill, December 4, 1840, in Williams and Barker, *Writings of Sam Houston*, 2:341, 343.

77. J. E. Ross to M. B. Lamar, June 10, 1839, in *Lamar Papers*, 3:16–17.

Chapter 6

1. "Rabbit Plays Pranks on Big Man-Eater," in Howard N. Martin, *Myths and Folktales of the Alabama-Coushatta Indians of Texas* (Austin, Tex.: Encino Press, 1977), 35–36.

2. Ibid.

3. George William Bonnell, *Topographical Description of Texas* (1840; repr., Waco, Tex.: Texian Press, 1961), 11; Frances Moore Jr., *Map and Description of Texas* (1840; repr., Waco, Tex.: Texian Press, 1965), 29–30.

4. According to various travelogues, in Texas cotton could be planted two to three weeks earlier in the spring than elsewhere and, in contrast to the United States, Texas's harvesting season continued into the fall. More importantly, Texans claimed that the soil was more productive than the "best Mississippi or Louisiana land," which enabled the average planter to cultivate a larger surplus. Bonnell, *Topographical Description of Texas*, 118–19, 118 (quote); Thomas Bell to John Bell, August 17, 1840, in Llerena Friend, ed., "Notes and Documents, Thomas W. Bell Letters," *Southwestern Historical Quarterly* 63 (October 1959), 299–310.

5. Texas's toleration of slavery also appealed to southern slave owners and those who aspired to be planters themselves. Those who relocated to Texas

were allowed to bring as many slaves as they wished. Moreover, the Texas Republic placed strict limitations on "free Negroes." Travelogues advertised that Texas laws banned such persons from the republic without a "special enactment of Congress," a privilege rarely granted. Given the rising tensions between the two cultures in the form of slave revolts in the Southeast and the endless abolitionist propaganda from the North, observers predicted that Texas would become a "land of refuge" for the American slaveholders. Bonnell, *Topographical Description of Texas*, 120–21; Frederic Gaillardet, *Sketches of Early Texas and Louisiana*, ed. and trans. James L. Shepherd III (Austin: University of Texas Press, 1966), 68.

6. Moore, *Map and Description of Texas*, 29–30 (quote); Bonnell, *Topographical Description of Texas*, 11.

7. Francis Paul Prucha, *Indian Policy in the United States: Historical Essays* (Lincoln: University of Nebraska Press, 1981), 153–57.

8. Bonnell, *Topographical Description of Texas*; Moore, *Map and Description of Texas*, 68.

9. Paul D. Lack, "The Córdova Revolt," in *Tejano Journey, 1770–1850*, ed. Gerald E. Poyo (Austin: University of Texas Press, 1996), 108 (quote); Mirabeau Lamar to Colonel Bowl and Other Head Men, May 26, 1839, in *The Papers of Mirabeau Bonaparte Lamar (Lamar Papers)*, ed. Charles Adams Gulick Jr. and Katherine Elliot, 6 vols. (Austin, Tex.: A. C. Baldwin and Sons, 1921–28), 2:590–94.

10. Mirabeau Lamar to Both Houses of Congress, December 21, 1838, in *Lamar Papers*, 2:353. For more detailed information regarding Lamar's Indian policy and his attitude toward them, see Anna Muckleroy, "The Indian Policy of the Republic of Texas: The Indian Policy of Lamar's Administration," *Southwestern Historical Quarterly* 25 (October 1922): 128–48; and A. K. Christian, "Mirabeau Buonaparte Lamar," *Southwestern Historical Quarterly* 24 (July 1920): 39–80. Although both are dated, these articles are among the few scholarly studies relating to Lamar's Indian policy.

11. Mirabeau Lamar to Colonel Bowl and Other Head Men, May 26, 1839, in *The Indian Papers of Texas and the Southwest, 1825–1916*, ed. Dorman H. Winfrey and James Day, 5 vols. (Austin: Texas State Library, Archives Division), 1:64.

12. M. B. Lamar to David G. Burnet, Albert Sidney Johnston, Thomas J. Rusk, I. W. Burton, and James S. Mayfield, June 27, 1839, in Winfrey and Day, *Indian Papers of Texas*, 1:67–69, 69 (quote).

13. Bonnell, *Topographical Description of Texas*, 148–50.

14. For more information about this battle and Lamar's Indian policy, see Gary Clayton Anderson, *The Conquest of Texas: Ethnic Cleansing in the Promised Land, 1820–1875* (Norman: University of Oklahoma Press, 2005), chap.

11; W. W. Newcomb Jr., *The Indians of Texas: From Prehistoric to Modern Times* (Austin: University of Texas Press, 1961), 347.

15. Report of K. H. Douglass to A. Sidney Johnston, July 16, 1839, in Winfrey and Day, *Indian Papers of Texas*, 76–77.

16. Treaty with the Shawnee Indians, Nacogdoches, August 2, 1839, MS. Indian Papers, Texas State Archives, Austin; Albert Sidney Johnston, Thomas J. Rusk, and Jason S. Mayfield to James Reily, August 1, 1839, in Winfrey and Day, *Indian Papers of Texas*, 1:78.

17. Christian, "Mirabeau Buonaparte Lamar," 39; Andreas V. Reichstein, *Rise of the Lone Star: The Making of Texas* (College Station: Texas A&M University Press, 1989), 162.

18. "Orders of the Day," November 19, 1839, in *Journals of the Fourth Congress of the Republic of Texas, 1839–1840, to Which Are Added the Relief Laws*, ed. Harriet Smither, 3 vols. (Austin, Tex.: Von Boeckmann-Jones Co., 1929), 1:48; Joseph L. Ellis to Thomas G. Western, December 8, 1844, MS. Indian Papers, no. 107, Texas State Archives.

19. "Orders of the Day," January 13, 1840, in Smither, *Journals of the Fourth Congress*, 1:239.

20. Ibid.; Reichstein, *Rise of the Lone Star*, 170; M. B. Lamar to "The Citizens of Liberty County, Residing Near The C[o]ushatta Towns And Villages," July 9, 1839, in *Lamar Papers*, 3:39.

21. J. E. Ross to M. B. Lamar, June 10, 1839, in *Lamar Papers*, 3:16.

22. M. B. Lamar to Colluta [Colita], July 9, 1839, in MS. Indian Papers, no. 39, Texas State Library.

23. Ibid.

24. M. B. Lamar to "The Citizens of Liberty County, Residing Near The C[o]ushatta Towns And Villages," July 9, 1839, in *Lamar Papers*, 3:39.

25. Ibid.

26. Liberty County to M. B. Lamar, August 1, 1839, in MS. Indian Papers, no. 48, Texas State Archives.

27. Moore, *Map and Description of Texas*, 31.

28. Liberty County to M. B. Lamar, August 1, 1839, in MS. Indian Papers, no. 48, Texas State Archives.

29. Bonnell, *Topographical Description of Texas*, 12–13, 22–23; Moore, *Map and Description of Texas*, 68.

30. "Orders of the Day," January 13, 1840, in Smither, *Journals of the Fourth Congress*, 1:239.

31. "Orders of the Day," The Meeting of the Fourth Congress of the Republic of Texas, November 19, 1839, 1:48; "Orders of the Day," November 20, 1839, 1:53; "Orders of the Day," November 23, 1839, 1:62–63; all in Smither, *Journals of the Fourth Congress*.

32. Ibid.

33. H. W. Karnes to A. Sidney Johnston, January 10, 1840, in Winfrey and Day, *Indian Papers of Texas*, 1:101.

34. "Orders of the Day," The Meeting of the Fourth Congress of the Republic of Texas, November 19, 1839, 1:48; "Orders of the Day," November 20, 1839, 1:53; "Orders of the Day," November 23, 1839, 1:62–63; "Orders of the Day," November 26, 1839, 1:66; "Orders of the Day," November 27, 1839, 1:74; "Orders of the Day," January 7, 1840, 1:212; "Orders of the Day," January 8, 1840, 1:225; "Orders of the Day," January 10, 1840, 1:233; all in Smither, *Journals of the Fourth Congress*.

35. Ibid.

36. An Act Authorizing the Survey of Land for the Coushatta and Alabama Indians, January 14, 1840, Winfrey and Day, *Indian Papers of Texas*, 1:102–3; Thomas G. Stubblefield to Abner L. Lipscomb, November 2, 1840, in Winfrey and Day, *Indian Papers of Texas*, 117–18; Records of James B. Shaw, Comptroller, January 14, 1840, in Smither, *Journals of the Fourth Congress*, 3:328; "Orders of the Day," January 14, 1840, in Smither, *Journals of the Fourth Congress*, 2:293; "Orders of the Day," January 20, 1840, in Smither, *Journals of the Fourth Congress*, 1:271; Report of the Hon. I. W. Burton, "Unfavorable To the Passage of the Cherokee Land Bill," January 22 1840, in Smither, *Journals of the Fourth Congress*, 1:276–80.

37. Moore, *Map and Description of Texas*, 31; "Petition of the Alabama Indians," December 13, 1853, Secretary of State's Memorials and Petitions, Texas State Archives, Austin.

38. Thomas Farrow Smith to Anson Jones, April 22, 1842, in Winfrey and Day, *Indian Papers of Texas*, 125–6.

39. Affidavit of Holland Coffee, May 6, 1842, in Winfrey and Day, *Indian Papers of Texas*, 1:127; Statement of J. G. Jowett in Relation to the Difficulties between the Indians of the United States, and the Citizens of Texas, May 7, 1842, in Winfrey and Day, *Indian Papers of Texas*, 1:128–29; David Rowlett's Affidavit, May 13, 1842, in Winfrey and Day, *Indian Papers of Texas*, 1:131–32; Deposition of R. W. Lee, April 22, 1842, Army Papers, Adjutant General Records, Group 401, Texas State Archives, Austin; Affidavit of Mark R. Robertts, May 7, 1842, MS. Indian Papers, Texas State Archives, Austin.

40. "Petition of the Alabama Indians," December 13, 1853, in Secretary of State's Memorials and Petitions.

41. Minutes of the Indian Council at Tehuacana Creek, March 28, 1843, in Winfrey and Day, *Indian Papers of Texas*, 1:156–63; Reichstein, *Rise of the Lone Star*, 170–71; W. P. Webb, "The Last Treaty of the Republic of Texas," *Southwestern Historical Quarterly* 25 (January 1922), 152–53.

42. M. L. Houston to Gen. Sam Houston, October 6, 1843, *The Personal*

Correspondence of Sam Houston, Volume I: 1839–1845, ed. Madge Thornall Roberts (Denton: University of North Texas Press, 1996), 1:294.

43. Joseph L. Ellis to Thomas G. Western, December 8, 1844, in MS. Indian Papers, no. 107, Texas State Archives, Austin; Thomas G. Western to Joseph L. Ellis, May 31, 1845, in MS. Indian Papers, no. 222.

44. Joseph L. Ellis to Thomas G. Western, December 8, 1844, in MS. Indian Papers, no. 107, Texas State Archives, Austin.

45. Reichstein, *Rise of the Lone Star*, 180–202.

46. J. P. Henderson to P. M. Butler, May 5, 1846, in Winfrey and Day, *Indian Papers of Texas*, 3:42.

47. "Death of Chief Colita," July 17, 1852, *Texas State Gazette*, Clements Center for Southwest Studies, Dallas, Texas.

48. The Alabamas and Coushattas taught their young not to fear death. Interview of Sissy Abbey, July 14, 1938, in Lyda Averill Taylor Papers, Center for American History, University of Texas at Austin; Gregory A. Waselkov, Brian M. Wood, and Joseph M. Herbert, *Colonization and Conquest: The 1980 Archaeological Excavations at Fort Toulouse and Fort Jackson, Alabama* (Montgomery, Ala.: Auburn University), 66–91; Geoffrey D. Kimball, *Koasati Dictionary* (Lincoln: University of Nebraska Press, 1994), 29; Jean-Bernard Bossu, *Jean-Bernard Bossu's Travels in the Interior of North America, 1751–1762*, trans. and ed. Seymour Feiler (Norman: University of Oklahoma Press, 1962), 145.

49. David La Vere, *Contrary Neighbors: Southern Plains and Removed Indians in Indian Territory* (Norman: University of Oklahoma Press, 2000), 85–86.

50. Ibid., 162; Newcomb, *Indians of Texas*, 352–57.

51. Ibid. For discussion of the Brazos Reservation, see La Vere, *Contrary Neighbors*, 148–66.

52. "Petition of the Alabama Indians."

53. Ibid.

54. Ibid.

55. Ibid.

56. Alabama Indians Land Grant, Center For American History, University of Texas at Austin; State of Texas, Tyler County, August 15, 1854, MS. Indian Papers, Texas State Archives, Austin; Deed Records of Polk County, October 14, 1854, and January 14, 1855, MS. Indian Papers.

57. Ralph Henry Marsh, "The History of Polk County, Texas," in *Alabama-Coushatta (Creek) Indians*, ed. David Agee Horr (New York: Garland, 1974), 288–89.

58. A. J. Harrison to F. M. Lubbock, December 5, 1861 (quote); A. J. Harrison to F. M. Lubbock, July 17, 1862, A. J. Harrison Letters, in MS. Indian Papers, Texas State Archives, Austin.

59. Ibid.

Conclusion

1. "The Alabamas Travel Westward," in Howard N. Martin, *Myths and Folktales of the Alabama-Coushatta Indians of Texas* (Austin, Tex.: Encino Press, 1977), 77–79.

2. Ibid.

Epilogue

1. They even offered to muster a company of men to defend their land against Union invasion during the American Civil War. See H. C. Pedigo for Chiefs Antone, Cilistine, Thompson, and John Scott, "Letter from Chiefs of the Alabama Indians to Sam Houston," December 29, 1859, in *The Indian Papers of Texas and the Southwest, 1825–1916*, ed. Dorman H. Winfrey and James M. Day, 5 vols. (Austin: Texas State Historical Commission, 1995), 389–90; A. J. Harrison to F. M. Lubbock, December 5, 1861, A. J. Harrison Letters, in MS. Indian Papers, Texas State Archives, Austin.

2. Ralph K. M. Haurwitz, "In East Texas, Tribe Blends Old and New Alabama-Coushatta Culture Alive Despite Centuries of Loss," *Austin (Texas) American-Statesman*, November 9, 2003; Howard N. Martin, *Myths and Folktales of the Alabama-Coushatta Indians of Texas* (Austin, Tex.: Encino Press, 1977), xi.

3. The story continues with the waters rising toward the sun. A woodpecker's head burned to a bright red, explaining the existence of redheaded woodpeckers, now the sacred symbol of the Alabama-Coushatta Tribe of Texas. Martin, *Myths and Folktales*, xi; Haurwitz, "In East Texas."

4. Martin, *Myths and Folktales*, preface.

5. Report of Inspector James McLaughlin (McLaughlin Report), in "Advisability of Purchasing Lands For Alabama and Coushatta Indians, Polk County, Texas," House of Representatives, 65th Congress, 3rd Session, September 14, 1918, no. 1579, 2–4, Texas State Archives.

6. McLaughlin Report, 2–4.

7. Ibid.

8. Ibid.; Haurwitz, "In East Texas."

9. Jonathan Hook, *The Alabama-Coushatta Indians* (College Station: Texas A&M University Press, 1998), 60, 84.

10. See my bibliography for Swanton's work on the Alabamas and Coushattas.

11. Martin, *Myths and Folktales*, preface.

12. Linguists agree that out of all Native languages, Koasati is most closely related to Alabama. The next closest are the languages spoken by the Seminoles (Mikasuki) and the Apalachees (whose language is now extinct). Compared to all other Muskogean dialects, the structure and grammar of the

Alabama and Koasati languages had the most in common with each other. Many of their words are identical, and differences are not consequential; the Alabamas speak with more detail, whereas Coushattas are more direct. Karen Jacque Lupardus, "The Language of the Alabama Indians" (Ph.D. diss., University of Kansas, 1982), 1, 4; Cora Sylestine, Heather K. Hardy, and Timothy Montler, *Dictionary of the Alabama Language* (Austin: University of Texas Press, 1993), xi–xii; Geoffrey D. Kimball, *Koasati Dictionary* (Lincoln: University of Nebraska Press, 1994), xi; Robert Leigh Wright, *The Only Land They Knew: The Tragic Story of the American Indians in the Old South* (New York: Free Press, 1981), 8–9.

13. Sylestine, Hardy, and Montler, *Dictionary of the Alabama Language*, foreword.

14. Ibid.; Kimball, *Koasati Dictionary*; Geoffrey D. Kimball, *Koasati Grammar* (Lincoln: University of Nebraska Press, 1991).

15. Mary Lee Grant, "Alabama, Coushatta Tribes Trying to Preserve Language," *Huntsville (Alabama) Times*, August 20, 2000.

16. Grant, "Alabama, Coushatta Tribes."

17. Hook, *Alabama-Coushatta Indians*, 40, 72–75.

18. Mark Babineck, "Time Not on Casino's Side," *Dallas Morning News*, July 16, 2002.

19. Ibid.

20. Ralph K. M. Haurwitz, "$270 Million Award for Tribe Stalled," *Austin (Texas) American-Statesman*, December 8, 2003.

21. Ralph K. M. Haurwitz, "East Texas Tribe Awaiting Its Due," *The Austin (Texas) American-Statesman*, December 26, 2005.

22. Haurwitz, "$270 Million Award."

23. Suzanne Gamboa, "Lobbyist Helped Line Up Indian Leaders to Meet with Bush," *Associated Press*, June 8, 2005; Gamboa, "Texas Tribe Names Abramoff, Reed in Suit," *Associated Press*, July 12, 2006.

24. Hook, *Alabama-Coushatta Indians*, 65, 101; Haurwitz, "In East Texas."

Bibliography

Unpublished Sources

Alabama Indians Land Grant. Center For American History, University of Texas at Austin.

"Archaeological Excavation of Alabama Burial Mound, East Texas." 1983. Richard Yarborough Collection. Center For American History, University of Texas at Austin.

Archives des Colonies. C13 Manuscript Series. Historic New Orleans Collection, New Orleans, La., and Center for Louisiana Studies, University of Louisiana, Lafayette.

Archivo General de Mexico. Fomento y Colonization. Center for American History, University of Texas at Austin.

Bexar Archives. Center for American History, University of Texas at Austin and Clements Center for Southwestern Studies, Southern Methodist University, Dallas.

British Public Records, Colonial Office, Class 5. London and the Library of Congress, Washington, D.C.

British Public Records Office, South Carolina Colonial Entry, South Carolina Department of Archives and History, Columbia.

Deed Records of Polk County, Texas State Archives, Austin.

Delisle, Guillaume. "Carte du Mexique et de la Floride, 1703." Historic New Orleans Map Collection.

Fer, Nicholas de. "Le Cours de Missisipii [*sic*], ou de St. Louis, 1718." Historic New Orleans Map Collection.

Gauld, George. "A Survey of the Coast of West Florida from Pensacola to Cape Blaise: Including the Bays of Pensacola, Santa Rosa, Saint Andrew, and Saint Joseph, with the shoals lying off Cape Blaise, 1766." Special Collections, University of West Florida, Pensacola.

Harrison, A. J. Papers. Texas State Archives, Austin.

McLaughlin, James. Report of Inspector James McLaughlin, in "Advisability of Purchasing Lands For Alabama and Coushatta Indians, Polk County, Texas," House of Representatives, 65th Congress, 3rd Session, September 14, 1918, no. 1579, 2–4, Texas State Archives, Austin.

Morse, Jedediah. "A Report to the Secretary of War of the United States on Indian Affairs, 1822." Richard Yarborough Collection. Center For American History, University of Texas at Austin.

MS. Indian Papers, 1825–1916. Texas State Library, Austin.

Nacogdoches Archives. Center For American History, University of Texas at Austin.

Nacogdoches Archives Calendar. Center For American History, University of Texas at Austin.

Panton and Leslie Papers. Microfilm. Auburn University. Auburn, Alabama.

"Petition of the Alabama Indians, 13 December 1853." Secretary of State's Memorials and Petitions. Texas State Archives, Austin.

Rusk, Thomas Jefferson. Papers. Center For American History, University of Texas at Austin.

Sylestine, James Papers. Texas State Archives. Austin, Texas.

Taylor, Lyda Averill Papers. Center For American History, University of Texas at Austin.

Texas State Gazette. Clements Center for Southwest Studies, Dallas, Texas.

Treaty with Cherokees and their associate bands residing in Texas, 23 February 1836, Manuscript Collection. Texas State Archives, Austin.

Published Sources

Abel, Annie Heloise, ed. *A Report From Natchitoches in 1807 by Dr. John Sibley*. New York: Museum of the American Indian: Heye Foundation, 1922.

Adair, James. *The History of the American Indians, Particularly Those Nations Adjoining to the Mississippi East and West Florida, Georgia, South and North Carolina, and Virginia*. Edited by Samuel Cole Williams. London: Charles Dilly, 1775. Reprint, New York: Argonaut Press, 1968.

Alden, John Richard. *John Stuart and the Southern Colonial Frontier: A Study of Indian Relations, War, Trade, and Land Problems in the Southern Wilderness, 1754–1775*. New York: Gordian Press, 1966.

Allain, Mathé. *"Not Worth A Straw": French Colonial Policy and the Early Years of Louisiana*. Lafayette: Center for Louisiana Studies, University of Southwestern Louisiana, 1988.

Almonte, Juan N. "Statistical Report on Texas." Edited by Carlos Casteneda. *Southwestern Historical Quarterly* 28 (1924): 177–222.

Anderson, David G. *Savannah River Chiefdoms: Political Change in the Late Prehistoric Southeast*. Tuscaloosa: University of Alabama Press, 1994.

Anderson, Gary Clayton. *The Conquest of Texas: Ethnic Cleansing in the Promised Land, 1820–1875*. Norman: University of Oklahoma Press, 2005.

Atkin, Edmond. *The Edmond Atkin Report and Plan of 1755*. Edited by Wilbur Jacobs. Lincoln: University of Nebraska Press, 1967.

Aubert, Guillaume. "'The Blood of France'": Race and Purity of Blood in the French Atlantic World," *William and Mary Quarterly* 61, no. 3 (2004): 439–78.

Axtell, James. *The European and the Indian: Essays in the Ethnohistory of Colonial North America*. New York: Oxford University Press, 1981.

Babineck, Mark. "Time Not on Casino's Side." *Dallas Morning News*. July 16, 2002.

Baker, D. W. C., comp. *A Texas Scrap Book*. New York: A. S. Barnes and Co., 1875.

Bannon, John Fancis, ed. *Bolton and the Spanish Borderlands*. Norman: University of Oklahoma Press, 1964.

Barker, Eugene C., ed. *The Austin Papers*. Annual Report of the American Historical Association, 1919. 2 Vols. Washington, D.C.: U.S. Government Printing Office, 1924.

——. *The Life of Stephen F. Austin: Founder of Texas*. Nashville, Tenn. and Dallas, Tex.: Cokesbury Press, 1925.

——. *Mexico and Texas, 1821–1835*. Dallas, Tex.: Turner Publishing, 1928.

Bell, Amelia Rector. "Separate People: Speaking of Creek Men and Women," *American Anthropologist* 92 (1990): 332–45.

Bell, Thomas W. "Thomas W. Bell Letters." Edited by Llerena Friend. *Southwestern Historical Quarterly* 63 (October 1959): 299–310.

Binkley, William C., ed. *Official Correspondence of the Texas Revolution*. 2 vols. New York: D. Appleton, 1936.

Blitz, John H. *Ancient Chiefdoms of the Tombigbee*. Tuscaloosa: University of Alabama Press, 1993.

Blitz, John H., and Karl G. Lorenz. *The Chattahoochee Chiefdoms*. Tuscaloosa: University of Alabama Press, 2006.

Blount, Lois Foster. "A Brief Study of Thomas J. Rusk Based on His Letters to His Brother, David, 1835–1856." *Southwestern Historical Quarterly* 34 (April 1931): 271–92.

Bollaert, William. *William Bollaert's Texas*. Edited by W. Eugene Hollon and Ruth Lapham Butler. Norman: University of Oklahoma Press, 1956.

Bolton, Herbert Eugene. *The Spanish Borderlands: A Chronicle of Old Florida and the Southwest*. New Haven: Yale University Press, 1921.

Bonnell, George William. *Topographical Description of Texas, to Which Is Added an Account of the Indian Tribes*. Austin, Tex.: Clark, Wing and Brown, 1840. Reprint, Waco, Tex.: Texian Press, 1961.

Bossu, Jean-Bernard. *Jean-Bernard Bossu's Travels in the Interior of North America, 1751–1762*. Translated and edited by Seymour Feiler. Norman: University of Oklahoma Press, 1962.

Bowne, Eric E. *The Westo Indians: Slave Traders of the Early Colonial South*. Tuscaloosa: University of Alabama Press, 2005.

Boyd, Mark F., trans. and ed. "Expedition of Marcos Delgado from Apalache to the Upper Creek Country in 1686." *Florida Historical Quarterly*, 16 (1937): 2–32.

Brasseaux, Carl., trans. and ed. *A Comparative View of French Louisiana, 1699 and 1762: The Journals of Pierre Le Moyne d'Iberville and Jean-Jaques-Blaise d'Abbadie*. Lafayette: Center For Louisiana Studies, 1979.

Braund, Kathryn E. Holland. *Deerskins and Duffels: The Creek Indian Trade with Anglo-America, 1685–1815*. Lincoln: University of Nebraska Press, 1993.

——. "Guardians of Tradition and Handmaidens to Change: Women's Roles in Creek Economic and Social Life during the Eighteenth Century." *American Indian Quarterly* 14 (Summer 1990): 239–58.

Brown, John Henry. *History of Texas from 1685 to 1892*. 2 vols. Austin, Tex.: Pemberton Press, 1970.

Burch, Marvin C. "The Indigenous Indians of the Lower Trinity Area of Texas." *Southwestern Historical Quarterly* 60 (July 1956): 36–52.

Calloway, Colin G. *The American Revolution in Indian Country: Crisis and Diversity in Native American Communities*. Cambridge: Cambridge University Press, 1995.

Candler, Allen D., Kenneth Coleman, and Milton Ready, eds. *The Colonial Records of the State of Georgia*. 28 vols. Atlanta: C. P. Byrd, 1904–16. Reprint, Athens: University of Georgia Press, 1974–76.

Cantrell, Gregg. *Stephen Austin: Empresario of Texas*. New Haven, Conn.: Yale University Press, 1999.

Carlton, Leslie. "Indians of Southeast Texas." M.A. thesis, North Texas State University, 1939.

Carson, James Taylor. "Ethnogeography and the Native American Past." *Ethnohistory* 49 (2002): 769–88.

———. *Searching for the Bright Path: The Mississippi Choctaws from Prehistory to Removal.* Lincoln: University of Nebraska Press, 1999.

Carter, Clarence Edwin, ed. *The Territorial Papers of the United States.* Vol. 19. *The Territory of Arkansas, 1819–1825.* Washington, D.C.: U.S. Government Printing Office, 1953.

Cashin, Edward J. *Lachlan McGillivray, Indian Trader: The Shaping of the Southern Colonial Frontier.* Athens: University of Georgia Press, 1992.

Castaneda, Carlos E., trans. and ed. *The Mexican Side of the Texan Revolution (1836) by the Chief Mexican Participants.* Washington, D.C.: Documentary Publications, 1971.

Chamberlain, C. K. "East Texas: Alabama-Coushatta Indian Reservation." *East Texas Historical Journal* 8 (March 1970): 109–77.

Chaudhuri, Jean, and Joyotpaul Chaudhuri, *A Sacred Path: The Way of the Muscogee Creeks.* Los Angeles: University of California, Los Angeles, American Indian Studies Center, 2001.

Christian, A. K. "Mirabeau Buonaparte Lamar." *Southwestern Historical Quarterly* 24 (July 1920): 39–80.

Claassen, Cheryl, and Rosemary A. Joyce, eds. *Women in Prehistory: North America And Mesoamerica.* Philadelphia: University of Pennsylvania Press, 1997.

Clarke, Mary Whatley. *Chief Bowles and the Texas Cherokees.* Norman: University of Oklahoma Press, 1971.

———. "The State of Two Tribes." *The Cattleman* 69 (August 1982): 158–62.

Clayton, Lawrence A., Vernon James Knight Jr., and Edward C. Moore, eds. *The De Soto Chronicles: The Expedition of Hernando De Soto to North America In 1539–1543.* 2 vols. Tuscaloosa: University of Alabama Press, 1993.

Clements, William M. and Frances M. Malpezzi. *Native American Folklore, 1879–1979: An Annotated Bibliography.* Compiled by William M. Clements and Frances M. Malpezzi. Athens, Ohio: Swallow Press, 1984.

Cohen, Robin. *Global Diasporas: An Introduction.* Seattle: University of Washington Press, 1997.

Corbitt, D. C., ed. "Papers from the Spanish Archives Relating to Tennessee and the Old Southwest, 1783–1800." *East Tennessee Historical Society Publications* 35 (1963–69).

Cottier, John W. "The Alabama River Phase: A Brief Description of a Late Phase in The Prehistory of South Central Alabama. Appendix to *Archaeological Salvage Investigation in the Miller's Ferry Lock and Dam Reservoir, 1968.* Moundville: University of Alabama, 1970.

Crane, Verner W. *The Southern Frontier, 1670–1732*. Durham, N.C.: Duke University Press, 1928.

Crawford, James. *The Mobilian Trade Language*. Knoxville: University of Tennessee Press, 1978.

Crosby, Alfred. *The Columbian Exchange*. Westport, Conn.: Greenwood Press, 1972.

Crouse, Nellis M. *Le Moyne d'Iberville: Soldier of New France*. Ithaca, N.Y.: Cornell University Press, 1954.

Davidson, William C. "Sam Houston and the Indians: A Rhetorical Study of the Man and the Myth." Ph.D. dissertation, University of Kansas, 1971.

Davies, Kenneth G., ed. *Documents of the American Revolution, 1770–1783*. 20 vols. Dublin: Irish University Press, 1972–79.

De la Pena, Jose Enrique. *With Santa Anna in Texas: A Personal Narrative of the Revolution*. Translated and edited by Carmen Perry. College Station: Texas A&M University Press, 1975.

De la Teja, Jesus F., ed. *A Revolution Remembered: The Memoirs and Selected Correspondence of Juan N. Seguin*. Austin, Tex.: State House Press, 1991.

Densmore, Frances. "The Alabama Indians and Their Music." In *Straight Texas*. Edited by J. Frank Dobie. Austin, Tex.: Texas Folklore Society, 1937.

DePratter, Chester B., Charles M. Hudson, and Marvin Smith. "The Hernando de Soto Expedition: From Chiaha to Mabila." In *Alabama and the Borderlands*. Edited by R. Reid Badger and Lawrence A. Clayton. Tuscaloosa: University of Alabama Press, 1985.

De Shields, James T. *Border Wars of Texas: Being an Authentic and Popular Account, in Chronological Order, of the Long and Bitter Conflict Waged Between Savage Indian Tribes and the Pioneer Settlers of Texas, Wresting of a Fair Land from Savage Rule A Red Record of Fierce Strife*. Austin: Texas Historical Association, 1912. Reprint, Austin, Tex.: State House Press, 1993.

Dobyns, Henry F. "Estimating Aboriginal American Population: An Appraisal of Techniques with a New Hemispheric Estimate." *Current Anthropology* 7 (1966): 395–416.

———. *Their Number Became Thinned*. Knoxville: University of Tennessee Press, 1983.

Dowd, Gregory. *A Spirited Resistance: The Native American Struggle for Unity, 1745–1815*. Baltimore: Johns Hopkins University Press, 1992.

Dresel, Gustav. *Houston Journal: Adventures in North America and Texas, 1837–1841*. Edited and translated by Max Freund. Austin: University of Texas Press, 1954.

Duncan, David Ewing. *Hernando de Soto: A Savage Quest in the Americas*. New York: Crown, 1995.

Ethridge, Robbie. *Creek Country: The Creek Indians and Their World*. Chapel Hill: University of North Carolina Press, 2003.

——. *From Chicaza to Chickasaw*. Chapel Hill: University of North Carolina Press, forthcoming.

——. "The Making of a Militaristic Slaving Society: The Chickasaws and the Colonial Indian Slave Trade." In *The Indian Slave Trade in Colonial America*. Edited by Alan Gallay. Lincoln: University of Nebraska Press, forthcoming.

Ethridge, Robbie, and Charles Hudson, eds. *The Transformation of the Southeastern Indians, 1540–1760*. Jackson: University Press of Mississippi, 2002.

Ethridge, Robbie, and Sheri M. Shuck-Hall, eds. *Mapping the Mississippian Shatter Zone: The European Invasion and Regional Instability in the American South*. Lincoln: University of Nebraska Press, forthcoming.

Everett, Dianna. *The Texas Cherokees: A People Between Two Fires, 1819–1840*. Norman: University of Oklahoma Press, 1990.

Fabel, Robin F. A. *Bombast and Broadsides: The Lives of George Johnstone*. Tuscaloosa: University of Alabama Press, 1987.

——. *Colonial Challenges: Britons, Native Americans, and Caribs, 1759–1775*. Gainesville: University Press of Florida, 2000.

Fabel, Robin F. A., and Robert Rea. "Lieutenant Thomas Campbell's Sojourn among the Creeks, November 1764–May 1765." *Alabama Historical Quarterly* 36, no. 2 (Summer 1974): 97–111.

Faulk, Odie B. *The Last Years of Spanish Texas, 1778–1821*. London: Mouton and Company, 1964.

Fehrenbach, T. R. *Lone Star: A History of Texas and the Texans*. New York: Macmillan, 1968.

Fitzpatrick, John. *The Merchant of Manchac: The Letterbooks of John Fitzpatrick, 1768–1790*. Edited by Margaret Fisher Dalrymple. Baton Rouge: Louisiana State University Press, 1978.

Flanagan, Sue. *Sam Houston's Texas*. Austin: University of Texas Press, 1964.

Flores, Dan, ed. *Jefferson and Southwestern Exploration: The Freeman and Custis Accounts of the Red River Expedition of 1806*. Norman: University of Oklahoma Press, 1984.

——. "The Red River Branch of the Alabama-Coushatta Indians: An Ethnohistory." *Southern Studies* 16 (Spring 1977): 55–72.

Frégault, Guy. *Pierre Le Moyne d'Iberville*. Montreal: Fides, 1968.

Friend, Llerena, ed. "Notes and Documents, Thomas W. Bell Letters." *Southwestern Historical Quarterly* 63 (October 1959): 299–310.

Friis, Herman R. "The Image of the American West at Mid-Century (1840–1860)." In *The Frontier Re-Examined*. Edited by John Francis McDermott. Chicago: University of Illinois Press, 1967.

Gaillardet, Frederic. *Sketches of Early Texas and Louisiana*. Translated and edited by James L. Shepherd III. Austin: University of Texas Press, 1966.

Gallay, Allan. *Indian Slave Trade: The Rise of the English Empire in the American South, 1670–1717*. New Haven, Conn.: Yale University Press, 2002.

Galloway, Patricia Kay. *Choctaw Genesis, 1500–1700*. Lincoln: University of Nebraska Press, 1995.

——. "Where Have All the Menstrual Huts Gone? The Invisibility of Menstrual Seclusion in the Late Prehistoric Southeast." In *Women In Prehistory: North America and Mesoamerica*. Edited by Cheryl Claassen and Rosemary A. Joyce. Philadelphia: University of Pennsylvania Press, 1997.

Gamboa, Suzanne. "Lobbyist Helped Line Up Indian Leaders to Meet with Bush." Associated Press. June 8, 2005.

——. "Texas Tribe Names Abramoff, Reed in Suit." Associated Press. July 12, 2006.

Gammel, H. P. N. *The Laws of Texas, 1822–1897*. 10 vols. Austin, Tex.: Gammel Book Company, 1898.

Garroutte, Eva Marie. *Real Indians: Identity and the Survival of Native America*. Berkeley: University of California Press, 2003.

Goetzmann, William H. *Exploration and Empire: The Explorer and the Scientist in the Winning of the American West*. New York: W. W. Norton, 1966.

Grant, Mary Lee. "Alabama, Coushatta Tribes Trying to Preserve Language." *Huntsville (Alabama) Times*. August 20, 2000.

Grantham, Bill. *Creation Myths and Legends of the Creek Indians*. Gainesville: University Press of Florida, 2002.

Green, Michael D. *The Politics of Indian Removal: Creek Government and Society in Crisis*. Lincoln: University of Nebraska Press, 1982.

Gregory, Jack. *Sam Houston With the Cherokees*. Norman: University of Oklahoma, 1967.

Gregory, James N. *The Southern Diaspora: How Great Migrations of Black and White Southerners Transformed America*. Chapel Hill: University of North Carolina Press, 2006.

Gullick, Charles Adams, ed. *The Papers of Mirabeau Buonaparte Lamar*. 6 vols. Austin, Tex.: A. C. Baldwin and Sons, 1922.

Hahn, Steven C. *The Invention of the Creek Nation, 1670–1763*. Lincoln: University of Nebraska Press, 2004.

Hatcher, Mattie Austin. *The Opening of Texas to Foreign Settlement, 1801–1821*. Austin: University of Texas Bulletin, 1927. Reprint, Philadelphia: Porcupine Press, 1976.

Hatley, Tom. *The Dividing Paths: Cherokees and South Carolinians through the Era of the Revolution*. New York: Oxford University Press, 1992.

Haurwitz, Ralph K. M. "In East Texas, Tribe Blends Old and New Alabama-Coushatta Culture Alive Despite Centuries of Loss," *Austin (Texas) American-Statesman*. November 9, 2003.

——. "$270 Million Award for Tribe Stalled." *Austin (Texas) American-Statesman*. December 8, 2003.

Hawkins, Benjamin. *The Letters, Journals, and Writings of Benjamin Hawkins*. Edited by C. L. Grant. 2 vols. Savannah, Ga.: Beehive Press, 1980.

———. *A Sketch of the Creek Country, in the Years 1798 and 1799*. 1848. Reprint, Savannah: Georgia Historical Society, 1916.

Higginbotham, Jay. *Old Mobile: Fort Louis de la Louisiane, 1702–1711*. Tuscaloosa: University of Alabama Press, 1977.

Himmel, Kelly. *The Conquest of the Karankawas and the Tonkawas, 1821–1859*. College Station: Texas A&M University Press, 1999.

Hinderaker, Eric, and Peter C. Mancall. *At the Edge of Empire: The British Backcountry in British North America*. Baltimore: Johns Hopkins University Press, 2003.

Hoig, Stanley. *The Cherokees and Their Chiefs: In the Wake of Empire*. Fayetteville: University of Arkansas Press, 1998.

Holm, Tom, J. Diane Pearson, and Ben Chavis. "Peoplehood: A Model for the Extension of Sovereignty in American Indian Studies." *Wicazo Review* (Spring 2003): 7–24.

Hook, Jonathan B. *The Alabama-Coushatta Indians*. College Station: Texas A&M University Press, 1997.

Horr, David Agee, ed. *Alabama-Coushatta (Creek) Indians*. New York: Garland, 1974.

Horsman, Reginald. *Race and Manifest Destiny: The Origin of American Racial Anglo-Saxonism*. Cambridge, Mass.: Harvard University Press, 1981.

———. "The Indian Policy of an 'Empire of Liberty.'" In *Native Americans and the Early Republic*. Edited by Frederick Hoxie, Ronald Hoffman, and Peter Albert. Charlottesville: University Press of Virginia, 1999.

———. *Expansion and American Indian Policy, 1783–1812*. East Lansing: Michigan State University Press, 1967.

Houren, A. "The Causes and Origin of the Decree of April 6, 1830." *Southwestern Historical Quarterly* 16 (1913): 378–442.

Houston, Sam. *The Writings of Sam Houston, 1813–1863*. Edited by Amelia W. Williams and Eugene C. Barker. 8 vols. Austin: University of Texas Press, 1938–43.

Hudson, Charles. *Conversations with the High Priest of Coosa*. Chapel Hill: University of North Carolina Press, 2003.

———. *The Juan Pardo Expeditions: Exploration of the Carolinas and Tennessee, 1566–1568*. Washington, D.C.: Smithsonian Institution Press, 1990.

———. *Knights of Spain, Warriors of the Sun: Hernando De Soto and the South's Ancient Chiefdoms*. Athens: University of Georgia Press, 1997.

———. *The Southeastern Indians*. Knoxville: University of Tennessee Press, 1976.

Hunt, John Gabriel, ed. *The Essential Thomas Jefferson*. New York: Gramercy Books, 1994.

Hunter, Donald G. "Their Final Years: The Apalachee and Other Immigrant Tribes on the Red River, 1763–1834." *Florida Anthropologist* (March 1994): 3–45.

Hunter, J. Marvin. "Treaty Made with Indian Tribes in 1844." *Frontier Times* 20 (December 1942): 53–55.

Jackson, Jason Baird. *Yuchi Ceremonial Life: Performance, Meaning, And Tradition in a Contemporary American Indian.* (Studies in the Anthropology of North American Indians). Lincoln: University of Nebraska Press, 2005.

Jefferson, Thomas. "Message from the President of the U.S. Transmitting a Letter from Gov. Claiborne on the Small Tribe of Alabama Indians on the Western Side of the Mississippi," December 30, 1808, *Pamphlets in American History* (Washington, D.C.: A.&G. Wat Printers, 1809), Group I: 962.

Jenkins, John H., ed. *The Military Papers of the Texas Revolution, 1835–1836.* 10 vols. Austin, Tex.: Presidial Press, 1973.

Jenkins, Ned J. "Early Creek Origins: The Moundville Connection." *Alabama Museum of Natural History Bulletin* (in press).

Jennings, Francis. *The Founding of America.* New York: W. W. Norton, 1993.

Jones, Anson. *Memoranda and Official Correspondence Relating to the Republic of Texas, Its History, and Annexation.* New York: D. Appleton and Co., 1859. Reprint, New York: Arno Press, 1973.

Jurney, David H., and Timothy K. Pertula. "Nineteenth Century Alibamu-Koasati Pottery Assemblages and Culinary Traditions." Paper presented at the 1995 Meeting of the Louisiana Archaeology Society, Natchitoches, Louisiana.

———. "Nineteenth Century Alibamu-Koasati Pottery Assemblages and Culinary Traditions." *Southeastern Archaeology* 14 (Summer 1995): 17–30.

Kavanaugh, Thomas W. *Comanche Political History: An Ethnohistorical Perspective, 1707–1875.* Lincoln: University of Nebraska Press, 1996.

Kelton, Paul. "The Great Southeastern Smallpox Epidemic, 1696–1700: The Region's First Major Epidemic." In *Transformation of the Southeastern Indians, 1540–1760.* Edited by Robbie Ethridge and Charles Hudson, 21–38. Jackson: University Press of Mississippi, 2002.

Kennedy, William. *Texas: The Rise, Progress, and Prospects of the Republic of Texas.* 2 vols. London: R. Hastings, 1841.

Kimball, Geoffrey D. *Koasati Dictionary.* With the assistance of Bel Abbey, Martha John, and Ruth Poncho. Lincoln: University of Nebraska Press, 1994.

———. *Koasati Grammar.* Lincoln: University of Nebraska Press, 1991.

King, Adam. *Etowah: The Political History of a Chiefdom Capital.* Tuscaloosa: University of Alabama Press, 2003.

Kinnaird, Lawrence, ed. *Spain in the Mississippi Valley, 1765–1794.* Annual Report of the American Historical Association for the Year 1945. Washington, D.C.: U.S. Government Printing Office, 1946.

Kniffen, Fred B., Hiram R. Gregory, and George A. Stokes. *The Historic Indian Tribes of Louisiana: From 1542 to the Present.* Baton Rouge: Louisiana State University Press, 1987.

Knight, Vernon James, Jr. "The Formation of the Creeks." In *The Forgotten Centuries: Indians and Europeans in the American South, 1521–1704.* Edited by Charles Hudson and Carmen Chavez Teaser (Athens: University of Georgia Press, 1994.

———, ed. *The Moundville Expeditions of Clarence Bloomingfield Moore.* Tuscaloosa: University of Alabama Press, 1996.

———. "Symbolism of Mississippian Mounds." In *Powhatan's Mantle: Indians in the Colonial Southeast.* Edited by Peter H. Wood, Gregory A. Waselkov, and M. Thomas Hatley, 279–91. Lincoln: University of Nebraska Press, 1989.

Knight, Vernon James, Jr., and Sherée L. Adams. "A Voyage to the Mobile and Tomeh in 1700, with Notes on the Interior of Alabama." *Ethnohistory* 28 (1981): 179–194.

Knight, Vernon James, Jr., and Vincas P. Steponaitis. "A New History of Moundville." In *Archaeology of the Moundville Chiefdom.* Edited by Vernon James Knight Jr. and Vincas P. Steponaitis. Washington, D.C.: Smithsonian Institution Press, 1998.

Lack, Paul D. "The Córdova Revolt." In *Tejano Journey, 1770–1850.* Edited by Gerald E. Poyo. Austin: University of Texas Press, 1996.

La Harpe, Jean-Baptiste Bénard de. *Historical Journal of the Settlement of the French in Louisiana.* Translated by Virginia Koenig and Joan Cain, and edited by Glenn R. Conrad. Lafayette, Louisiana: University of Southwestern Louisiana, 1971.

Lamar, Mirabeau B. *The Papers of Mirabeau Buonaparte Lamar.* Edited by Charles A. Gulick Jr., Katherine Elliott, and Harriet Smither. 6 vols. Austin: Von Boeckmann-Jones, 1921–27.

La Vere, David. *The Caddo Chiefdoms: Caddo Politics and Economics, 700–1835.* Lincoln: University of Nebraska Press, 1998.

———. *Contrary Neighbors: Southern Plains and Removed Indians in Indian Territory.* Norman: University of Oklahoma Press, 2000.

———. *Life among the Texas Indians: The WPA Narratives.* College Station: Texas A&M Press, 1998.

Lavie, Samdar, and Ted Swedenburg, eds. *Displacement, Diaspora, and Geographies of Identity.* Durham, N.C.: Duke University Press, 1996.

Laws of the Republic of Texas. 2 vols. Houston: Office of the Telegraph, 1838.

Lewis, Barry R., and Charles Stout, eds. *Mississippian Towns and Sacred Spaces: Searching for an Architectural Grammar.* Tuscaloosa: University of Alabama Press, 1998.

Lewis, David, Jr., and Ann Jordon, *Creek Indian Medicine Ways: The Enduring*

Power of Muskoke Religion. Albuquerque: University of New Mexico Press, 2002.

Lewis, Thomas M. N. *The Prehistory of the Chickamauga Basin in Tennessee.* Vol. 1. Knoxville: University of Tennessee Press, 1995.

Lipscomb, Terry W., and R. Nicholas Olsberg, eds. *The Colonial Records of South Carolina: The Journal of the Commons House of Assembly, November 14, 1751–October 7, 1752.* Columbia: University of South Carolina Press, 1977.

Lupardus, Karen Jaque. "The Language of the Alabama Indians." Ph.D. Dissertation, University of Kansas, 1982.

Malone, Prairie View. *Sam Houston's Indians: The Alabama-Coushatti.* San Antonio, Tex.: Naylor Company, 1960.

Martin, Calvin. *Keepers of the Game: Indian Animal Relationships and the Fur Trade.* Berkeley: University of California Press, 1978.

——. *Sacred Revolt: The Muskogees' Struggle for a New World.* Boston: Beacon Press, 1991.

Martin, Howard, N. "Alabama-Coushatta Tales." In *Mexican Border Ballads and Other Lore.* Edited by Mody Coggin Boatright. Austin: Texas Folklore Society, 1946.

——. "Ethnohistorical Analysis of Documents Relating to the Alabama and Coushatta Tribes of the State of Texas." In *Alabama-Coushatta (Creek) Indians.* Edited by David Agee Horr, 179–256. New York: Garland, 1974.

——. *Folktales of the Alabama-Coushatta Indians.* Livingston, Tex.: by the author, 1946.

——. "Folktales of the Alabama-Coushatta Indians." In *Mexican Border Ballads and Other Lore.* Edited by Mody C. Boatright, 65–80. Austin: Texas Folklore Society, 1946.

——. *Myths and Folktales of the Alabama-Coushatta Indians of Texas.* Austin, Tex.: Encino Press, 1977.

——. "Polk County Indians: Alabamas, Coushattas, Pakana Muskogees." *East Texas Historical Journal* 17 (1979): 3–23.

——. "Texas Redskins in Confederate Gray." *Southwestern historical Quarterly* 70 (April 1967): 586–92.

McClain, Rotha Berry. "Alabama and Coushatta Indians of Texas." *Texas Geographic Magazine* 12 (Fall 1948): 19–23.

McDowell, William L., Jr., ed. *The Colonial Records of South Carolina: Documents Relating to Indian Affairs, 1750–1765.* 2 vols. Columbia: South Carolina Department of Archives and History, 1958, 1970.

——, ed. *The Colonial Records of South Carolina: Journals of the Commissioners of the Indian Trade, September 20, 1710–August 29, 1718.* Columbia: South Carolina Department of Archives and History, 1955.

McWilliams, Richard Gaillard, ed. *Iberville's Gulf Journals.* Tuscaloosa: University of Alabama Press, 1981.

Moore, Alexander, ed. *Thomas Nairne's Muskhogean Journals: The 1708 Expedition to the Mississippi River*. Jackson: University of Mississippi Press, 1988.

Moore, Francis, Jr. *Map and Description of Texas Containing Sketches of its History, Geology, Geography, and Statistics: With Concise Statements, Relative to the Soil, Climate, Productions, Facilities of Transportation, Population of the Country; and Some Brief Remarks Upon the Character and Customs of its Inhabitants*. Philadelphia: H. Tanner Jr., 1840. Reprint, Waco, Tex.: Texian Press, 1965.

Muckleroy, Anna. "The Indian Policy of the Republic of Texas: The Indian Policy of Lamar's Administration." *Southwestern Historical Quarterly* 25 (April 1922): 229–260; 26 (July 1922):1–29; (October 1922): 128–48; (January 1923), 184–206.

Muir, Andrew Forest, ed. *Texas in 1837, An Anonymous, Contemporary Narrative*. Austin: University of Texas Press, 1988.

Muller, Jon. *Mississippian Political Economy*. New York: Plenum Press, 1997.

Murdock, George Peter. *Social Structures*. New York: Free Press, 1965.

Nance, Joseph Milton. *Attack and Counter-Attack: The Texas-Mexican Frontier, 1842*. Austin: University of Texas Press, 1964.

——. *After San Jacinto: The Texas-Mexican Frontier, 1836–1841*. Austin: University of Texas Press, 1963.

Nasatir, Abraham P., ed. *Before Lewis and Clark: Documents Illustrating the History of the Missouri, 1785–1804*. 2 vols. St. Louis: St. Louis Historical Documents Foundation, 1952.

——. *Borderland in Retreat: From Spanish Louisiana to the Far Southwest*. Albuquerque: University of New Mexico Press, 1976.

Neely, Mary Ann Oglesby. "Lachlan McGillivray: A Scot on the Alabama Frontier." *Alabama Historical Quarterly* 36, no. 1 (Spring 1974): 5–14.

Neighbours, Kenneth Franklin. *Robert Simpson Neighbors and the Texas Frontier, 1836–1859*. Waco, Tex.: Texian Press, 1975.

Newcomb, W. W., Jr. *The Indians of Texas: From Prehistoric to Modern Times*. Austin: University of Texas Press, 1961.

Newell, Chester. *History of the Revolution in Texas, Particularly of the War of 1835 and '36; Together With the Latest Geographical, Topographical, and Statistical Accounts of the Country, From the Most Authentic Sources*. New York: Wiley and Putnam, 1838. Reprint, New York: Arno Press, 1973.

O'Brien, Greg. *Choctaws in a Revolutionary Age, 1750–1830*. Lincoln: University of Nebraska Press, 2002.

Okpewho, Isidore, Carole Boyce Davies, and Ali Alamin Mazrui, eds. *The African Diaspora: African Origins and New World Identities*. Bloomington: Indiana University Press, 2001.

O'Neill, Charles. *Church and State in French Colonial Louisiana*. New Haven, Conn.: Yale University Press, 1966.

Owsley, Frank L., Jr. *Struggle for the Gulf Borderlands: The Creek War and the Battle of New Orleans, 1812–1815*. Gainesville: University Press of Florida, 1981.

Padilla, Juan Antonio. "Texas in 1820: Report on the Barbarous Indians of the Province of Texas." Translated by M. A. Hatcher. *Southwestern Historical Quarterly* 32 (July 1919): 47–68.

Peebles, Christopher S. "Moundville from 1000 to 1500 A.D. as seen from 1840 to 1985." In *Chiefdoms in the Americas*. Edited by Robert D. Drennen and Carlos A. Uribe. Lanham, MD: University Press of America, 1987: 21–41.

———. "The Rise and Fall of the Mississippian in Western Alabama: The Moundville and Summerville Phases, A.D. 1000 to 1600." *Mississippi Archaeology* 22 (1987): 1–31.

Pénicaut, André. *Fleur de Lys and Calumet: Being the Pénicaut Narrative of French Adventure in Louisiana*. Translated and edited by Richebourg Gaillard McWilliams. Tuscaloosa: University of Alabama Press, 1988.

Perdue, Theda. *Cherokee Women: Gender and Culture Change, 1700–1835*. Lincoln: University of Nebraska Press, 1998.

———. "Writing the Ethnohistory of Native Women." In *Rethinking American Indian History*. Edited by Donald Fixico, 73–115. Albuquerque: University of New Mexico Press, 1997.

Perttula, Timothy. "Material Culture of the Koasati Indians of Texas." *Historical Archaeology* 28 (1994): 65–77.

Piker, Joshua. *Okfuskee: A Creek Indian Town in Colonial America*. Cambridge, Mass.: Harvard University Press, 2004.

Pound, Merritt B. *Benjamin Hawkins, Indian Agent*. Athens: University of Georgia Press, 1951.

Power, Susan C. *Early Art of the Southeastern Indians: Feathered Serpents and Winged Beings*. Athens: University of Georgia Press, 2004.

Pluckhahn, Thomas J. *Kolomoki: Settlement, Ceremony, and Status in the Deep South, A.D. 350–750*. Tuscaloosa: University of Alabama Press, 2003.

Prucha, Francis Paul. "American Indian Policy in the 1840s." In *The Frontier Challenge: Responses to the Trans-Mississippi West*. Edited by John G. Clark. Lawrence: University Press of Kansas, 1971.

———. *The Great Father*. Lincoln: University of Nebraska Press, 1984.

———. *Indian Policy in the United States: Historical Essays*. Lincoln: University of Nebraska Press, 1981.

Purser, Joyce. "The Administration of Indian Affairs in Louisiana, 1803–1820." *Louisiana History* 5 (Fall 1964): 401–19.

Reichstein, Andreas V. *Rise of the Lone Star: The Making of Texas*. Translated by Jeanne R. Willson. College Station: Texas A&M University Press, 1989.

Reid, John Phillip. "The Cherokee Thought: An Apparatus of Primitive Law." In *Ethnology of the Southeastern Indians: A Source Book*. Edited by Charles Hudson, 281–302. New York: Garland, 1985.

——. *A Law of Blood: The Primitive Law of the Cherokee Nation.* New York: New York University Press, 1970.

Reinhartz, Dennis, and Gerald D. Saxon, eds. *The Mapping of the Entradas into the Greater Southwest.* Norman: University of Oklahoma Press, 1998.

Remini, Robert. *The Legacy of Andrew Jackson: Essays on Democracy, Indian Removal, and Slavery.* Lincoln: University of Nebraska Press, 1988.

Robertson, Archibald. *Archibald Robertson: His Diaries and Sketches in America, 1762–1780.* Edited by Harry M. Lydenberg. New York: New York Public Library, 1971.

Rodriguez, Mark S., ed. *Repositioning North American Migration History: New Directions in Modern Continental Migration, Citizenship and Community.* Rochester, N.Y.: University of Rochester Press, 2004.

Robbins, Lester Eugene. "The Persistence of Traditional Religious Practices Among Creek Indians." Ph.D. Dissertation, Southern Methodist University, 1976.

Roberts, Madge Thornall, ed. *The Personal Correspondence of Sam Houston, 1839–1845.* Vol. 1. Denton: University of North Texas Press, 1996.

Robinson, Orrin W. *Old English and its Closest Relatives: A Survey of the Earliest Germanic Languages.* Stanford: Stanford University Press, 1992.

Rogers, J. Daniel, and Bruce D. Smith, eds. *Mississippian Communities and Households.* Tuscaloosa: University of Alabama Press, 1995.

Romans, Bernard. *A Concise Natural History of East and West Florida.* Facsimile Reproduction of the 1775 Edition. Florida Facsimile and Reprint Series. Gainesville: University of Florida Press, 1962.

Rowland, Dunbar, ed. *General Correspondence of Louisiana.* New Orleans: Polyanthos, 1976.

——, ed. *Mississippi Provincial Archives: English Dominion, 1763–1766.* Nashville: Brandon Printing Company, 1911.

Rowland, Dunbar, and A. G. Sanders, trans. and eds. *Mississippi Provincial Archives: French Dominion.* Vols. 1–3. Jackson: Mississippi Department of Archives and History, 1927–32.

Rowland, Dunbar, A. G. Sanders, and Patricia Galloway, trans. and eds. *Mississippi Provincial Archives: French Dominion.* Vols. 4–5. Baton Rouge: Louisiana State University Press, 1984.

——, ed. *Official Letter Books of W. C. C. Claiborne, 1801–1806.* 6 Vols. Jackson: Mississippi Department of Archives and History, 1917.

Salley, Alexander S., Jr., ed. *Journal of the Commons House of Assembly of South Carolina for 1701.* Columbia: Historical Commission of South Carolina, 1925.

——, ed. *Journal of the Commons House of Assembly of South Carolina for 1703.* Columbia: Historical Commission of South Carolina, 1934.

——, ed. *Journals of the Commons House of Assembly of South Carolina for the*

Four Sessions of 1693. Columbia: Historical Commission of South Carolina, 1907.

———, ed. *Journal of the Grand Council of South Carolina, August 25, 1671–June 24, 1680*. Columbia: Historical Commission of South Carolina, 1907.

Saunt, Claudio. *A New Order of Things: Property, Power, and the Transformation of the Creek Indians, 1733–1816*. New York: Cambridge University Press, 1999.

Scarry, John F. "The Apalachee Chiefdom: A Mississippian Society on the Fringe of the Mississippian World." In *The Forgotten Centuries: Indians and Europeans in the American South, 1521–1704*. Edited by Charles Hudson and Carmen Chaves Tesser. Athens: University of Georgia Press, 1994: 327–56.

———, ed. *Political Structure and Change in the Prehistoric Southeastern United States*. The Ripley P. Bullen Series. Gainesville: University Press of Florida, 1996.

Service, Elman R. *Primitive Social Organization*. New York: Random House, 1962.

Sheehan, Bernard W. *Seeds of Extinction: Jeffersonian Philanthropy and the American Indian*. Chapel Hill: University of North Carolina Press, 1973.

Sheldon, Craig T. "The Mississippian-Historic Transition in Central Alabama." Ph.D. Dissertation, University of Oregon, 1974.

Shoemaker, Nancy. *A Strange Likeness: Becoming Red and White in 18th Century North America*. Oxford University Press, 2004.

Shuck-Hall, Sheri Marie. "Diaspora and Coalescence of the Alabamas and Coushattas in the Southeastern Shatter Zone." In *Mapping the Shatter Zone: The European Invasion and Regional Instability in the American South*. Edited by Robbie Ethridge and Sheri M. Shuck-Hall. Lincoln: University of Nebraska Press, forthcoming.

———. "Borderlands and Identity in Imperial Texas: The Alabamas and Coushattas in the Anti-Comanche Union, 1820–1839." *International History Review* 25, no. 3 (September 2003): 563–91.

———. "Power-Brokers of the Spanish Borderlands: The Alabamas and Coushattas, 1805–1809." *Gulf South Historical Review* 14, no. 1 (Fall 1998): 158–80.

Sibley, John. "Historical Sketches of Several Indian Tribes in Louisiana South of the Arkansas River, and Between the Mississippi and the River Grande, 5 April 1805." In *American State Papers: Indian Affairs, Class II, 1789–1814*. Washington: Gales and Seton, 1832.

Siegel, Stanley. *A Political History of the Texas Republic, 1836–1845*. Austin: University of Texas, 1956.

Smith, Marvin T. *Archaeology of Aboriginal Culture Change in the Southeast*. Athens: University of Georgia Press, 1987.

——. *Coosa: The Rise and Fall of a Southeastern Mississippian Chiefdom.* Gainesville: University Press of Florida, 2000.

Smith, F. Todd. *The Caddo Indians.* College Station: Texas A&M University Press, 1995.

——. *From Dominance to Disappearance: The Indians of Texas and the Near Southwest, 1786–1859.* Lincoln: University of Nebraska Press, 2005.

——. *The Wichita Indians: Traders of Texas and the Southern Plains, 1540–1845.* College Station: Texas A&M University Press, 2000.

Smither, Harriet. "The Alabama Indians of Texas." *Southwestern Historical Quarterly* 36 (October 1932): 83–108.

——, ed. *Journals of the Fourth Congress of the Republic of Texas, 1839–1840.* 3 vols. Austin, Tex.: Von Boeckmann-Jones, 1930.

——, ed. *Journals of the Sixth Congress of the Republic of Texas, 1841–1842.* 3 vols. Austin: Von-Boeckmann-Jones, 1940–45.

Snapp, J. Russell. *John Stuart and the Struggle for Empire on the Southern Frontier.* Baton Rouge: Louisiana State University Press, 1996.

Snyder, Christina. "Captives of the Dark and Bloody Ground: Identity, Race, and Power in the Contested American South." Ph.D. dissertation. University of North Carolina, Chapel Hill, 2007.

Stenberg, Richard. "The Western Boundary of Louisiana, 1762–1803." *Southwestern Historical Quarterly* 35 (October 1931): 95–108.

Steponaitis, Vincas P. *Ceramics, Chronology, and Community Patterns: An Archaeological Study at Moundville.* New York: Academic Press, 1983.

Swan, Caleb. "Position and State of Manners in and Arts in the Creek, or Muscogee Nation in 1791." In *Historical and Statistical Information Respecting the History, Condition, and Prospects of the Indian Tribes of the United States.* Edited by Henry Rowe Schoolcraft. Vol. 5. Philadelphia: J. B. Lippincott, 1855.

Swanton, John Reed. "Animal Stories from the Indians of the Muskhogean Stock." *Journal of American Folklore* 26 (1913): 193–218.

——. *Early History of the Creek Indians and Their Neighbors.* Bureau of American Ethnology Bulletin No. 73. Washington, D.C.: U.S. Government Printing Office, 1922.

——. *The Indians of the Southeastern United States.* Bureau of American Ethnology Bulletin No. 137. Washington, D.C.: U.S. Government Printing Office, 1946.

——. *Myths and Tales of the Southeastern Indians.* Bureau of American Ethnology Bulletin No. 88. Washington, D.C.: U.S. Government Printing Office, 1929.

——. "Social Significance of the Creek Confederacy." In *Ethnology of the Southeastern Indians.* Edited by Charles Hudson. The North American Indian Series. New York: Garland Publishing, 1985.

Sweet, Julie Ann. *Negotiating for Georgia: British-Creek Relations in the Trustee Era, 1733–1752*. Athens: University of Georgia Press, 2005.

Sylestine, Cora, Heather Hardy, Timothy Montler. *Dictionary of the Alabama Language*. Austin: University of Texas Press, 1993.

Tate, Michael L. *The Indians of Texas: An Annotated Research Bibliography*. Native American Bibliography Series, no. 9. Metuchen, N.J.: 1986.

Taylor, Theodore W. *The States and Their Indian Citizens*. Washington, D.C.: U.S. Department of the Interior, Bureau of Indian Affairs, 1972.

Thomas, Daniel H. *Fort Toulouse: The French Outpost at the Alabamas on the Coosa*. With an introduction by Gregory A. Waselkov. Tuscaloosa: University of Alabama Press, 1989.

Thompson, William Bird. "A History of the Alabama and Coushattis Indians." M.A. Thesis, Stephen F. Austin State University, 1947.

Trennert, Robert A., Jr. *Alternative to Extinction: Federal Indian Policy and the Beginnings of the Reservation System, 1846–1851*. Philadelphia: Temple University Press, 1975.

Tyson, Carl Newton. *The Red River in Southwestern History*. Norman: University of Oklahoma Press, 1981.

Usner, Daniel H. Jr. *Indians, Settlers, and Slaves in a Frontier Exchange Economy: The Lower Mississippi Valley before 1783*. Chapel Hill: University of North Carolina Press, 1992.

Van Hear, Nicholas. *New Diasporas: The Mass Exodus, Dispersal and Regrouping of Migrant Communities*. Seattle: University of Washington Press, 1998.

Van Ruymbeke, Bertrand, and Randy J. Sparks, eds. *Memory and Identity: The Huguenots in France and the Atlantic Diaspora*. Columbia: University of South Carolina Press, 2003.

Vidrine, Jacqueline Olivier, ed. *Love's Legacy: The Mobile Marriages Recorded in French, Transcribed with Annotated Abstracts in English, 1724–1786*. Lafayette: University of Southwestern Louisiana, 1985.

Wade, Mary Donalson. *The Alabama Indians of East Texas*. Livingston, Texas: Polk County Enterprise, 1936.

Wallace, Anthony F. C. "The Obtaining Lands: Thomas Jefferson and the Native Americans." In *Thomas Jefferson and the Changing West: From Conquest to Conservation*. Edited by James P. Rhonda. Albuquerque: University of New Mexico Press, 1997.

Ware, John D. *George Gauld: Surveyor and Cartographer of the Gulf Coast*. Revised and completed by Robert Rea. Gainesville: University Press of Florida, 1982.

Waselkov, Gregory and Kathryn E. Holland Braund, eds. *William Bartram on the Southeastern Indians*. Lincoln: University of Nebraska Press, 1995.

Waselkov, Gregory A., Brian M. Wood, and Joseph M. Herbert. *Colonization and Conquest: The 1980 Archaeological Excavations at Fort Toulouse and Fort Jackson, Alabama.* Report to the Alabama Historical Commission and the National Park Service/Heritage Conservation and Recreation Service (Fort Toulouse, Phase IVB). Montgomery, Ala.: Auburn University, April 1982.

Webb, Walter Prescott. "The Last Treaty of the Republic of Texas." *Southwestern Historical Quarterly* 25 (January 1922): 151–73.

Weber, David J. *The Mexican Frontier, 1821–1846: The American Southwest Under Mexico.* Albuquerque: University of New Mexico Press, 1982.

Welch, Paul D. *Moundville's Economy.* Tuscaloosa: University of Alabama Press, 1991.

White, Richard. *The Middle Ground: Indians, Empires, and Republics in the Great Lakes Region, 1650–1815.* Cambridge: Cambridge University Press, 1991.

———. *Roots of Dependency: Subsistence, Environment, and Social Change among the Choctaws, Pawnees, and Navajos.* Lincoln: University of Nebraska Press, 1983.

Williams, John Hoyt. *Sam Houston: A Biography of the Father of Texas.* New York: Simon and Schuster, 1993.

Winfrey, Dorman H. "The Alabama-Coushattas." In *Indian Tribes of Texas.* Waco, Tex.: Texian Press, 1971.

Winfrey, Dorman H., and James M. Day, eds. *The Indian Papers of Texas and the Southwest, 1825–1916.* 5 vols. Austin: Texas State Historical Commission, 1995.

Wright, Amos, Jr. *Historic Indian Towns in Alabama, 1540–1838.* Tuscaloosa: University of Alabama Press, 2003.

Wright, Robert Leitch. *The Only Land They Knew: The Tragic Story of the American Indians in the Old South.* New York: The Free Press, 1981.

Wood, Peter H., Gregory A. Waselkov, and M. Thomas Hatley, eds. *Powhatan's Mantle: Indians in the Colonial Southeast.* Lincoln: University of Nebraska Press, 1989.

Woods, Patricia Dillon. *French-Indian Relations on the Southern Frontier, 1699–1762.* Studies in American History and Culture No. 18. Ann Arbor, Mich.: University Microfilms International Research Press, 1980.

Young, Mary E. *Redskins, Ruffleshirts, and Rednecks.* Norman: University of Oklahoma Press, 1961.

Index

271